The Letters of Hildegard of Bingen

The Letters of Hildegard of Bingen

VOLUME II

Translated by

Joseph L. Baird
Radd K. Ehrman

New York *Oxford*
OXFORD UNIVERSITY PRESS
1998

Oxford University Press

Oxford   New York
Athens   Auckland   Bangkok   Bogotá   Buenos Aires   Calcutta
Cape Town   Chennai   Dar es Salaam   Delhi   Florence   Hong Kong   Istanbul
Karachi   Kuala Lumpur   Madrid   Melbourne   Mexico City   Mumbai
Nairobi   Paris   São Paulo   Singapore   Taipei   Tokyo   Toronto   Warsaw

and associated companies in
Berlin   Ibadan

Library of Congress Cataloging-in-Publication Data
Hildegard, Saint, 1098–1179.
[Correspondence, English]
The letters of Hildegard of Bingen / translated by
Joseph L. Baird, Radd K. Ehrman.
p. cm.   Includes bibliographical references and index.
ISBN 0-19-508937-5 (v. 1)
ISBN 0-19-512010-8 (v. 2)
1. Hildegard, Saint, 1098–1179—Correspondence.   2. Christian
saints—Germany—Bingen (Rhineland-Palatinate)—Correspondence.
3. Bingen (Rhineland-Palatinate, Germany)—Biography.   I. Baird,
Joseph L.   II. Ehrman, Radd K.   III. Title.
BX4700.H5A3   1994
282'.092—dc20
[B]   93-33715

1 3 5 7 9 8 6 4 2

Printed in the United States of America
on acid-free paper

Acknowledgments

Once again, we are pleased to have the opportunity to express our appreciation to the many people who contributed in various ways to this work. As before, special thanks are due to Professor Barbara Newman of Northwestern University, who has been generous with her time and advice. We are grateful for her continuing interest in our work. A special note of appreciation is due to Professor Anne L. Clark of the University of Vermont for sharing her knowledge and advice on the correspondence between Hildegard and Elisabeth of Schönau before the publication of her edition of Elisabeth's letters. We wish to thank also Professor Kathryn Kerby-Fulton, who read the manuscript of this work and made many helpful suggestions.

We would also like to express our appreciation to our friends and colleagues at Kent State University: to Professors Ron Crawford and Harold Fry for their assistance with matters German; to Professor Rick M. Newton, chair of the Department of Modern and Classical Language Studies, who has enthusiastically supported this project from the start; to Professors Geoffrey Koby and Gregory Shreve for general advice and computer assistance; and, last but not least, to Professor Ehrman's daughter Julia, who was present at the inception of this project and more than once answered our call to make tea.

Once again, we express our appreciation to the Kent State University Research Office for continuing support of this project.

Finally, aside from the general scholarly debt, we are personally indebted to the late Lieven Van Acker, editor of the Latin texts of these letters, who always promptly answered any queries we directed to him. We—and the scholarly world—will sorely miss you, sir.

Contents

Heilsbronn

Herkenrode(?)

Himmerod(?)

Hirsau

Hördt

Ilbenstadt

Koblenz

Cologne (St. Martin)

Cologne (St. Agatha(?)/Bonn)

Cologne (St. Ursula)

Cologne (The Holy Apostles)

Krauftal

Lubolzberg(?)

Lutter

Mainz (St. Victor)

Mainz (Altmünster)

Mainz (St. Martin)

Mainz(?)

Maulbronn

Metz (St. Glodesindis)

Metz

Neuenburg

Neuss (St. Quirin)

Otterberg

Park

The Letters of Hildegard of Bingen

Introduction

This, the second volume of the translation of Hildegard of Bingen's correspondence, contains 176 letters, all of which are directed to, or received from, figures in the Church—abbots and abbesses, monks, nuns. Twenty-three of the letters are unilateral, that is, they are from correspondents to Hildegard, for which we have no corresponding letter from the saint, either initiatory or in response. This lack may, of course, be the result of simple failure in transmission of the texts, but there is also sufficient evidence from the letters themselves to indicate that, owing to the press of her duties and writing, Hildegard was not always up to the task of responding. It was, for example, only after a barrage of letters that the persistent Guibert of Gembloux was able to make the contact with the saint that he so desperately desired. Or compare the following plaintive cry from the monks of St. Michael in Siegburg:

> He Who knows all secrets is aware with what an extraordinary feeling of love we have chosen you as our spiritual mother and have brought you into the circle of our prayers, and you yourself, beloved lady, have been able to observe this from the sheer number of messages we have sent to you. Yet you have never shown us any sign of motherly affection. And despite our desire, you have never even sent us a letter of admonition, which you should have done even against our will, just as a mother gives wholesome advice to her children.

This is an especially interesting letter, since it attests both to a failure in transmission (where are all those earlier letters that they sent to her?) and, apparently, to Hildegard's occasional negligence in keeping up with her correspondence. Given the circumstances of the time, it could, of course, be that those letters simply did not reach her, which would account too for their not being preserved, but there are numerous other complaints from writers who received no reply to their request, and Hildegard herself confesses to Guibert of Gembloux that the heavy press of her duties has kept her from responding. On the whole, however, Hildegard was quite attentive to her epistolary duties, and we are very fortunate that so large a body of her correspondence has come down to us.

Perhaps the most important group of letters in this collection is those exchanged between Hildegard and Guibert of Gembloux. This Walloon monk, who was later to become Hildegard's secretary, was unrelenting in his efforts to get the saint to respond to his specific questions about her life and visions. And, unlike his contemporaries, he asked the kind of questions that concern us all. Do you, he wanted to know, receive your visions in Latin? Or do they come to you in German, with someone else translating them into Latin as you utter them? Do you receive these visions in a dream while you are asleep, or in an ecstatic state while awake, and do you indeed, as is widely reported, promptly forget the entire vision once you have given voice to it? What is the basis of your learning? Is it from diligent study, or has everything come to you through divine inspiration? Modern scholarship owes much to this farsighted monk who saw fit to ask such specific and detailed questions, and would not rest without receiving some sort of answer.

Other notable letters in this collection are those addressed to her own nuns at Mount St. Rupert; those from the young mystic, Elisabeth of Schönau, along with Hildegard's response; Letter 169r, Hildegard's treatise against the heresy of the Cathars in response to a request from the monks in Mainz; the letter from Volmar, Hildegard's first secretary, who served her faithfully for some thirty years in that capacity; Hildegard's brief letter to her blood brother Hugo; the letters to and from Ludwig, abbot of St. Eucharius.

But the book lies open before you. Read and enjoy.

We cannot take leave of this work without expressing our deep regret on the passing of Lieven Van Acker, the editor of the Latin text of these letters, on which this translation is based. Professor Van Acker's prodigious work on Hildegard's correspondence was truly a labor of love, which he continued even in the midst of his last illness until his death on 16 December 1994. We are deeply regretful that he did not live to see his work through to completion. It was a monumental undertaking, executed with meticulous care and precision. We mourn his loss. The world of scholarship owes him an inestimable debt.

The Letters

Ellwangen

91

Abbot Adelbert to Hildegard

Before 1170

In this brief letter of high praise for Hildegard, Adelbert asks the seer to consult the divine oracle for assistance with his problems, for, as he notes in very general terms, he is surrounded on every side by enemies. Adelbert is apparently fearful of committing specifics to written form, for he indicates that the messenger will supply further information.

Adelbert, abbot (unworthy though I am) of Ellwangen, to Hildegard, beloved bride of Christ, with a prayer that she may share the joys of the citizens of heaven once she has left this vale of tears [cf. Ps 83.7].

Although separated from you by so great a distance, blessed lady, we gladly send our greetings, embracing in you the mighty works of God [cf. Ecclus 18.5; Acts 2.11], for, through God's grace, the sanctity of your exceptionally pure life shines above all others, and the spirit of prophecy, with which you are divinely endowed beyond human understanding, enables you to comprehend the present, unveil the past, foresee the future.[a] Thus doubly honored by an unheard-of gift of God, you are truly the object of wonder and veneration by the people of this age. Indeed the Dawn has visited us [cf. Luke 1.78] and has placed His hand upon this tottering age[b] since, even in the midst of the storm clouds of this evil generation [cf. Gal 1.4], He has graciously given such a one as you to bring light to our time. As a result of this divine intervention, therefore, we rejoice to be able to comprehend the divine ordering of things, and to obtain forgiveness for our sins, remedy for our pains, and consolation for our grief.[c]

Yet our conscience still accuses us, our guilt terrifies us, and our sins rebuke us. We are troubled within, endangered without. Security eludes us, for the enemy hosts resound on every side. A deceitful friend lies in ambush on the right; a savage adversary besieges us on the left.

About these matters, and others, which our messengers will inform you of, holy mother, consult the divine oracle [cf. II Sam 21.1], and write back to inform us what we may expect from the mercy of God.

91r

Hildegard to the Abbot Adelbert

Before 1170

Whatever specifics the messenger may have supplied, Hildegard nevertheless answers the general letter in very general terms, admonishing Adelbert that he is too weak and indulgent in correcting the vices of his subordinates.

He Who sees and is subject to no change says: You do not yet have wings to fly, O human being, wings to bear up under storms or even to glide in serene weather. But you are like a pillar without a pedestal standing in the street, and so you are splattered by all the mud. You are too indulgent, for you do not have the keen and critical eye necessary to condemn the black and wicked ways of mankind. All the same, God in His grace is mindful of you, for you are not afflicted with hardness of the heart, but are merely asleep in undisciplined listlessness so that you do not attend God zealously.

Do not regard your Lord as your servant, but look to Him faithfully like an honorable knight who, armed with helmet and breastplate, fights bravely in the battle. These times are the times that cast God into oblivion, times weary of waging Christ's battle. Through the vain love of novelty and change, lies fly abroad, as if the people see God—and yet they know Him not.[1] [a]

Where, therefore, are the people who walk in the straight path [cf. Prov 14.2]? They are few indeed. But He Who Is [cf. Ex 3.14; Apoc 1.4] says: No man, for all his babbling, can draw the sword of my vengeance from the sheath before the appointed time of my vengeance. Therefore, O human being, rise up and bring light to your spirit through me, so that you may vigilantly search me out. Then you will have life.

Note

1. This characterization of her own age as a degenerate time, a time of a falling away from God—which she frequently denominates as a womanish age—is a recurrent theme in Hildegard's work.

92

Hildegard to the Abbot Adelbert

Before 1170

Another letter of advice to Adelbert, this one stressing the monastic virtue of stability. In response, apparently, to an inquiry about a religious pilgrimage, Hildegard advises the abbot to attend to his duties and govern his flock with proper responsibility.

Bear your burden faithfully in the straight paths, and keep your sheep in line to the best of your ability. For this is better for you than pilgrimages to foreign lands, because God has the same power over the works of man in all places.[1] And with God's help, keep your mind from wandering about, like the day that shifts capriciously between bright sunshine and violent storm. For sometimes your mind is, as it were, in such a heightened state of holiness that you can scarcely bear it, but, at others, it is troubled by weariness and other such hindrances.[a]

Now, therefore, rise up into the proper warmth of the purest sun, because although you are in many ways restricting your sacrifice to Him, God still wants you [cf. Ps 21.9], because He has established you as His very eye.[b] Therefore, do not withdraw from Him.

Note

1. This passage calls to mind St. Jerome's famous dictum: "Non Hierosolymis fuisse, sed Hierosolymis bene uixisse laudandum est," that is, "It is praiseworthy not to have been in Jerusalem but to have lived well in Jerusalem," where the second Jerusalem clearly stands for "the holy," or "heavenly" Jerusalem. Jerome's admonition was frequently cited in the twelfth century, especially in seeking to dissuade monastics from engaging in spiritual travel, for pilgrimage, in one sense at least, was in sharp conflict with the monastic emphasis on *stabilitas*. See Giles Constable, *Religious Life and Thought*, especially the chapters "Monachisme et pèlerinage au Moyen Age" and "Opposition to Pilgrimage in the Middle Ages."

Erfurt

93

A Certain Provost to Hildegard

Before 1173

The provost testifies to the widespread fame of Hildegard's sanctity, and expresses the desire to see her in person.

To the lady Hildegard, beloved bride of Christ, A., provost of Erfurt, although unworthy, sends all his devout prayers and devoted obedience.

We never cease lifting up our thanks to you, because your sanctity has spread far and wide, and because you greet so many with the sweet salutation of your letters. With our whole heart we long to see you, and we hope and pray to take delight some day in the kindly words of your consolation, and, enflamed by seeing you face-to-face, to be made joyous through you. May divine mercy, which has begun so holy and so magnificent a work in you, fulfill this our desire, and, in response to your assiduous prayer, make us participants in that goodness of yours.

Now, therefore, blessed lady, we faithfully commend to your love the bearer of this letter, our friend who has made this trip for God's love and yours. May he be mercifully received by you, and merit to hear the words of the Holy Spirit speaking through your mouth.

Erfurt (St. Cyriacus)

94

An Abbess to Hildegard

Before 1173

The abbess entrusts herself and her nuns to the prayers of Hildegard, who, she believes, has been specially anointed by the Lord.

To Hildegard, the mirror of sanctity, N., unworthy abbess of Christ's handmaidens dwelling on Mount St. Cyriacus in Erfurt, with our prayers that she may partake of the joys of eternal brightness.

"Glorious things are said of thee" [Ps 86.3], servant of God. Therefore, although I am heavily burdened with sin, I ask you to reach out the hand of your prayer to me, imitating in this way your Beloved, who stretched out His hand to the leper [cf. Mark 1.40–42]. I know that you have been anointed "with the oil of gladness above thy fellows" [Ps 44.8]. Therefore, on bended knees I beseech you to show compassion on my distress when, having entered the Holy of Holies, you have laid hold of the celestial and eternal. I adjure you to implore your Bridegroom—and mine—for my sake, a poor little woman, that my faults may be reconciled to His grace. Indeed, beloved of Christ, how can it be said that you have divine love if you have not sympathy for the weakness of others? Therefore, let me and the sisters entrusted to me be commended to you. Pray that our feet will stay on the straight paths [cf. Ps 25.12; Ecclus 51.20] so that, made perfect in our journey, we may reach the day of bliss. Intercede with Him who has hidden us "in the secret of His face, from the disturbance of men" so that He may deign to "protect us in His tabernacle from the contradiction of tongues" [Ps 30.21]. And may He "Who keepeth truth for ever" [Ps 145.7] grant us to be willing, and able, to perform all that He commands.

We, therefore, commit the whole of our community to you, holy lady, and we pray from the bottom of our hearts that we may have the assurance of your prayer. May your glory, saintly lady, grow, flourish, and be strong.

94r

Hildegard to the Abbess

Before 1173

Hildegard admonishes the abbess to be more moderate in the governance of her nuns, for affliction of the body by overzealous abstinence can cause vices to flourish.

O daughter of God, you are surrounded by Christ's love. Still, the bitterness of the flesh inhibits your spirit, and so you rebel by lashing out at the devil. I see that your people are well grounded in the faith, and this is pleasing to God. I see also that they are rising up strenuously into the better part [cf. Luke 10.42] and that although they are not fully established in the religious way of life, they are nevertheless growing vigorously.[a] Therefore, let your spirit rejoice in God, and remain devoutly in Him.[1]

Nevertheless, you are ignorant of the way to break the bonds of those who are entangled [cf. Ps 106.14], those, that is to say, who wander aimlessly as the object of mockery [cf. Ps 106.40]. And you cannot figure out what to do. Why do I say this? A certain person kept watch over a large tower to see that it did not shift, but his efforts were in vain. Therefore, he cried out in his distress, "Oh woe, woe is me." And so the people mocked him, saying, "What does it profit you to constantly wage war against those who reject you?"[b] [2]

So look to the lofty mountain, to Him who will respond to you with steadfast love: "My daughter, my daughter, what is it that you want? Whatever you seek from me for your soul's sake, I will grant."

Now, let your mind be at ease, and take peace unto yourself. For I see in the True Light that this will be salutary for your spirit. But see to it that you show proper concern for your little garden,[3] being careful not to overwork it, lest the viridity of the herbs and aromatic virtues fail, so that they become incapable of bearing seed because they have been worn down by the plow of your toil. I frequently see that when a person afflicts the body by overzealous abstinence, weariness sets in, and, as a result, vices flourish more than if the body had been nourished properly.[4]

A compassionate, loving mind has been planted in you. Therefore, beware lest you heed the commands to wound the body too frequently. But announce the times properly appointed for the balm of salvation to those committed to your care, and then you will live forever.

I see your spirit shining brightly in pure light.

Notes

1. The entire first half of this letter poses a number of difficulties for a reader, perhaps even a twelfth-century reader. See the endnotes for the Latin text.

2. We have broken the paragraph at this point to indicate the end of Hildegard's illustrative anecdote. It could be, however, that the anecdote continues through the end of the next paragraph.

3. Hildegard's word here is *terram*, which, apparently, in the immediate context stands for the body, but should, perhaps (as the next paragraph suggests), be broadened to include the entire community. The abbess/abbot (gardener) overseeing (cultivating) the community of those souls committed to her/his care (the garden) is an image dear to Hildegard.

4. Hildegard's sense of moderation is one of her more attractive characteristics: she is neither a body-denying ecstatic nor a flesh-scourging ascetic.

Erlesbüren(?)

95

Hildegard to an Abbess

1166–70(?)

Hildegard admonishes the abbess to follow the Rule of St. Benedict assiduously, and singles out a particular nun whom she should "nourish with the milk of consolation."

O blessed soul, you have climbed the ladder of celestial desire to seek the kingdom of God, according to His command: "Seek ye first the kingdom of God," and so forth [Matt 6.33]. For when you first submitted yourself to God's service, you were given the desire for heaven which would lead you to the heavenly abode.

Then through the prompting of the devil, the winds of vice came rushing upon you, but even they could not move you from your desire.

Therefore, daughter of God, act like those on board a ship who heed the ship's pilot so that he can bring them safely to harbor. For God will give you all things that pertain to the salvation of your soul if, through your holy calling to obedience, you observe the Rule of Saint Benedict as best you can. The pilot of the ship is, in fact, the teaching of the blessed Benedict, who, inspired by the Holy Spirit, gave the precepts of spiritual life. In the spirit of those precepts, gather the daughters of God to yourself, for they have been entrusted to you through Benedict's authority. Among those is the daughter of God, Elizabeth, whom you must keep in your heart with blazing love, and continually nourish with the milk of consolation. See also that you preserve yourself from the baleful wind of vainglory and from your own self-seeking will, for such desires are deadly to human beings. And do this in genuine humility, for humility always rises upward, since it considers itself the least. But vainglory always falls, since it seeks to exist on itself alone.

May the Holy Spirit now gird you with the girdle of sanctity, so that you may build a habitation for yourself in the eternal mansion of the heavenly Jerusalem [cf. Heb 12.22].

Esrum

96

Hildegard to the Monk Frederick

Before 1170

Hildegard admonishes Frederick to show mercy to his brother Rudolph, who is suffering great distress at the moment, for his soul will be in even greater danger if Frederick refuses to allow him to stay in the monastery where he has sought refuge.

I heard Wisdom say these words: The sun shines brightly, but then dark clouds cover it over. Why? Because the situation of the sun is unstable, since it is frequently blasted by dangerous winds. Still, the sky clears up again, happily, and the sun shines once more. So it is with a person's mind. How? When the virtues of God ascend into the temple, that is, into the heart of man, then many times, through the deceptions of the devil, a whirlwind of vices comes and brings darkness in the temple. But can night and storm prevent the sun from ever shining again? Of course not. The same is true of a holy spirit. For although set amidst great dangers and worn down by the vicissitudes of life, it is still capable of good works, and is indeed eager to rise up to them. Therefore, dear son, be not afraid, because God wants your soul in the sacrifice of praise [cf. Ps 49.14, 23] offered through the sacrificial victim of the ram [cf. Gen 22.13]. And you will be a stone without blemish in the temple of God.

Also with respect to the aforementioned afflictions, be mindful of your brother Rudolph, who endures great suffering in your country, and see to it that you do not prevent him from staying in that holy monastery where he presently is. And know for certain that if you pull him out of that place, his soul will be overshadowed by great distress. As for you, live, and cause your talent to grow [cf. Matt 25.14–23; Luke 19.12–26] in your Lord.

Flonheim

97

A Certain Provost to Hildegard

Before 1173

The provost writes Hildegard to repeat his petition that she pray God to reveal to her anything that pertains to him.

To the Lady Hildegard of Bingen, saintly and reverend mother in Christ, H., unworthy provost of Flonheim, offers the great devotion of his prayers and obedience.

God, Who sees all hearts, knows how gladly I would honor you with my expressions of allegiance, saintly lady, if only divine providence had provided an opportunity. In the meantime, accept my devotion, and, as I asked you some time ago, pray to the Lord for me that He might reveal to you all things that pertain to me, so that I may offer thanks for the good, and may, before I die, merit to render satisfaction to God with the fruits worthy of penitence [cf. Matt 3.8; Luke 3.8] for the evil. Please be kind enough to inform me in writing whatever the Lord reveals to you about me, and keep me in your prayers. I would have written more fully and intimately to you if the weakness of my body had not prevented me from doing so.

Frankfurt

98

A Certain Provost to Hildegard

Before 1173

A brief letter asking Hildegard to keep the writer in her prayers.

To Hildegard, his beloved lady in Christ, G., unworthy provost in Frankfurt, sends his wish that she share the labor of Martha and the consolation of Mary [Luke 10.38ff].

I have greatly desired to see you in person, but various matters of business have prevented me. Now, at least, God has granted me the opportunity to embrace you and greet you in a letter. We would not have you ignorant of your good reputation, but at the same time we are unwilling to embrace you with our greeting beyond what is proper. We will intercede to God for you to the best of our ability both day and night.[a][1]

Therefore, compassionate lady, please remember me, sinner that I am, before the merciful majesty of God. Farewell, while it is called "today" in heaven [cf. Heb 3.13].

Note

1. There are problems with translation of the almost opaque Latin here, numerous problems, and we cannot be assured that we have solved all of them satisfactorily. The emendations of the *Patrologia* editor, who makes all passive infinitives active and all second person plural pronouns first person plural, will perhaps indicate something of the desperateness of the passage. Van Acker, nevertheless, preserves the MS reading intact with no indication whatsoever of any problem. See endnote for the Latin text.

98r

Hildegard to the Provost

Before 1173

Hildegard replies to the provost with a letter of general consolation.

In a true vision I heard and saw these words: Sometimes the first light of day shines brightly, but, later, dawn is stripped away because the sky becomes overshadowed with great storm clouds. Then the eagle soars high and sighs deeply, because the earlier part of the day was beautiful and free from the turbulence of the storms.

Therefore, O man, you who have knowledge of good and evil [cf. Gen 2.21], consider what kind of person you are and give thought to all the things you have done in God's sight since childhood. Take heed to such things, lest the zeal of the Lord strike you, and lest your spirit say on its departure from the body, "Woe is me! What lies before me, and where will I go?" Or, "What have my days been like, and what, my works? They are such as the millhouse of my body has revealed to me."[a] Beware also, lest you shake with fear when the citizens of heaven say to you, "See what kind of God God is."

Now, live forever.

Gandersheim

99

Hildegard to the Abbess Adelheid

1152–70

Addressed as it is to a nun[1] formerly under Hildegard's governance, and indeed a nun that she fought to retain, this letter of general consolation and admonition surprises with its objective and generalized tone. Note Adelheid's more personal tone in the letter that follows.

The Serene Light says to you: Day excels the night, but night speaks knowledge [cf. Ps 18.2]. How is this so? Day gives proof to the visual and auditory senses of what ought to be rejoiced in and celebrated, while night provides the opportunity to make useful choices, and waits upon the day. Sometimes, however, a storm precedes the day, and only afterward does the day appear clear and bright.

You have been in the first light, O daughter of God, and you have been trod down in the winepress [cf. Is 63.3; Lam 1.15]. But, later, you have walked on broad paths. Now, be careful not to leave the good paths, because God wants you and knows you, and, if you look to Him, He will speedily aid you. But when you reach out to the vanity of the world, it overwhelms you. Therefore, choose from these two directions what is good for you, because if, by seeing and hearing, you call upon God, He will not abandon you.

May God so help you that the day shines in you, and the night withdraws from you, so that you may become a jewel amid virtues. Then you will live forever.

Note

1. Adelheid was the niece of Richardis, Hildegard's favorite nun (see Introduction, Vol. 1, p. 18, and Letters 4, 12, 13, 13r, 18, and 64). Adelheid was a nun along with Richardis in Hildegard's community at Mount St. Rupert. During that time both girls were elected abbess of other communities, an election in both cases that Hildegard strongly opposed. Adelheid took up her duties in 1152.

100

The Abbess Adelheid to Hildegard

1152–73

Alluding to her early years under Hildegard's tutelage, Adelheid writes Hildegard in the name of "ancient friendship," begging to renew earlier ties.

Adelheid, unworthy abbess of the church at Gandersheim, to Hildegard, beloved mother of Mount St. Rupert, with a prayer that she, as the bride of free Jerusalem [cf. Gal 4.26], receive the kisses of the Bridegroom.

A good tree is known by its good fruit [cf. Matt 12.33], and ought never to be cast into oblivion, because by producing sweet fruit it has earned the sweet love of good men. A person, therefore, who does not properly embrace things that are truly delightful will, rightly, be regarded as lower than brute beasts.[a] And so, unsullied dove [cf. Hos 7.11] of Christ, great and pure in spirit, just as good does not create evil, nor light bring forth darkness, nor sweet produce bitterness, so too you never depart from my heart. Likewise, you ought to keep me frequently in mind, since, as is well known, I am joined to you in intimate closeness of love and devotion. I do not want the flower, nursed so gently in former days, to dry up in your heart, the blossom that once vitally flourished between the two of us at the time when you were gently educating me. By that love and by the love of your beloved Spouse, I beseech and implore you to send up prayers and supplications to God both for me and for my flock and for the community that was entrusted to me by your permission. Also, I ask that you deliver us up to the prayers of all your sisters. I pray also that you work out a kind of alliance[b] between your sisters (nay, mine also) and mine, and, when a messenger becomes available, send us a letter informing us, in Christ, what you feel about this matter, as well as any other. I myself, God willing, will not delay a visit to you when the time becomes available, so that we may speak face-to-face, and, hand in hand, do what is good. In this way, our ancient friendship will be strengthened. May God, Who is love [cf. I John 4.16], make it strong!

O you "who live in gardens" [Cant 8.13], give heed, and, as cordially as possible, greet for me all those who dwell with you, that is to say, my sisters, and make me joyful with your approving letter.

101(100r?)

Hildegard to the Abbess Adelheid

1152–73

Van Acker's initial sense that this letter is not in answer to the preceding one is, surely, correct. Thus his number in parentheses with a question mark comes as something of a surprise. This letter, in its rather cool admonitory tone, is scarcely an appropriate answer to Adelheid's passionate plea for closer emotional ties. The letter was, it would appear, written at a much later time than the preceding one. Note Van Acker's suggested twenty-year time frame for the two.

O daughter of God, your mind is distressed by great anxiety in two ways. For on account of a certain kind of worry you are wasting away, almost to the point of despairing of your life. Thus although you sometimes scale the mountain of assured faith to reach God, you nevertheless question Him as if you do not know what to do in this state of doubt. But I say to you, walk in pure faith doing good works in the day of your prosperity, and give God what is His [cf. Matt 22.21; Mark 12.17; Luke 20.25]. For, in truth, you see the sun—an honor which God will not yet take away from you—and also with sighs and with awe for God's law, you hold the world in contempt, like the moon in the night. In both ways, therefore, serve God, because He desires your sacrifice, and because He demands good works from you before you die.

May the light of God's grace cover you, and may He anoint you with the ointment of His mercy, just as He anointed David, who, having confessed his sins, saw God [cf. II Sam 12.13]. May He anoint you with the viridity of the Holy Spirit, and may He work good and holy works in you through that devotion with which true worshipers worship God [cf. John 4.23]. Now, keep God's commandments, and you will live forever.

Gembloux

102

The Monk Guibert to Hildegard

1175

This extraordinary monk[1] was to become Hildegard's last secretary, taking on the position in 1177, when the saint was seventy-nine years old, and remaining in that capacity until her death two years later. This letter is his first contact with her. Note his extravagant praise: save for the Blessed Virgin, her grace is "unique among women"; she is the equal of the great women prophets of the Old Testament, et cetera. Still, he feels it necessary to warn her, at length, of the dangers of pride in one's holiness. Then, he poses the first group of his famous questions to Hildegard, about the language in which she receives her visions; about her learning, whether the result of personal study or divine revelation, etc.

To the servant of Christ, Hildegard, most excellent of name and merit, with reverence, Brother Guibert, least among the brothers at Gembloux, with a prayer that, with the virgins in eternal beatitude, she receive the crown of glory [cf. I Pet 5.4] from the Bridegroom of virgins.

When, venerable mother, we reflect on the singular gifts bestowed upon you by the Holy Spirit, gifts scarcely heard of through all the ages up to the present day, all of us who have seen your writings offer thanks out of our poor gifts to the Author of gifts. For although, on account of our sins, we do not merit to receive these gifts ourselves, nevertheless, through you, we drink of them frequently, because you are like a pure vessel into which they are poured, and, overflowing, you distill them to us. Truly, "thy breasts are better than wine"

[Cant 1.1] to us, your fragrance better than the "best ointment" [Cant 1.2], for on coming forth from the cellars of contemplation where the eternal King often brings you as His bride [cf. Cant 1.3], you make us participants through your writings of those holy visions which, with unveiled face [cf. II Cor 3.18], you see while in the embraces of your Bridegroom, and you draw us after you, running in the fragrance of your ointments [cf. Cant 1.3]. Who indeed reads those visions, or even the exposition of them, without being delighted as in great riches? Or who tastes how sweet and sound your Catholic doctrine is, without immediately crying out about you: "Thy lips are as a dropping honeycomb, honey and milk are under thy tongue" [Cant 4.11]; "thy plants are a paradise of pomegranates with the fruits of the orchard" [Cant 4.13]?

Truly, holy mother, rivers of living water flow to us from your belly [cf. John 7.38], according to the promise of the Lord, and for the joy of the city of God (which is the Church) you have become "the fountain of gardens" in the Church, "the well of living waters, which run with a strong stream from Libanus" [Cant 4.15]. From Libanus, indeed, for they flow to us not *from* you, but *through* you, from Libanus, from the mountain, that is to say, covered and made white by all the virtues, from the mountain which the Father lifted not only above the hills but above the tops of the highest mountains, from the many-peaked and fat mountain [cf. Ps 67.16]. And He also does not fail to abundantly irrigate you, among the other mountains (whence cometh our help [cf. Ps 120.1]), with the showers of His benediction from the peaks.

Truly, save for her through whose Son we attain our salvation, your grace is unique among women. For although we find in the Scripture some songs and prophecies of Miriam, the sister of Aaron and Moses, or of Deborah or Judith, you seem to us coequal, if I may say so, to those contemplators of the highest mysteries through visions or revelations from the Lord, bedewed much more by the floods of the Spirit. O the wondrous and unceasing mercy toward humankind of our gracious Redeemer! For through the same sex by which death entered the world, life has been restored—through His mother. And the same hand that served us the deadly cup of perdition has now poured out for us the antidote of recovery through your salvific teaching.[a]

Still, saintly lady, I must warn you—not argumentatively, certainly, but reverently—to be cautious and persevering. I know that I need not advise you about spiritual progress, since you have already reached the heights of perfection. All the same, remember that you bear your treasure in a fragile vessel, and that it is not the reeds and twigs (which easily bounce back) but the mighty trees that are uprooted by the winds. Look to David and Peter, and "do not aspire too high, but fear" [Rom 11.20], and however high you are, humble yourself in all things, so that the grace that you now have may be preserved whole until the end. Be aware, too, that the way is filled with traps and scandals, and that dangers abound; and, therefore, proceed cautiously until you complete the journey. And never rest secure until the accounting of the talents entrusted to you has been settled with the great Creditor. And do not boast about these talents as if they were your own, save in accordance with the Scripture: "Whoever boasts, let him boast in the Lord" [I Cor 1.31]. It is true that you need not fear that ter-

rible power or strength which is described as being in the loins or the belly of
the Leviathan [cf. Job 40.11] since you have crushed the head of the evil one [cf.
Gen 3.15], that is to say, the principal inducement to lechery, beneath the foot
of chastity. Still, you should bear in mind that in Apocalypse the tail of the dragon
not only carried off the fields of the earth, but also a third part of the stars of
heaven [cf. Apoc 12.4]. One reads there too that the horses had the power of
injuring, not only in their mouths, but also in their tails. For "their tails are like
to serpents, and with them they hurt" [Apoc 9.19]. Therefore, holy mother, now
that you have escaped the head of the ancient serpent, take care that you are not
struck by the tail, and, as far as you can, with God's protection, guard your heel,
that is, your departure from life, from the serpent's treachery.

I do not fear that you will accuse me of presumption in speaking to you thus,
for my advice does not stem from temerity but from my sincere devotion to you.
Besides, I have taken the time simply for the happy occasion of being able to
talk with you freely. That advice was for *your* benefit. On my side, I, who "stick
fast in the mire of the deep" [Ps 68.3], and whose "sores are putrified and corrupted, because of my foolishness" [Ps 37.6], I pray through the sweetness of the
almighty God that you deign to count me among the number of your close friends,
and that you will not refuse to keep in mind the one who is always mindful of
you. Thus lifting up pure hands in prayer [cf. I Tim 2.8], I beseech the immense
goodness of the blessed Redeemer, that He will not be slow to grant me forgiveness of my past sins, emendation of my present ones, and warning about any future
lapses. But because I am a monk, and have neither the opportunity nor the means
of visiting you so that I can discuss with you in person the matters I wish to learn
from you, I pray that you will deign to give diligent attention to the questions I
have candidly set before you through the present messenger.[2] I am asking for a
revelation of the spirit to aid me in these and other personal concerns. Please do
not delay in informing me what course of action I am to take, and in responding
to my queries in writing. We—my friends and I—wish to know whether it is
true, as is commonly said, that you completely forget what you have spoken in
a vision once it has been taken down by your amanuenses at your bidding. Personally, I can scarcely believe it. We also desire to know whether you dictate
those visions in Latin, or whether, after you have uttered them in German, someone else translates them into Latin. We wish to know too whether you have
mastered letters or the Holy Scriptures through study, or whether you have
learned through divine anointing alone, which chooses those it would inspire.

But because, my lady, I do not yet deserve to see your face, resplendent, as
I believe, with divine light, at least let me hear your voice, so sweet to me, through
a letter, so that I may have a memorial of you, in which the image of your saintliness will shine back to me like a reflection in a mirror. Thus, the closer it is, the
more frequently your memory will remain in my heart.

May the Lord deign to preserve the manifestation of your sanctity unimpaired
for years to come, reverend mother, for the honor and profit of His Church. Amen.

The lord abbot and our prior, along with the entire church at Gembloux
entrusted to them, greet you, and pray God for your health, requesting that you
do the same for them. I, the writer of this letter to you, greet you with all my
heart, as does too my beloved brother, also named Guibert, who took the dicta-

tion. And we all especially ask for your prayers. Greeting you also are those whom you love and who love you too, men whom you know personally: Lord Siger de Waura and Nicholas, a young knight from Niel, whom you saw when the two of them visited you during Lent. Brother Franc, the recluse, an upright son in Christ of our church, sends his greetings. So too does Brother Robert, who is sick of body, but sound of mind, currently in the infirmary at Mount St. Guibert, as it is called. Lord Emmo, parochial priest of our church, sends greetings, as does a certain young man whom I care for greatly. His name and the course of action I am prescribing for him will be fully revealed to you by this penitent woman,[3] a woman whom I cherish highly.

All of these people, saintly lady, would gladly impart to you their own special requests about their needs if they could speak to you face-to-face. But, here, we do not have the space. However, since they cannot meet with you at present, we ask that you intercede with God—to Whom all things are known and for Whom all things are possible—for each of them, so that He may come to their aid in these tribulations, and especially for those who are beset by dangers. Thus may the merciful Helper, Who knows our needs, come at the appropriate time, bringing help to these, and, moreover, remission of sins, correction of morals, and eternal joy. May He Who is blessed above all, God forever, grant all these things from His beneficence for the sake of your prayers both for me and for those for whom I pray. Amen.

Farewell in Him, my most beloved lady.

Notes

1. This and the following letters from Guibert of Gembloux (Nos. 104, 105, 106, 107, 108, and 109) are translated from the edition by Derolez (*Guiberti Gemblacensis Epistolae*, pp. 216–57). Van Acker supplies the numbers, but refers the reader to Derolez for the text.

2. The gender of "messenger" (*latricem*) is feminine, and indeed in his next letter (103), Guibert identifies her as "Sister Ida."

3. That is, Sister Ida, the messenger.

103

The Monk Guibert to Hildegard

1175

Guibert expresses disappointment that Hildegard has postponed sending answers to his previous questions, and then sets about asking new ones.

To Hildegard, the most reverend lady and mother in Christ, Guibert, least of God's servants, with a prayer that the coming Bridegroom find her ready with lamp trimmed among the wise virgins [cf. Matt 25.1ff].

Blessed lady, I and friends of yours who dwell with us recently sent a letter to you, delivered by our Sister Ida, and we waited with eager anticipation for what responses you, worthy lady, would give to our queries. But when she returned, we learned that our hope, while not entirely disappointed, was nevertheless not fully realized, at least not to our complete satisfaction. For she reported that you had been pleased with the salutation of our letter and that you had listened to the rest of it intently when it was read to you at your command a number of times. Still, you put off answering my inquiries, those things I had requested to be revealed to us either in a letter or in a verbal response through Sister Ida, the bearer of our letter. You postponed your reply until such time as it should please God to answer your prayers about what response should be made. Sister Ida also informed us that although you could have easily answered some of the questions immediately, you preferred to delay your response because you were unwilling to answer others out of your own perceptions alone. You added, however, that after the Feast of the Assumption of the Perpetual Virgin[1] you would answer all the questions at once if, according to a sign you had given, we would send a reliable messenger to you.

When we heard this, we were somewhat saddened by the delay, but, in anticipation of the more abundant fruit of happiness which Sister Ida promised would come from your response, saintly lady, we rejoiced greatly, humbly giving thanks to the heavenly dispensation and to your kindness. In the meantime, with the aforementioned Feast day at hand, we were anxiously searching for someone to send to your sweet presence, not an easy task during harvest season. Then, unexpectedly, help came from one of your especial friends, a nobleman who lives in our district. Lord Siger de Waura, who had previously declined to go, suddenly changed his mind, and sent one of his servants to inform us that he planned to make the trip to see you on that very Feast day of the Assumption of the Mother of Christ, and that if I wanted to write he would take the letter to you. I gave thanks to my friend for his kindness, and especially to God, by Whose will I was able to accomplish, without cost, what I could scarcely have achieved on my own, even with great exertion and expense.

Immediately on the Vigil of that Feast day I have mentioned so frequently, I began to write the letter you now read, with the fervent hope that since I have received no response to my previous letter you will deign to answer the questions I pose here, along with those earlier ones. Do you, for example, receive your visions in a dream while asleep, or do they come to you in an ecstatic state [cf. Acts 11.5] while awake? Also, is it by divine revelation or merely for the sake of ornamentation that you have your virgins wear crowns?[2] And, further, how are we to interpret the distinctions among the various crowns, for we have heard that they are not all the same? Also, how is the title of your book *Scivias* to be interpreted? Does it mean "Knowing the Ways," or is there a better translation? And, finally, have you written other books? By the faith you owe God, I pray you not to be slow in disclosing these matters to me, along with the other questions I asked in my previous letter.

Taking advantage of the opportunity, your friends here greet you as enthusiastically as they had in the earlier letter, beseeching you to intercede with God for their needs. For my part, I especially pray and beseech through the name and love of Jesus Christ, that you double your prayers and petitions for me, your humble servant, so that God's compassion may be the more gracious to me the more disobedient to His commands and useless I am, and thus all the more indebted to Him. For so far I have lived a life of bestial sensuality. I am a priest wearing the monk's habit, but I act without priestly purity and without the obedience and humility incumbent on a monk, and thus am bringing on myself a harsher judgment. While singing hymns in the choir or assisting at the holy altar, my mind is forever turning to foul and disgusting matters, idle things. I do not revere fully the very present majesty of God nor the presence of His angels. Set in a very dangerous place in the midst of spiritual enemies, I am indolent and sluggish, neither prepared to resist the enemy nor bold enough to take up arms against him. I am the foolishly secure person who owed 10,000 talents [cf. Matt 18.23ff], without fear of the account which I must some day give to the Judge, or of the chains or prison which awaits the sluggish.

And so pray for me that the compassion of almighty God chasten me with a proper, salutary fear, and compel me to understand the many great dangers I am in, and, once they are understood, to fear them utterly. Pray that with some restorative bitterness He will totally dissolve the pact I have made with my flesh and this present life, for it is a bargain sweetened to my ill. Pray that He will cause me—even though forced and compelled—to flee unto Him, and pray that He will take this fugitive into the open arms of His favor. Also, please pray for that friend of mine I mentioned, without giving his name, in my earlier letter. Pray that he cease his aimless wandering and that the grace of His spirit enkindle in him an appetite for the eternal.

Farewell in Christ, reverend mother.

Notes

1. August 15.
2. On the crowns and other ornaments worn by Hildegard's nuns, see the hostile report by Tengswich in Letter 52.

103r

Hildegard to the Monk Guibert

1175

Hildegard writes in answer to the insistent Guibert of Gembloux. Much of this letter is taken up with answers to some, though not all, of the questions posed by Guibert.

The words I speak are not my own, nor any human being's. I merely report those things I received in a supernal vision. O servant of God, you gaze into the mirror of faith in order to know God, and through the formation of man in whom God established and sealed His miracles, you have become a son of God. For just as a mirror, which reflects all things, is set in its own container, so too the rational soul is placed in the fragile container of the body. In this way, the body is governed in its earthly life by the soul, and the soul contemplates heavenly things through faith. Hear, then, O son of God, what the unfailing Light says.

Man is both heavenly and earthly [cf. I Cor 15.47–49]: through the good knowledge of the rational soul, he is heavenly; and through the bad, fragile and full of darkness. And the more he recognizes the good in himself, the more he loves God. For if someone looks in a mirror and finds that his face is very dirty, he will want to wash it clean. So too, if he understands that he has sinned and been caught up in vain pursuits, let him groan and cry out with the Psalmist because his good knowledge makes him aware that he is polluted: "O daughter of Babylon, miserable" [Ps 136.8]. Here is the sense of this verse: human desire was tainted through the poison of the serpent. Thus it is impoverished and wretched, for despite the fact that it tastes the glory of eternal life through its good knowledge, it nevertheless fails to seek that glory from God with true desire—for which reason it has a low reputation in philosophical thought.[a] But blessed is he who understands that he has his life from God, and blessed is he whose knowledge teaches him that God created and redeemed him. For through this divinely given freedom, he breaks the evil habit of his sins, and poor as he is in celestial riches, he dashes his wretchedness upon the rock that is the foundation of beatitude.[b] For when a person knows that he is filthy and cannot resist tasting sin whatsoever, black birds completely befoul him. But then also the rational soul, which he neither sees nor knows, leads him to put his faith in God by believing. Yet although he knows that this is his nature, and knows too that he will live forever, he still cannot keep himself from sinning over and over again. And so: O how lamentable is the fact that God makes such fragile vessels which cannot refrain from sin, save through the grace of God. And yet how wondrous that these same vessels are sometimes adorned with the stars of His miracles. For even Peter, who vowed vehemently that he would never deny the Son of God, was himself not safe [cf. Matt 26.33ff; Mark 14.29ff; Luke 22.33ff; John 13.37f]. The same was true of many other saints, who fell in their sins. Yet these were all, afterward, made more useful and more perfect than they would have been if they had not fallen.

O faithful servant, I—poor little woman that I am—say these words to you again in a true vision: If God were to raise my body as He does my spirit in this vision, my mind and heart would still not be free from fear, because, although I have been cloistered from childhood, I am fully aware that I am only human. For many wise men have been so miraculously inspired that they revealed many mysteries, and yet they fell, because in their vanity they ascribed all these miracles to their own power. On the other hand, those who have drunk deeply of God's wisdom in elevation of spirit while still regarding themselves as nothing—these have become the pillars of heaven. Paul was such a one, for although he was a far better preacher than all the other disciples, he still counted himself as nothing [cf. II Cor 12.11; Eph 3.8]. Likewise, the evangelist John was mild and humble, and therefore drank deeply of divine revelations [cf. Apoc 1.1–2].

And how could God work through me if I were not aware that I am but a poor little creature? God works His will for the glory of His name, not for the glory of any earthly person. Indeed I always tremble in fear, since I know that I cannot safely rely on my own innate capacity.[c] But I stretch out my hands to God so that He might raise me up like a feather,[1] which, having no weight of its own, flies on the wind. Still, I cannot fully understand those things I see, as long as I am an invisible spirit in a fleshly body, because man was injured in both these faculties.[2]

I am now more than seventy years old. But even in my infancy, before my bones, muscles, and veins had reached their full strength, I was possessed of this visionary gift in my soul, and it abides with me still up to the present day. In these visions my spirit rises, as God wills, to the heights of heaven and into the shifting winds, and it ranges among various peoples, even those very far away. And since I see in such a fashion, my perception of things depends on the shifting of the clouds and other elements of creation.[d] Still, I do not hear these things with bodily ears, nor do I perceive them with the cogitations of my heart or the evidence of my five senses. I see them only in my spirit, with my eyes wide open, and thus I never suffer the defect of ecstasy in these visions.[3] And, fully awake, I continue to see them day and night.[4] Yet my body suffers ceaselessly, and I am racked by such terrible pains that I am brought almost to the point of death. So far, however, God has sustained me.

The light that I see is not local and confined. It is far brighter than a lucent cloud through which the sun shines. And I can discern neither its height nor its length nor its breadth. This light I have named "the shadow of the Living Light,"[e] and just as the sun and moon and stars are reflected in water, so too are writings, words, virtues, and deeds of men[5] reflected back to me from it.

Whatever I see or learn in this vision I retain for a long period of time, and store it away in my memory. And my seeing, hearing, and knowing are simultaneous, so that I learn and know at the same instant. But I have no knowledge of anything I do not see there, because I am unlearned.[f] Thus the things I write are those that I see and hear in my vision, with no words of my own added. And these are expressed in unpolished Latin, for that is the way I hear them in my vision, since I am not taught in the vision to write the way philosophers do. Moreover, the words I see and hear in the vision are not like the words of human speech, but are like a blazing flame and a cloud that moves through clear air. I can by no means grasp the form of this light, any more than I can stare fully into the sun.

And sometimes, though not often, I see another light in that light, and this I have called "the Living Light."[6] But I am even less able to explain how I see this light than I am the other one. Suffice it to say that when I do see it, all my sorrow and pain vanish from my memory and I become more like a young girl than an old woman.

But the constant infirmity I suffer sometimes makes me too weary to communicate the words and visions shown to me, but nevertheless when my spirit sees and tastes them, I am so transformed, as I said before, that I consign all my sorrow and tribulation to oblivion. And my spirit drinks up those things I see and hear in that vision, as from an inexhaustible fountain, which remains ever full.

Moreover, that first light I mentioned, the one called "the shadow of the Living Light," is always present to my spirit. And it has the appearance of the vault of heaven in a bright cloud on a starless night.[7] In this light I see those things I frequently speak of, and from its brightness I hear the responses I give to those who make inquiry of me.

In a vision I also saw that my first book of visions was to be called *Scivias*,[8] for it was brought forth by way of the Living Light and not through any human instruction. I also had a vision about crowns. I saw that all the orders of the church have distinct emblems according to their celestial brightness, but that virginity has no such distinguishing emblem save the black veil and the sign of the cross. And I saw that a white veil to cover a virgin's head was to be the proper emblem of virginity. For this veil stands for the white garment which man once had, but subsequently lost, in Paradise. Furthermore, upon the virgin's head is to be set a circlet of three colors joined into one. For this circlet stands for the Holy Trinity. To this circlet four others are to be joined: the front bearing the Lamb of God; the right, a cherubim;[9] the left, an angel; and the one behind, man.[10] For all of these are pendants to the Trinity. This sign given by God will bless God, for He once clothed the first man in the whiteness of light. All of this is fully described in the *Scivias*. And I wrote this *Scivias*, as well as other volumes, according to a true vision, and I continue my writing up to the present day.

Body and soul, I am totally ignorant, and I count myself as nothing. But I look to the living God and relinquish all these matters to Him, so that He, Who has neither beginning nor end, may preserve me from evil. And so pray for me, you who seek these words of mine, and all of you who long to hear them in faith— pray for me that I may remain God's servant in true happiness.

O child of God, you who faithfully seek salvation from the Lord, observe the eagle flying toward the clouds on two wings. If one of those wings is wounded, the eagle falls to earth and cannot rise, no matter how hard it tries. So too man flies with the two wings of rationality, that is to say, with the knowledge of good and evil. The right wing is good knowledge, and the left, evil. Evil knowledge serves the good, and good knowledge is kept in check by the evil, and is even made more discerning by it. Indeed the good is made wise in all things through the evil.[g]

Now, dear son of God, may the Lord raise the wings of your knowledge to straight paths so that although you come into contact with sin through the senses—since man's very nature makes it impossible not to sin—you nonetheless never willingly consent to sin. The heavenly choir sings praises to God for the person who acts in this way, because, although made from ashes, he loves God so much that, for His sake, he does not spare himself, but, totally despising the self, preserves himself from sinful works. O noble knight, be so valiant in the battle that you may take your place in the heavenly choir, so that God will say to you: "You are one of the sons of Israel, because in your great desire for heaven you direct the eyes of your mind to the lofty mountain."

As for all those you called my attention to in your letter, may they be guided by the Holy Spirit and inscribed in the Book of Life [cf. Apoc 20.12]. Moreover, O faithful servant of God, speak specifically to Lord Siger, and warn him not to turn from the right hand to the left [cf. Deut 5.32; Prov 4.27]. For if someone resists a vow that he has made, let him put on the breastplate of faith and the helmet of celestial desire [cf. Eph 6.14ff], and fight manfully. Then, he will successfully complete his journey. And let him consider the fact that when the first man obeyed the voice of his wife rather than the voice of God, he perished in his presumption [cf. Gen 3.17], because he consented to her. But if the tribulation appears to exceed their powers, let them remember the Scripture: "God is faithful, who will not suffer you to be tempted above that which you are able: but will make also with temptation issue, that you may be able to bear it" [I Cor 10.13]. Thus strengthened by this blessed promise, let him and his wife be of one mind, and let them follow whatever course of action is best, whether suggested by the husband or the wife. And let them not fall prey to that first deception, with the man accusing the woman, and the woman, the man. But let them settle this whole matter according to the will of God. I pray that the fire of the Holy Spirit so enkindle their hearts that they never withdraw from Him.

Notes

1. This image of herself as a feather borne up by the breath of God is a frequent one in the letters and in the *Scivias*. See Letter 2, n. 3.

2. Hildegard's phrasing here is quite curious: *quamdiu in corporali officio sum et in anima inuisibili, quoniam in his duobus homini defectus est.*

3. Hildegard always insists that her visions are not the result of ecstasy, that she receives them in full consciousness, "with eyes wide open." See Vol. 1, p. 29, n. 4. Elsewhere, Hildegard stresses the uniqueness of this fully conscious visionary state. Compare the very different mystical experience of Elisabeth of Schönau, who apparently has her visions *only* in a state of ecstasy. See Letter 201.

4. This entire paragraph and most of the preceding one (beginning "God works His will for the glory of His name") are cited in the *Vita Hildegardis* I.8.

5. Hildegard's words are *scripture, sermones, uirtutes, quedam opera hominum. Scripture* could, of course, be rendered as "the Scriptures," and *sermones* perhaps as "sermons."

6. Does Hildegard remember here the verse from Psalms 35.10, "*Et in lumine tuo videbimus lumen,*" "And in thy light we shall see light"?

7. *et illud uideo uelut in lucida nube firmamentum absque stellis aspiciam.* Whatever Hildegard means by this strange image, it certainly captures the immensity of her vision.

8. This, the first of Hildegard's mystical works, takes its title apparently from a shortened form of the phrase *Sci* (or *Scito*) *Vias* (*Domini*), "Know the Ways (of the Lord)."

9. The plural *cherubim* used for the singular is a common medieval error.

10. In *Scivias* II.v.7 the "chorus of virgins" wear white veils, "because those who strive for the glory of virginity are to protect their minds from all noxious heat, and, adorned with the beautiful splendor of chastity, hold on to the warmth of innocence by their faith." In Letter 52r, Hildegard justifies the veils and crowns that her virgins wear on feast days in answer to charges of immodesty and feminine vanity from a certain Tengswich.

104

The Monk Guibert to Hildegard

1175

Guibert joyfully writes to inform Hildegard that an opportunity has arisen for him to come to see her. Also, with what can only be described as a kind of wild, irrepressible exuberance, he expresses his ecstasy on receiving her first letter. Then, Guibert reports reading the letter before a large group of people, one of whom proclaims Hildegard to be the equal of the greatest theologians in France. After this, Guibert recounts in direct discourse a long commentary by "another person," presumably Guibert himself, again filled with high praise, but this time accompanied by specific details about Hildegard's life. Finally, Guibert cannot, once again, refrain from warning Hildegard of the dangers of pride. This letter is a good example of the inflated and ostentatious rhetoric that is characteristic of Guibert's style.

To the lady and mother, Hildegard, whom I will always receive with the most sincere affection, Guibert, her servant, with a prayer that she obtain lasting health of body and soul from the God of our salvation [cf. Ps 67.20].

In the first letter that I sent to you, blessed and worthy lady, I asked certain questions and made some personal observations, and thus quite naturally looked forward to a written response from you. In that letter, I also declared, unequivocally, that I had no hope of being able to come to see you—which, most certainly, I would not have done, if, at that time, I had had any notion or intention of seeking you out, lest my own words should convict me of trifling or of untrustworthiness. Still, I know—I am indeed certain—that things impossible for human beings are nonetheless possible with God [cf. Matt 19.26; Mark 10.27; Luke 18.27], to Whom immediately, whenever He wishes, things are possible [cf. Wisdom 12.18].

Moreover, I uttered those words of hesitation not out of any distrust of divine assistance (for it often gives comfort even to the ignorant), but because I am still uncertain whether it would be good for me to make this journey. For experience has taught me very well that God, in His great mercy, has frequently thwarted the ill-considered impulses of my foolish will. Yet, on the other hand, by bringing certain arguments to bear, He has quickened the slothfulness of my soul and recalled me to better things, even when I was striving in precisely the opposite direction. And it is this latter, revered mother—I confess in my great joy—that has happened to me by His grace and by your merits. For although I was doing nothing about seeking you out, or even thinking about it, He, Who, in the abundance of His mercy, exceeds the desires and merits of our prayers, and sometimes even adds what our prayers do not presume to ask,[1] He, I believe, planted the resolve in me and enkindled the desire, when an opportunity and means of visiting you came our way. And He did this, I believe, because He knew that it would be good for me.

Hear briefly the upshot of these matters. Our mutual friend, Lord Siger, a man of notable family, all the more notable for his very clear devotion to God, had delivered my second letter to you, and, having returned from your presence, saintly lady, had been home scarcely a single night before sending word to me. For, behold, the very next morning, he sent a horse for me by a young man I knew well, and summoned me into his presence. And although I did not find him at home when I arrived, his wife, Elizabeth, herself a very fervent worshiper of God, gave me the letter you had sent me through him, sweet lady, and I received it with reverence and joy. Suspecting that the letter contained something remarkable and magnificent (as indeed turned out to be true), I did not dare to read it until I had prayed. Indeed—if I may reveal the complete agitation of my soul—I was terribly afraid that divine wrath, angered at my sins, would pour some kind of destruction upon me through your mouth immediately, or would at least threaten it for the future.

Therefore, I entered the church next to the house and placed your letter upon the altar. Then, falling to my knees, I prayed the Holy Spirit to make me worthy to read it and to so strengthen the weakness of my heart that I could accept what I would read. Moreover, if any danger lay in store on account of my sins, I asked Him to show me a way to avert it through the prayers of the saints. Then I took up your letter again and read it two or three times in silence. And in sheer wonder at the words, I was, as it were, completely changed and brought almost into ecstasy, for the things said there surpassed my poor powers, and seemed to be more the voice of the Spirit or the speech of angels than of a human being. And so from the bottom of my heart, I blessed the Father of lights [cf. James 1.17], Who spoke and caused light to shine in the darkness [cf. Gen 1.3ff], and Who has filled your spirit with such great brightness that (as you unerringly note in this letter) you are inundated with a double light, ineffable and unending. One of these is with you constantly, that is to say with no intervening fluctuation; the other, only at certain times. Truly, by a special privilege among the women of our time, the light of God's visage has been sealed upon you [cf. Ps 4.7], in order that He might diffuse a salvific joy in your heart.

Truly, in this respect, my lady, your glory is unique! Unique, excepting always, of course, that eminent woman from whom the Sun of Righteousness arose [cf. Mal 4.2], He Who in the radiance of the holy ones was born from the womb of the Father before Lucifer.[a] As the mother of such a one, that woman is rightly called the gate of perpetual light and the resplendent star of the sea. With the exception of her, I say, no other woman in the history of the world save you has ever brought it about that the female sex, which brought the darkness of death into the world, has been marked with the privilege of a greater gift or suffused with such great brightness.

Moreover, I poured out my thanks to our munificent Savior for that other gift, bestowed on you by heaven, for He has poured such grace forth upon your lips that, irrigated in certain parts by the distillation of your words and doctrine, the soil of the Church rejoices, putting forth shoots and producing worthy fruit, through God's kindness. And so let the Church sing a hymn to His name for this voluntary rain which God set apart for His heritage, for He has so magnified your name that your praise will never cease from the lips of men.

Finally, I am very grateful to you, sweet lady, commending you to God. For I have been granted my highest desire, since, as I gather from your words, you have deigned to give me a high place among your special friends, unworthy and undeserving though I am. Thus when you unlocked the chapel of your radiant heart to me, you made known to me the manner and quality of your enlightening more clearly than to anyone else so far, as may be inferred by those who have read your writings.

Assuredly, you have weighed my request and your generosity in your honest scales [cf. Lev 19.36; Job 31.6; Ezech 45.10], judging it right to open the chamber of love to the eye of love and to make me a participant of that exultation, of that delightful secret, not as a spy but as one who takes delight in your joy. You willingly did this for me because the door is opened to the one who knocks [cf. Matt 7.7]. Why, therefore, should my heart not exult in the Lord, my mouth be filled with jubilation, my lips rejoice, since I was uttering with my mouth, proclaiming with my lips, and turning over in my heart those words that were sent out especially to me, words which you could not have learned from your own self, nor from any other human being, but which could only have come in a supernal vision?

Now, however—to turn from my expression of admiration for you to speak, for a moment, of myself—I was burning with no little embarrassment, and my heart was palpitating with fear when, in one part of your letter, the weakness of my conscience and the inconstancy of my character were laid bare, while, in another—with me reading these words in open public[2]—you called me, variously, "servant of God" or "son of God" or "worthy knight." Venerable mother, may almighty God have mercy on you![3] What kind of burden have you imposed on me, an inept and indolent creature? You will see in what spirit you have made such pronouncements. Where, after all, do such qualities as these appear in me? If anyone but you were saying such things, I would reject them out of hand, accounting them as lies or mere flattery. Yet I do not dare to contradict your words, which flow, as you assert, from the supernal fountain. Still, I suffer some little agony of turmoil about myself within my being when I contrast what I hear from you with what I know to be true about myself. Nevertheless, because I believe that you are neither willing nor able to lie, let it be done to me according to thy word [cf. Luke 1.38], whatsoever my real condition. That is to say, with the Lord's help may I become a servant, serving with my whole heart, and a son in my devoted imitation of His Son. And, since the life of man on this earth is a state of war, may I become an approved knight of God, recovering from my weakness and made strong in battle, fighting manfully against vice and the demons that instigate vice. And so that I may not lack your aid also in this battle, pray to Him, Who "knoweth the high afar off" [Ps 137.6], and regards humble things up close, both in heaven and on earth, pray to Him that He not allow my heart to be destroyed by a calamitous outcome, on the one hand, nor, on the other, to exult when the battle goes my way. And pray that He keep my eyes from being lifted up in pride with a desire to walk among the mighty or meddle in things too high for me [cf. Ps 130.1], but may He make me humble and poor in spirit, trembling at His word [cf. Is 66.2], so that He may deign to gather me with the meek of the earth and regard me with compassion.

Meanwhile, when day was beginning to turn to evening, Lord Siger returned home, and when he saw me, smiled graciously and directed to me the greetings you had entrusted to him. And when he learned that I had read your letter, he said, "I pray that you will expound it to me in French, lest I be like the ass that carries the wine but does not taste it." And although he kept urging his request, with some little difficulty I got him to put the matter off until the next day, for it was already evening. Later, seeking to fulfill his desire to the best of my ability, I attempted to satisfy him in this difficult matter, in the presence of a number of people, both clergy and laity. Then, awe seized everyone, and, filled with wonder, they all gave thanks to Wisdom, and to the Spirit that was speaking through its instrument, that is, your mouth. All of these people, of varying rank and age, kept insisting—indeed demanding—that I fulfill this difficult task of translation, unwilling though I was. Yet how gladly they listened to that letter of yours, how eagerly they had copies made, how enthusiastically they read and praised it— not just individual readers but almost the entire church!

Hence it is that when that letter was read to Lord Robert, former abbot of Val-Roi and a man of great reputation and learning, he sat quietly, shaking his head time and again. He was so moved that he burst out in a way that could scarcely have been anticipated, though still with dignity, and he testified that the words he had heard could have come from none other than the Holy Spirit. "I believe," he said, "that not even the greatest theologians in France today, however great their intelligence, could completely comprehend the power and depth of some of the words found in this letter, except through the revelation of that same Spirit which inspired them.[b] They prattle with parched heart and blathering cheeks, reveling in questions and battles, from which quarrels arise. And, all the while, they don't have the slightest idea what they are talking about. Thus they enmesh themselves—and others—inextricably in the entangling coils of contention.[4] But this blessed lady, constantly disciplined, as I hear tell, by the whip of infirmity, and restrained by her own will, contemplates the one thing that is alone necessary, the glory of the Blessed Trinity, in the utmost simplicity of heart. Mild and gentle in heart, she drinks from that fullness within herself and pours it out of herself to relieve the thirst of those who thirst."

Another person added comments that quite agreed with this. "It is nothing new or unusual," he[5] said, "for the souls of men to be illumined by the various gifts of the Holy Spirit. As the Apostle says, 'every one hath his proper gift from God; one after this manner, and another after that' [I Cor 7.7], and in another passage, 'now there are diversities of graces, but the same Spirit' [I Cor 12.4], 'dividing to every one according as he will' [I Cor 12.11]. A new sign of sanctification at length shone forth among our predecessors, about which we solemnly sing:

> Today He has bestowed
> upon Christ's apostles
> a singular gift,
> unheard of
> in any generation.[6]

This refers, of course, to the flickering tongues of fire sitting on each one of the apostles, from whose mouths came forth all manner of tongues [cf. Acts 2.3–4]. Just so, beyond doubt, this too is a new kind of illumination by which this lady is granted clear sight. And unlike others who see divine things in sleep, or in dreams, or in ecstasy, she perceives those things shown to her, wondrous to say, fully awake, irradiated, as she herself declares, in a certain eternal light, which she calls the shadow of the Living Light. And during such visions, she is always alert and self-controlled. Furthermore, if she sees certain things in enigmatic terms, there are many more that she observes with a pure, veracious understanding, with all mystic appearances removed, and she is so much at peace in either mode that she cannot be drawn away from the contemplation of inner things by noticing exterior things.

"Moreover, this gift of hers exceeds the illumination of all others, because the words that she hears in those visions have the double effect of fire in her: she both burns and shines in them. And, also, in that Light (by which she has been illumined from childhood, and which she still enjoys to this day) her spirit is exalted and expanded, since she not only gains an understanding of the Holy Scriptures but is also made capable of seeing into certain (if not all) works of men, however far distant they are from her. The blessed Gregory testifies to the uniqueness of her gift by his evidence to the contrary,[7] for he maintains that the spirit of prophecy does not always irradiate the minds of the prophets, citing two passages from the Scripture in proof: in one David asks Nathan about the building of the temple, and Nathan at one moment grants, at the next forbids it [cf. II Sam 7.2ff]. It is clear that he would not have done this if the spirit were continually present. In the other passage Elisha speaks to Giezi concerning the Sunamite: 'Let her alone for her soul is in anguish, and the Lord hath hid it from me, and hath not told me' [II Kings 4.27]. And since 'deep calleth on deep' [Ps 41.8] in the height of divine revelations, it follows that this illumination in her is totally new, and surpasses all others up to the present time. For on those rare occasions when she enters the mystery of the Living Light, as she herself testifies, she seems to herself to be completely transformed, as it is written 'thy youth shall be renewed like the eagle's' [Ps 102.5]. And just as she feels herself to be a young girl again, she completely forgets all troubles that have befallen her—infirmity, sadness, pain, and the feebleness of her advanced years—and carried away by the sweetness of the symphonic harmony, a delight inexpressible to her and inconceivable to us (since, although well known to her, it surpasses our senses), she, mentally, grows quiet and sleeps in peace in that Light, while, physically, she is fully awake [cf. Ps 4.9].

"Moreover, returning to ordinary life from the melody of that internal concert, she frequently takes delight in causing those sweet melodies which she learns and remembers in that spiritual harmony to reverberate with the sound of voices, and, remembering God, she makes a feast day from what she remembers of that spiritual music. Furthermore, she composes hymns in praise of God and in honor of the saints, and has those melodies, far more pleasing than ordinary human music, publicly sung in church.[8] Who has ever heard such things said about any other woman?

"And so what does it matter if she is ignorant of the liberal arts and grammar? And what does it matter if she does not know anything about the agreement of cases, inflections, genders, numbers, degrees, or anything else of that kind?[9] She is, for all that, refulgent with such extraordinary learning, and possesses such a great understanding of the Scriptures that, as we read of St. Martin, she is ready to answer biblical questions on the spot. And in ordinary conversation she is articulate and lucid, always ready to answer whatever is asked of her. Nor has it been her custom to do this impudently and petulantly, as one might, but, quite the contrary, when she has a ready answer, she pours forth what has been distilled to her without delay. If, however, she is not prepared to answer immediately, she prays, with seemly delay and humble devotion, for things which are unclear to her or of which she is ignorant to be opened up to her by the One Who reveals mysteries. And when she receives what she seeks from the largess of the One Who breathes where and when He will [cf. John 3.8], in absolute faith she imparts to those who question her the abundance of blessing she has received—without ill-will or refusal.

"This woman abundantly proves St. Gregory's dictum that 'the gift of the Holy Spirit is not constrained by law.'[10] And rightly so, since she neither allows herself to be separated from the One because of the love of another, nor to be bound by the law by subjecting herself to the power of a man through marriage. Rather, called to freedom of spirit, she keeps the faith to that One alone, to Whom she has proved herself and Whom she desires to please with a holy body and spirit. In this way, she surpasses other women, who bear the burdens of marriage.

"The Apostle does not allow a woman to teach in church [cf. I Tim 2.12], but, through the gift of the Spirit, this woman is absolved from that prohibition, and, having been taught by His instruction, she has come to know that Scripture very well in her heart: 'Blessed is the one whom thou shalt instruct, O Lord: and shalt teach out of thy law' [Ps 93.12]. And ignorant perhaps in word, but not in knowledge, she teaches many through her sound doctrine, pouring forth abundantly from her two breasts, as it were, the milk of consolation for the ignorant and the wine of correction for the strong. But although the divine anointing teaches her within about all things, and commands her, as we find in her writings, to disclose faithfully and openly for the instruction of her hearers what the Spirit intimates to her secretly, she nevertheless bears in mind her sex, her appropriate condition, and especially the Apostle's aforementioned prohibition. She is obedient to the Spirit, and does not contradict the Apostle sent by the Spirit, but, rather, she educates the Church with books and sermons wholly consonant throughout to the Catholic faith, teaching in the Church, but not after the fashion of those who are accustomed to harangue the people.

"The Apostle also commands women to cover their heads with veils [cf. I Cor 11.5ff], not only out of respect for discipline but also as a commendation either to some mystery or to the submission they are obliged to observe. Yet this woman is not obliged to wear the kind of veil that wives commonly wear, although some kind of veil is required. For in her great loftiness, she transcends the lowly condition of women. And she is to be compared to the most eminent of men, for 'beholding the glory of the Lord with unveiled face, she is transformed

into the same image from brightness unto brightness, as by the Spirit of the Lord'
[II Cor 3.18].

"How appropriate 'from brightness unto brightness' is for one whose spirit
is always illuminated by the various shifts and welcome approaches of that Light,
which, as we said above, she has learned to call the shadow of the Living Light,
and, carried off into that same Light of Life, she gives thanks to God, saying, 'Thou
shalt fill me with joy with thy countenance' [Ps 15.11], and 'the light of thy coun-.
tenance, O Lord, is signed upon us' [Ps 4.7], 'for with thee is the fountain of light;
and in thy light I see light' [Ps 35.10]. When, on those rare occasions, she is inundated and carried off by the radiance of that Living Light, she is so totally,
miraculously, changed, as her friends as well as her writings testify, that from
the very gain in spiritual and bodily strength, one can tell to the minute when
that fiery torrent flows into her, of which torrent it is written, 'suddenly there
came a sound from heaven, and like a torrent of wind it filled the whole house'
[Acts 2.2], and 'A divine fire came, a fire not burning but illuminating, blazing
but not consuming, and it found the hearts of the disciples to be clean vessels,
and it imparted to them the gifts of the spirit.' Then she becomes more lively in
spirit, more spirited in expression, sharper in perception, readier with her words,
and more agile in her body. Thus although at other times she never went any-
where without being assisted by one or two nuns, at that time, miraculously
strengthened, she walks easily without any assistance whatsoever, to the great
wonder and joy of those who are present.

"But why should one wonder if by that Majesty, by whose nod all things
move, she is able to do that which, by herself, she is not able to do? Do not the
words of that Lady, blessed above all women, apply here, if not literally, at least
as a very clear sign? That Lady, through whom the restored human race rejoices,
said while gestating our salvation in her womb, 'Daughters of Jerusalem, why do
you marvel at me? This mystery which you see is divine.'

"Another miraculous thing is reported of her, which her friends, who have
frequently witnessed it, assert to be true: sometimes she fails to obey a divine command to write something or to go out to other monasteries, far or near, in order to
admonish the faithful or, where necessary, to correct certain problems. And whether
this failure of hers is due, God forbid, to sloth or obstinacy, or whether it is to be
blamed on feminine dread or virginal shamefastness (lest it be said that she did it
through presumption or through her own will), whatever the reason, she is immediately scourged doubly by the whip of illness, and by a clear sign she utterly closes
up the mouths of those who speak evil of her [cf. Ps 62.12], for her body suddenly
becomes so totally rigid that it appears not to be human flesh but unbending wood,
and this rigidity is never relaxed until she fulfills those commands."[11]

After your letter was read, and he saw the astonishment of those who heard
it, he became not an envious, but a well-wishing preacher of your glories, reverend mother, and he spoke of grace divinely bestowed upon you, making those
listeners even more fervent in praise of God and in admiration of you. Everyone
agreed that that same God, Who is always marvellous in His saints [cf. Ps 67.36],
was manifested in you. And by His gift and the glory of virginity, you shine
unburnt in the middle of the Babylonian furnace [cf. Dan 3.19ff], and, having

drunk of the fountain of life, you pour forth sweet honey and rich butter to us who hunger.

Now, concerning those things which many people say about you in our region, holy mother, this will suffice at present. For if I go beyond measure in this matter, someone who does not know my heart might think I am currying favor with you through flattering words, and you, either troubled by this praise or terrified by it, might become angry with me. Indeed, if I may speak the truth, it is better for you to be terrified than to be delighted, for it is certainly true that to wish to have a praiseworthy name without a praiseworthy life is certain damnation. That man of the highest perfection[12] says, "I do not consider that I have achieved anything" [Phil 3.13] in any Christian battle. Also it is written, "when a man hath done, then he begins" [Ecclus 18.6]. Moreover, as a certain wise man says, praise of a man, if true, is a proclamation, if false, a condemnation. Thus it follows that nobody, although conscious of no crime or sin in himself, should take pride, but should fear. And anyone in a good situation should desire and seek more earnestly to have good work than to have a good name, and he should not boast in himself to his ruin, but in the Lord to his benefit, for not the one who commends himself but the one whom God commends is worthy [cf. II Cor 10.18].

Farewell in Christ, venerable mother, and keep me and those who are mindful of you in your prayers.

Notes

1. The latter part of this sentence about God's mercy is from *Oratio Dominica XI post Pentecosten*. See P. Bruylants, *Les Oraisons*, n. 770.

2. Guibert anticipates himself a bit here. But he does read the letter in public, as he makes clear below.

3. With this expression of humility, cf. Gregory, *Dialogues* 2.33. *PL* 66, 196 A.

4. Here again, one can see the friction developing between the old monastic order and the new spirit developing in the universities, which will come to full flower in the age of scholasticism.

5. Derolez notes that this is "sans doute Guibert lui-même."

6. Notker Balbulus, *In Pentecoste*, 23. In *Analecta Hymnica*, 53, p. 120.

7. See Gregory, *Dialogues*, 2.21. *PL* 66, 174 A.

8. Barbara Newman (*Symphonia*, p. 9) writes of Hildegard's music: "We know that the *Ordo Virtutum* was intended for performance by Hildegard's nuns, and after that artistic triumph, she may well have prepared additional if less ambitious 'dramatic programs' to enhance the monastic liturgy. I suggest that she composed her songs not to fulfill a conceptual scheme but to suit particular occasions, integrating them with suitable homilies, prophecies, and dramatic exchanges."

9. See Introduction, Vol. 1, pp. 6–7.

10. Cf. Gregory, *Dialogues* 1.1. See *PL* 77, 156 C.

11. When Kuno, abbot of St. Disibod, refused to give his permission for her move to Mount St. Rupert, Hildegard took to her sickbed with a paralyzing illness. Lying rigid and stiff, she could not be moved, even though Kuno attempted with all his strength. Convinced, Kuno granted his permission, and Hildegard rose from her sickbed immediately. *Vita S. Hildegardis* I.v.34–43.

12. That is, St. Paul.

105

The Monk Guibert to Hildegard

Guibert reports having visited Hildegard in the fall. On the way back, he notes, he stopped at the abbey at Villers, where he read the letter he had received from Hildegard earlier, adding details he had learned while visiting at Mount St. Rupert. The monks were so impressed that they wrote their own letter, along with thirty-five questions (which Guibert appends) for Hildegard to answer.

To the holy mother and lady Hildegard, Guibert sends filial service with proper reverence.

When I returned from my visit with you last autumn, blessed lady, before returning to the chamber of my mother, that is, the church at Gembloux, I turned aside to the abbey at Villers to visit my most reverend brothers and masters. In the presence of the abbot and those brothers, I read and reread that letter I had received from you through the agency of Lord Siger. I added also that information which, from your God-given wisdom, you imparted to me during my brief stay with you, for, at that time, day and night, I hung on your every word. When they had heard all these things, their spirits were enkindled with such great ardor of learning from you that they unanimously formulated the appended questions for you to resolve for them, and directed me as your particular friend to get them to you, along with the following brief letter:

> To the virgin and servant of Christ, Hildegard, the brothers of the monastery at Villers.
>
> O most holy mother, beloved of God and men, your presence is lovely and gracious, and your memory is ever blessed, because through you and in you the Lord has done a new thing on earth. For He has illumined you miraculously with a new kind of sanctification, not with the untaught words of human wisdom but with the teaching of the Spirit, and He has filled you with the spirit of understanding [cf. Ecclus 39.8] so that through you He might open up the secrets and mysteries of His wisdom [cf. Ps 50.8] to the faithful. Casting ourselves at your feet, revered lady, we sincerely pray that, to the best of your God-given powers, you will deign to give us answers to the appended questions through the love of Jesus Christ. In this way, you will "give knowledge of salvation" [Luke 1.77] to us who "sit in darkness, and the shadow of death so that we may direct our feet in the way of peace" [Luke 1.79]. Farewell.

To their petition I add my own. Your faithful servant, I join these and the many others who make supplication to you, beseeching you to gird yourself for this task we most earnestly hope you will undertake, since divinity itself has been called to our assistance, and to perform without delay this labor which will benefit the whole Church. It will, of course, be up to your judgment to sort out—and therefore touch upon only briefly—the easier questions or those already discussed by the fathers from the more obscure ones not yet fully elucidated that will require more of your attention, such as those concerning the soul, or those that deal with the distinction between the *nativity* of the Son and the *procession* of the Holy Spirit, as well as others of this kind. By earnestly considering these matters and fully resolving them so that even the simplest soul can understand them, you will make available the goods of your house to the poor so that they may eat and be satisfied [cf. Ps 21.27]. Thus you yourself will provide them with the material for praise, and their praises to the Lord will reflect your success. So to the glory of His name, Who makes His miracles memorable and gives food to those who fear Him [cf. Ps 110.4–5], let it be said of them, "So they did eat, and were filled exceedingly, and he gave them their desire: they were not defrauded of that which they craved" [Ps 77.29–30]. Not content with just once, I advise, I pray, I beseech you again and again to knock at the door of the Lord with untiring prayer for the solution of each of these questions, until, admitted into His sanctuary, you understand all of them, and then, coming forth to us again with radiant face, you illumine the darkness of our ignorance with the splendor of God's revelations.

Sometimes holy prophets, when they are consulted, offer things out of their own spirit merely from the habit of prophesying, although they are thought to speak from the spirit of prophecy—as St. Gregory himself testifies.[1] This, above all, you must beware of, lest when you are strong with the great grace of the Spirit, you have too little discernment of spirits, and whatever you see in your spirit, you immediately impute to the Holy Spirit, saying, "I heard and saw these things in the Spirit." Beware of this, unless He who scrutinizes even the high things of God indicates what you are to say by a clear manifestation. Thus in accordance with him who said, "The Lord hath hid it from me, and hath not told me" [II Kings 4.7], it is much safer and much more praiseworthy to humbly confess one's ignorance in matters so obscure and remote from human comprehension than to ill advisedly build up something new that is not subject to proof.

If you are, by chance, aware that you have already answered some of those questions in one of your written works, would you please tell us where that answer is to be found, or, as I prefer, have it copied out for us just as it appears in the original.

Recently, after the Feast of the Purification of St. Mary,[2] when I went to Villers, once again, to visit your sons Siger and Anselm, who are novices in Christ's army, the monks there demanded to know whether or not I had sent those questions to you that we have been discussing. When I tried to excuse myself on the grounds that no dependable messenger had been available to me, they rejected my every excuse and accused me of laziness, for they were greatly distressed that I had delayed so long.

In the meantime, while I was staying there, Peter, a cleric of Villa Monasterias, a man of my acquaintance, arrived on his way back from Jerusalem. And since he had passed through your region on his return, he unexpectedly brought a letter from you. In this letter you send gracious consolation to those aforementioned novices, but underlying all was the mournful sorrow of your soul at the death of Volmar, your provost.[3] When we read the letter, we rejoiced at the zealous kindness and diligence you have shown your friends, even though they dwell far from you. At the same time, however, we groaned in commiseration at the misfortune of your house on the loss of that staff which provided support for you. With due observance of masses and prayers for your friend who has returned to his home in heaven, we have, however, fulfilled your request—and we continue to do so. Also, we have asked all our friends and associates to do the same.

When I returned to the monastery at Gembloux, I heard, quite unexpectedly, that our lord abbot was preparing to go to St. Quirin to pray, and that he was arranging, if possible, to return through your region. I was filled with great joy when I heard this. I immediately began to work on this letter, intending to send it to you by way of those who were accompanying him on the trip. But, although such a thing was beyond my hopes, the crown of rejoicing [cf. Ecclus 1.11], so to speak, was set on my head, because, for whatever reason, I was chosen to accompany him on the journey. Thus I could be confident that soon I would be able to hand that letter to you personally, from my hands, as they say, to yours.

The following are the questions[4] which the reverend brothers are sending to you, saintly lady, for answers:

1. How is the Scripture "He that liveth for ever created all things at once" [Ecclus 18.1] to be understood, since it is written elsewhere that God divided his works over a period of six days [cf. Gen 1]?

2. What is the meaning of the Scripture "He divided the waters that were under the firmament, from those that were above the firmament" [Gen 1.7]? Are we to believe that the waters above the firmament are physical waters?

3. How is the passage "A spring rose out of the earth, watering all the surface of the earth" [Gen 2.6] to be understood?

4. Before the first human being sinned, he saw God with his bodily eyes. Will we also see Him with our physical eyes, although the Apostle says that in the resurrection we will be given spiritual bodies [cf. I Cor 15.44ff]?

5. What kind of speech and form did God employ when He appeared to the first human being to give him a command [cf. Gen 2.16–17], and what form did He assume when He walked in the garden after mankind's sin [cf. Gen 3.8]?

6. What sort of eyes were opened in our first parents after their sin, since they both had sight beforehand, for the Scripture says, "the woman saw the tree" [Gen 3.6]?

7. What did the Lord mean when He said, "Behold Adam is become as one of us, knowing good and evil" [Gen 3.22]?

8. What is the meaning of this passage: "Sevenfold vengeance shall be taken for Cain: but for Lamech seventy times sevenfold" [Gen 4.24]?

9. Since, as we believe, both Enoch and Elijah were bodily taken into the earthly paradise [cf. Gen 5.24; II Kings 2.11; Ecclus 44.16; Heb 11.5], are we to believe that they had need of physical food and clothing in a place of such bliss?

10. In what part of the earth are we to believe that paradise was situated?

11. What is the meaning of the Lord's words to Noah and his sons "I will require the blood of your lives at the hand of every beast, and at the hand of man" [Gen 9.5], and again in the next verse, "Whosoever shall shed man's blood, his blood shall be shed" [Gen 9.6]?

12. What kind of bodies did those angels who appeared to Abraham have, those whom he served with the finest flour, a calf, butter, and milk [cf. Gen 18.1ff]? Do angels have physical bodies like human beings? And are they breathing creatures like men, save that they are immortal, a state which human beings have not yet achieved? Moreover, do angels alter and change their bodies into whatever shape or form they wish when they desire to be seen, by condensing and solidifying them as much as they like? Further, since in their essence they are impalpable and invisible to our sight because of their rarified nature, do they exist as an uncompounded spiritual material, taking on physical bodies when necessary and then putting them aside when their duty has been fulfilled, reverting to their original essence?

13. Why does Abraham command his servant, and, likewise, Jacob command his son to take the oath by placing their hands under the thigh [cf. Gen 24.9; Gen 47.29]?

14. Why were the holy patriarchs so desirous of being buried in the double cave that Abraham bought from the sons of Heth [cf. Gen 23.8–9; Gen 25.9–10; Gen 49.29]?

15. Was it a real fire that Moses saw burning but not consuming the bush [cf. Ex 3.2], and, similarly of that one which blazed on Mt. Sinai [cf. Ex 19.18], or the one which fell like tongues on the disciples at Pentecost [cf. Acts 2.3], or the one which appeared on the head of St. Martin as he was celebrating the sacraments?

16. What is the meaning of the passage about the ark in the book of Kings: "There was nothing in the ark except the tables of the covenant" [cf. I Kings 8.9], while in the Epistle to the Hebrews, we find, "After the second veil, the tabernacle, which is called the holy of holies: having a golden censer, and the ark of the testament covered about on every part with gold, in which was a golden pot that had manna, and the rod of Aaron, that had blossomed, and the tables of the testament" [Heb 9.3–4]?

17. Are we to believe that Samuel was called back to life at the summons of the sorceress [cf. I Sam 28.7ff]? What is the meaning of the verse about Jonathan eating the honey: "His eyes were enlightened" [I Sam 14.27]?

18. What does the Apostle mean when he says that he was snatched up into the third heaven, not knowing whether he was in the body or out of it [cf. II Cor 12.2–3]? Did he go out of the body when his spirit was snatched there, or did he arrive there while still in the body, and thus vivify it?

19. And what does the Apostle mean when he says, "Every sin that a man doth, is without the body; but he that committeth fornication, sinneth against his own body" [I Cor 6.18]?

20. What does he mean when he says, "If I speak with the tongues of men, and of angels" [I Cor 13.1]? What are the tongues of angels?

21. What is the meaning of "length," "height" and "depth" in Ephesians [cf. Eph 3.18]?

22. What is the meaning of the passage about the Lord, "And the angels came and ministered to him" [Matt 4.11]? In what way did they minister to him? What sort of ministering was involved?

23. Where are we to believe the Lord was from the day of the Resurrection to the day of the Ascension when he was not with the disciples?

24. Since we believe that new souls are newly created from nothing by the providence of the Creator, and that these animate the bodies of infants still in the womb of the mother, how do they contract the pollution of original sin, and how can they be justly punished?

25. What is the Apostle's meaning when he says, "For in him we live, and move, and are" [Acts 17.28]? Likewise, what does he mean by this, "A night and a day I was in the depth of the sea" [II Cor 11.25]? Finally, why does he say, "I am the least of the apostles" [I Cor 15.9] when he worked harder than any of the others?

26. In the Gospel, the Lord says of Himself, "From God I proceeded, and came" [John 8.42], and of the Holy Spirit, "The spirit, who proceedeth from the Father" [John 15.26]. What is the difference between the "procession" of the Son and the "procession" of the Holy Spirit. For He is called the Son, which cannot, and ought not, to be said of the Holy Spirit. What is the difference, then, between the begetting of the Son and the "procession" of the Holy Spirit, since both of them come from the Father?

27. What do the grace of God and free will have in common? What are the unique qualities of each?

28. How are we to understand this passage, "Thou hast ordered all things in measure, and number, and weight" [Wisdom 11.21]?

29. What is the nature and quality of that harmony of elements, about which it is said, "While the elements are changed in themselves, as in an instrument the sound of the quality is changed" [Wisdom 19.17]? Does not what the Lord says in another passage relate to this, "Who can make the harmony of heaven to sleep" [Job 38.37]? Since wicked thoughts frequently come forth from the human heart [cf. Matt 15.19], is it possible to know which come from our own corrupt, depraved nature, and which from the instigation of the fallen angels?

30. Can bodily things be seen with spiritual eyes, and, vice versa, can spiritual things be known through bodily sight?

31. Does the fire of hell [cf. Matt 5.22] have a physical nature or not? If it is physical, as many of the faithful maintain, are we to believe that it is compounded from the four elements?

32. Regarding the various parables in the Gospels, such as that about the man who fell in with thieves [cf. Luke 10.30ff], or about the king who made a wedding feast for his son [cf. Matt 22.2ff], or about the ten vir-

gins [cf. Matt 25.1ff], etc. Did these events actually happen, or are they used only as a simile to make a point about something else?

33. Since in terms of the soul alone, Abraham and Lazarus are at rest, and the rich man is in hell [cf. Luke 16.19ff], what do the "bosom" of Abraham, the "finger" of Lazarus, and the "tongue" of the rich man signify?

34. What special significance is there that, according to the writings of Bishop Gregory of Tours, St. Martin was shown so many times in the midst of fire?

35. If the blessed Nicholas did not appear in his own body to the sailors, some sleeping, some waking, as well as to both Constantine and the prefect,[5] then in what sort of body did he appear? Also, when Peter and Paul and other saints, whose bodies have been interred, are seen by people, some sleeping, some waking, in what kinds of bodies do they come?

Notes

1. *Homiliae in Hiezechihelem Prophetam*, I.i. 304–7.
2. February 2.
3. Actually, Volmar died some three years earlier, in 1173. The reference here is apparently a mistake for Gottfried, Volmar's successor as Hildegard's provost and secretary, who died early in 1176.
4. With these difficult and sometimes seemingly frivolous questions, one might compare the *Problemata* Heloise sends to Abelard for answers. The questions are quite similar, especially with respect to seeming contradictions in the Scripture.
5. For the Nicholas legends, see Jones, *Saint Nicholas*.

106

The Monk Guibert to Hildegard

1176

Guibert writes to inform Hildegard that his anticipated visit with her during the Lenten season has been interrupted—by the devil, as he supposes. Nevertheless, he has, he hastens to add, sent along by messenger the questions posed by the monks of Villers, and they all hope for a speedy answer.

To the most holy mother Hildegard, Guibert.

The joy of seeing and visiting with you during Lent in the company of my abbot has been taken away from me, at least temporarily—by the envy of the devil, as I believe—a joy that I thought had been bestowed upon me from heaven. For when we had traveled as far as Cologne, Satan and the sinful deceits of his carnal disciples put an obstacle in our intended path, and we were prevented from traveling further. But I hope that, once the obstacles have been removed, divine grace will restore to me at a more opportune time that which, to my sorrow, has been taken away.

In the meantime, since my journey was interrupted, I entrusted the questions of the brothers at Villers to Baldwin, a young man very dear to me, with instructions to carry them to you, and now I am anxious to know whether or not you have received them. If so, all of your friends in our region cast ourselves at your feet in the Spirit, and pray you to faithfully embark on the sea of the solution of those questions, not fearing to entrust your sails to the breeze of the Holy Spirit. Relying on such a guide, you will soon glide into a safe harbor without any difficulty. With regard to those questions, when you write with answers to them in response to my letter and the brothers', I pray that some will be made the more pleasing through the others, and will shine the more brightly.

Since you are learning of our affairs from the present messengers, inform us also of yours so that we may either sympathize with you in your grief or rejoice with you in your jubilation. After all, friends should have all things in common.

Farewell in Christ. Please pray for us.

106r

Hildegard to the Monk Guibert

1176

After an allegorical opening on the virtues and an admonition for the monk to live humbly, avoiding pride of spirit, Hildegard informs him that she has had to delay answering the questions sent her on account of ill health and administrative duties. But she assures him that she is indeed still working on them.

Love, which, in concert with Abstinence, establishes Faith, and which, along with Patience, builds up Chastity, is like the columns that sustain the four corners of a house. For it was that same Love which planted a glorious garden redolent with precious herbs and noble flowers—roses and lilies—which breathed forth a wondrous fragrance, that garden on which the true Solomon was accustomed to feast his eyes.

This garden designates those virtues that God Who is true Love [cf. I John 4.8] established in the rod of Jesse [cf. Is 11.1], that is to say, in Mary, who flowered in chastity and brought forth that most noble flower. And from that flower "the voice of the turtledove is heard" [Cant 2.12], which called forth virginal nature. The lily signifies this nature, for it puts forth white flowers with magnificent fragrance from its stalk, just as virginity itself is honored in the world on account of the sweet fragrance of its good reputation. Hermits and monks, who have renounced the world for Christ's sake, ought to live without contact with worldly pomp, just as a virgin, after her vow, ought to live without thought of a man. For virgins and monks are alike among the angelic orders: just as the angels desire nothing other than to gaze upon the face of God [cf. Matt 18.10], so also these, having cast off all earthly pomp, follow the Lamb of God (that is, Christ), bearing His cross [cf. Luke 14.27]. And in these the crimson flowers of the Lord's Passion flourish because of their true contempt for the world.

Now, O son of God, set in the valley of true humility, walk in peace without pride of spirit, which, like a precipitous mountain, offers a difficult, or near-impossible, ascent or descent to those who attempt to scale it, and on its summit no building can be built. For a person who tries to climb higher than he can achieve possesses the name of sanctity without the substance, because, in name alone without a structure of good works, he glories in a kind of vain joy of the mind.

But, now, look to that glorious garden which love planted, and gather to yourself every virtue in true humility and simplicity of heart. And although you find yourself among men of various states of mind, learn how patient and how long-suffering divine goodness has been to us all. Flee also the inconstancy of the slothful servant who serves one master today, another tomorrow; and gird yourself manfully with the sword of God's word by the example of those bold knights who, standing round about, guard the bed of the true Solomon [cf. Cant 3.7–8]. And, with vigilant eyes, commend the sincerity of your mind again and again to the omnipotent God, lest you begin to sleep in doubt; and be an upright and beloved knight of the true Solomon, who loves and crowns you for the victory of the daily battle.

May the Holy Spirit enkindle you with the fire of His love so that you may persevere, unfailing, in the love of His service. Thus you may merit to become, at last, a living stone in the celestial Jerusalem [cf. I Pet 2.4–5; Heb 12.22].

But concerning the questions you sent me to answer, I looked to the True Light praying that I might be given a drink of that river flowing from the living fountain [John 4.10ff] so that I could write back to you providing some answers. Nevertheless, I was suffering from an infirmity of the body—and still am—and I cannot yet refrain from tears, for I do not have the staff of my consolation [cf. Ps 22.4]. And yet I still have great joy of spirit in the Lord, for I am sure of His reward. Still, deprived as I am of such a great consolation, as I have said, and thoroughly taken up with governing our monastery, as much as I can through the grace of God, I am working to answer your questions.

107

The Monk Guibert to Hildegard

1176

Guibert, once again, exhorts Hildegard to answer the questions sent to her, and also thanks her for her book that she sent to them.

Guibert of Gembloux and the brothers and sons of the church at Villers to Hildegard, the spiritual mother of the faithful, and luminous servant of Christ. May yours be the palm and flower of immortal glory in the heavenly Jerusalem [cf. Heb 12.22].

Blessed be God, holy mother, Who has, we believe, not only destined you for singular glory in Heaven, but has beforehand endowed you with special grace, so that, through you, those who are proficient in the faith may be even more greatly strengthened in the Lord; so that sinners may be lifted up by the hope of forgiveness; so that the fainthearted may be consoled [cf. I Thess 5.14]; and so that the ignorant and erring may be instructed by your holy admonitions. Rejoicing in the blessed happiness of this sacred hope, holy lady, we sent a letter to you, seeking definitive knowledge, which we greatly desired, concerning certain secrets, mysteries, and matters of great import. We humbly beseech you to respond to our queries. We ask also that you give full consideration to the questions asked and completely satisfy our expectation, omitting nothing necessary in such great matters, nor for the sake of brevity hastily passing over anything that ought to be spoken. Indeed, if you enlighten the Church of God about matters the world has been ignorant of until now, it will be to the glory of Christ and to your eternal memory. Therefore, so that you may shine like the radiance of the firmament [cf. Dan 12.3] to future generations, open your mouth in the law of the Almighty so that receiving from your fullness we may understand and know the hidden secrets of God's wisdom [cf. Ps 50.8].

We who have gathered these questions together cast ourselves at your feet, pouring forth our prayers. So also do your sons among us: brothers Anselm, Siger, and John, those whom you have loved and cherished from the beginning and whom you have molded by your wholesome admonitions. All of these, along with our dear brother Eustachius—who, although he has never seen you in person, greatly loves you all the same in Christ—and our whole church greet you with affectionate good will and commend themselves with faithful supplication to your prayers. They make this one request with special devotion, that you keep pursuing until you fulfill your outstanding work, holy and worthy of all blessing, that work in which the grace of your sanctity and the uniqueness of that splendid truth shines forth as in a mirror.

For the glory of God and the prosperity of His church, therefore, be vigilant, O luminous spirit. Undertake this work of spirituality with all your might, and launch the little ship of your inner wisdom, emblazoned with the merits of your excellence, on the great and spacious sea so that with the sails of your eloquence filled and billowing with the Holy Spirit, we may sail on the powerful teaching of your words in the serenity of peace and the light of truth.

About the seat and placement of our abbey, our judgments and counsel waver and fluctuate. How I wish that something might be revealed through your prayers about what, in accordance with God's will, ought to be done concerning this uncertain matter so that through your solution our vows may come together again, and our desires grow quiet.

We joyfully received your book that you sent out to us, holy lady, and we are reading it zealously and embracing it affectionately. We bless God, the bestower of all grace, giving thanks to Him for those gifts with which he sustains you on every side and calls you to salvation. It is He Who with blessed grace inspired you to write that book, for the emendation of those who read or hear it.

Farewell. Do not cease to pray God's compassion for us.

108

The Monk Guibert to Hildegard

1176

Informing Hildegard that Siger is again preparing for a pilgrimage to St. Rupert, through whom presumably this letter will be conveyed, Guibert, again, exhorts Hildegard to address their queries, and send the answers back to them through this messenger. Note once again the high praise of Hildegard, where Guibert uses scriptural echoes of the words used to the Holy Virgin.

Brother Guibert of Gembloux along with the brothers and sons of the church at Villers to Hildegard, the beloved bride of Jesus Christ, with their prayer that she walk in the spirit and humility of the Mother Virgin, and fulfill the time of the separation from the body in the holiness and justice of the blessed virgins.

We bless the God of Heaven, who has not despised our times, and through the radiance of your splendor has put to rout the darkness of this world, lest our generation lack a miracle of virtue or a model of future glorification. The Holy Spirit has miraculously illumined you with visions, inspiring you with the means of expounding them and with pure judgments, wholly consonant with our Catholic faith. And through you He has revealed the hidden secrets of His wisdom to His little ones [cf. Ps 50.8] in various ways. Through the grace of God you have become His chosen vessel [cf. Acts 9.15], dear to God, pleasing to the angels, indispensable to men, and beloved to those who direct the feet of others onto the path of life so that they might learn the magnificence of God's eternal power. For they understand that the female sex has been divinely honored through the sacred merits of your excellence, and they see your glory, the glory of a woman given new life by the Father, full of grace and truth [cf. John 1.14].

Hail, therefore, lady full of grace, after Mary, the Lord is with you. Blessed are you among women [cf. Luke 1.28] and blessed the speech of your mouth, which conveys the secrets of invisible things to men, and couples the heavenly to the earthly, and joins the divine to the human. Believing this with our whole heart, we confess with our mouth that you are the fountain of gardens, the well of living water that flows from Libanus [cf. Cant 4.15]. We earnestly beseech you in the name of Him who has made you such a one—turn the streams of your learning to the profundities of our queries and, pouring forth the cup of life to our desires, infuse our thirsting spirits with the sober inebriation of the Spirit. Know, beloved lady, that your intent scrutiny of this abstruse matter will be pleasing to us, "above thousands of gold and silver" [Ps 118.72].

Your beloved son, brother Siger, is here with us, and, marvelously freed, has heeded your counsel and announced his contempt for the glory of this world. He is preparing to make a devout pilgrimage once again to the sweet breasts of your consolation. Through him, we, in our humility, send our greetings to you in the love of Christ, and commend ourselves to your holy prayers with full devotion. Furthermore, we beg wholeheartedly that you send back the responses to our questions through him as envoy. We await the reply to our inquiries with the joy of exultation. Now, for the glory of Christ and the profit of the whole Church, ponder diligently and send forth your response so that the expression of thanks and the voice of praise will resound from generation to generation.

108a

The Monk Guibert to the Community of St. Rupert

1176

Although it is not addressed specifically to Hildegard, this letter[1] is included here as a kind of addendum to the preceding one, outside the regular numbering system, because of its inherent interest. Guibert writes, rather, to the nuns of St. Rupert, because he has heard that Hildegard has died. It is perhaps typical of Guibert that he opens the letter not on the death of the saint but on the matter of the questions submitted to her. He does add, however, that it is mere rumor that they have heard, and that perhaps it is not true. But even if true, he knows that her soul is with the Lord.

Brother Guibert of Gembloux, monk, to the holy sisters of the church of the Blessed Mary and of St. Rupert in Bingen, with his prayer that they enjoy perpetual fellowship with the holy virgins in Heaven.

Without my knowledge, the brothers at Villers, on different occasions, sent two copies of that letter previously written under my name to my lady, your holy mother Hildegard. The first was entrusted to a certain elderly lady, while I was still at Gembloux, and the second to Lord Siger, their brother and our mutual friend, while I was spending time at Bingen with you. When Siger discovered that I was there, as he had hoped, he was very glad, and he had me present that letter to my lady and to you, as you will recall.

But, to return to the other messenger. The old lady I mentioned came from Villers to Gembloux the previous year, and showed me the first copy from the brothers, as well as certain secret matters, which required our assistance. After I had read the letter I was really quite exhilarated, both on account of the pleasing words of the senders and on account of their reverence for the recipient. Furthermore, I rejoiced that, finally, we were about to receive answers to those questions we had posed to our lady, as soon as this elderly messenger returned.

I am really surprised, however, that we were not informed of the death of my venerable lady, your holy abbess Hildegard, which had been reported to us some days ago, unless, by chance, the report is false. Indeed, even if it were true, those brothers would have discounted it, since no reliable messenger from your monastery had reported it. In fact, even if we were hidden away in the forest, I believe that a rumor of this sort could not have been kept secret, this rumor that has been noised far and wide among us and has distressed many people and caused their ears to tingle [cf. I Sam 3.11; II Kings 21.12; Jer 19.3].

All the same, my grief is not excessive because, on the one hand, the rumor has not yet been confirmed, and, on the other, even if it is true, I know that the luminous soul of that holy woman has been brought to the Father of lights [cf. James 1.17] and has been embraced by His Son, her Bridegroom, Jesus Christ, and is now enjoying eternal brightness. It is for this reason, dear sisters, that I am directing the present letter not to an individual, as has been my habit, but to your entire community. We pray that you will write us to confirm this matter one way or the other, so that if, on the one hand, the light of your eyes is still among you, we may rejoice with you, but if, on the other, that light of the world has been removed, we may share in your sorrow, while, at the same time, rejoicing with her for the crown of justice [cf. II Tim 4.8] she has received, in this way fulfilling the duties of affection and friendship.

But if indeed the blessed mother is still alive, please urge and beseech her, as requested by the brothers of Villers, to give full consideration to the questions asked and completely satisfy our expectation, omitting nothing necessary in such great matters, nor for the sake of brevity hastily passing over anything that ought to be spoken.[2] If, however, she is really dead, please write back to inform us on what day she parted the body, in what place, and by what persons she was given burial. Moreover, please be kind enough to send back to us both the present letter and the one I sent her on the previous Lent, along with the appended questions and whatever answers she had given to any of them before her death. For I would like to combine into one volume both our letters to her and hers to us, so as to provide for our eyes and ears a pleasing remembrance of her.

With all the affectionate veneration due you, we have received the *Book of Life's Rewards*, which your holy mother wrote and which you sent, out of your love for us. We consider it worthy of the greatest admiration. The brothers at Villers first feasted well on its marvelous doctrine at their table, and now we too are taking delectable sips from reading the collection.[3]

May God Almighty keep you from all evil and always grant you the aid of His protection. Amen. Farewell.

Notes

1. Since it is not addressed to Hildegard herself, Van Acker does not include a space for this letter in his edition. Because of its striking content, however, we felt compelled to include it here.

2. Guibert employs the same phrases used in 107.

3. There seems to be a play on words here. *Collatio* has two meanings: "a meal in the monastery," at which the work would have been read to the brothers, and "collection," as in a collection of visions.

109

The Monk Guibert to Hildegard

1177

Guibert expresses his great joy that Hildegard is still alive, and, inevitably, asks her to continue working on the answers to the questions while she is still among the living. He also expresses his desire to gather all the letters that have passed between the two of them into a single volume.

Guibert to his most holy mother, Hildegard, with his prayer that she gain eternal salvation in the Lord.

The sword of grief that pierced my soul when the news of your death was spread among us was at last, after some long delays, removed when sister Mathilde returned from your presence, blessed lady. After long delays, I say, because when she left us to seek you out before the Festival of All Saints, we thought that she would return no later than the Octave of St. Martin. Yet, impeded by some misfortune, she was delayed until the Octave of Epiphany.[1] Because of so long a delay, therefore, we thought that she had either fallen ill or had died on her journey. Then, returning unexpectedly and reporting that you had recovered from a serious illness, she poured joy and happiness into my ears, rejoiced my spirit, and opened my mouth to give thanks after such great grief. For, although I do not deserve it, I earnestly hope and desire, God willing, to be nourished by the breasts of your maternal consolation [cf. Is 66.11] for a long time still.

And so, O mother and lady, while you have life and wisdom, I beseech you to press on with the work you have undertaken of answering those questions, and never cease to pray continually to our Lord for my innumerable sins. He knows how far short I have fallen, and how much I need His great mercy and aid.

Once again I commend that young man to you whom I commended to you in my first letter, saintly lady, this time even more earnestly, because Satan has sought him out for special temptation, and he has been sifted in the sieve of temptation for a long time. And, alas, he has yielded to the tempter in many things, fearlessly pursuing a young man's desires. Be mindful of that young man whom the blessed evangelist John mercifully restored to the Church, and even put him in high office, after he had been drawn away from his lawlessness and absolved by his subsequent penitence and many good works.[2] Just so, please pray constantly for this young man that God, "Who commanded the light to shine out of darkness" [II Cor 4.6], will take back that lost vessel, wash it of its pollution, and make it a vessel of election and grace in His house [cf. Acts 9.15], for God patiently suffers vessels of wrath and disgrace, even vessels deserving death [cf. II Tim 2.20]. Pray also that God will grant that young man the strength to avoid deadly delights. And if God chooses to reveal it to you, I would like to know what I myself should do in his case. For if it is foreknown that he will continue in the hardness of heart [cf. Ecclus 16.11] that now holds him down, I would neither throw a saint to the dogs, nor cast the pearls of Christ's word before swine [cf. Matt 7.6], in my fear to counter God's judgment. And I would not want to cultivate barren soil that has been cursed, though God forbid that this be true in his case! But if I knew that he was to share in the inheritance of the saints [cf. Col 1.12], I would more frequently salve his many festering wounds with the tough medicine of exhortation, so that he could be brought back to health. Moreover, through my spiritual friends I would bring about a continual outpouring of prayers to God for him, so that with that balm poured around his wounds, his yoke would be broken [cf. Is 10.27], and he would shatter those fetters of impiety that now hold him tightly bound. Thus called back to the liberty of the glory of God's sons, he will be able to sing in exultation [cf. Ps 115.16]. O Lord, "thou hast broken my bonds: I will sacrifice to thee the sacrifice of praise" [Ps 115.16].

Moreover, there are two clerics that I love very much. One is William of Namur, a man of ethical life, gracious and highly honored, not just by me (lest I seem to be deceived from some personal interest) but also by everyone who makes his acquaintance. For he is a man of solid integrity, one truly to be venerated. The other, Bovo by name, is a very mild-tempered young man among the community here at Gembloux. I beseech you to pray to God that, in His benevolence, He may deign to so mold them that they will illumine and aid either our monastery or some other.

I pray also that you not cease to pour out your prayers for my beloved Robert, the scribe of the present letter. For recently by God's grace and our admonition he has turned from the vanity of the world and now labors under the banner of Christ's army. Thus your prayers may call forth the mercy of the Eternal King, Who may look upon the first service of His future soldier with kindly favor. Then he will be protected from all the weapons that the malicious disturber, the devil, uses to terrify tender novices, and he will be able to direct his course through the crises of the present life as faith billows his sails, and the Holy Spirit grants him a welcome, favoring breeze until he is brought safely through every danger and is anchored in the peaceful harbor, that is, in the security of eternal beatitude, which he longs for in answer to his vows.

Through your sweet mouth, let me dutifully greet the sacred convent of those sisters who serve God under your direction. Please have them pray for me and for all those whom I have entrusted to Christ's mercy. Beseech the Holy Spirit especially to remove carnal desires from us and to cause our hearts, which have so far been dark and slothful, to burn with the heat of His love and to radiate with His light.

Would you please send the present letter back to me, and also whatever letters I or the brothers of Villers have sent to you at various times up to the present. For it is my intention to gather all our letters, yours to me and mine to you, into one volume and to preserve them not only for my consolation but also as a means of exciting divine wonder for His gifts to me in those who will by chance deign to read them.[a] Farewell in Christ to you and yours.

Notes

1. The delay was long indeed. She left before November 1 (All Saints Day) and did not return until January 13 (the Octave of Epiphany). The brothers had reasonably expected her to return at least by November 18 (the Octave of St. Martin).

2. See *Virtutes Iohannis*, iii.66–82. In *Acta Iohannis*.

109r

Hildegard to the Monk Guibert and the Monks of Villers

1177

Hildegard cites Canticles 2.4–5, and expounds upon it at length as the love of God, that love which sustains the angels who look directly on the face of God and are never satiated, and that love which sustained the martyrs and brought them through to paradise. Then, she applies the verse specifically to the monks, who are "martyred" through their vows repudiating the world. Finally, she addresses the matter of the questions sent to her, noting that she has answered fourteen of them, but has advanced no further because of illness and the press of her administrative duties.

In a spiritual vision of my soul, I saw and heard these words: O sons of Love, you who have drunk from that sparkling, inexhaustible fountain [cf. John 4.14], and who have been enkindled by that inextinguishable lamp so that without tedium and in pure faith you seek the things that are His and desire to find them, these words are said to you: The king "brought me into the cellar of wine, he ordained love in me. Stay me up with flowers, comfort me with apples: because I languish with love" [Cant 2.4–5].

This verse is to be understood thus: God established the Old Law like the mold which an artisan makes out of mud in order to produce his metal work. For the Old Law was the shadow of that noble flower which God, according to His ancient plan, had ordained would come forth from the Virgin Mary [cf. Is 11.1]. This flower is the Son of God and the resplendent sun, which illuminates the whole world, and He provided us with the best wine when, through the clothing of His humanity, we knew His beautiful form through knowledge, and we learned the true doctrine of pure faith in wisdom. And so "He ordained love" in us. Love is an inextinguishable fire, the love which enkindles the sparks of true faith. And those sparks burn in the hearts of the faithful, who are enkindled to the faith through the love of God, faith which they could never have unless they loved Him in their hearts first. And so love has been ordained in us.

Through these sparks those martyrs who poured out their blood for Christ and the true faith flew to celestial desire burning with the inextinguishable fire of love, and, sustained by the flowers of martyrdom, attained eternal glory. And that same love filled the minds of a host of the faithful with the sparks of the true faith, for they hunger and thirst for the justice of God [cf. Matt 5.6] and can never be satiated with it, just as the angels, who gaze forever on the face of God, can never be satiated, for He is that love [cf. I John 4.8] which has neither beginning nor end. These blessed ones are comforted, as with apples, by the confident hope of the innumerable benefits of eternal beatitude, and they always sigh for God, for they have contempt for fleshly appetite in themselves, conquering it through martyrdom, that appetite which entered mankind through the taste of the fruit at Adam's fall [cf. Gen 3.6]. For the living fountain has so shed His grace upon them that, having died to the delight of the flesh, they languish in the love of Him with an everlasting hunger and thirst for the justice of God, until at last they are blessedly satisfied in eternal life with the magnitude of His glory.

O sons of God, you are sealed in this love because you have repudiated your worldly flesh for the love of the true sun, that is, the Son of God, Who flowered forth as true man from the flesh of Mary, and Who ordained His love in you. Now, may the purest light of the true sun illumine you, and may it teach you to persevere in the holy way of life to a happy end so that you may live in eternity in true bliss.

I am a poor little untaught form of a woman, who is subject to the governance of your profound wisdom. In response to the faithful petition of your love, I looked to the True Light, and as far as I could through the grace of God, I labored on the answers to your questions. But I have not yet completed the writing I began because of the press of my affairs and because of the great infirmity that I have suffered for a long time by the will of God. I have answered only fourteen of those questions so far, but, to the best of my ability through the grace of God, I will gladly work on the others.

Gerbstädt

110

An Abbess to Hildegard

Before 1173

Because the "fragrance" of Hildegard's virtues has spread throughout the Church, "even into our regions," the abbess writes the holy lady with a petition that she be included in her prayers.

To the venerable lady Hildegard, a burning and shining lamp, R., by the grace of God abbess in Gerbstädt, although unworthy, with a prayer that she run in the race until she achieves the eternal reward [cf. I Cor 9.24].

Since, as the Apostle witnesses, each member of the Church is a part of every other member [cf. Rom 12.4–5], there is much for the individual children of the Church to rejoice about, because the fame of your sanctity, flying everywhere, has spread the fragrance of your virtues throughout the whole Church. And so wafting even into our regions, it has greatly excited our hearts to render thanks to the Author of all good. Therefore, desiring to be made a participant of your merits, I, the least among the faithful, pray as fervently as possible that I may merit to be included in your prayers. And if you will grant my petition, I promise to send my prayer promptly, worthless as it is.

Wherefore, I appeal to your nurturing nature, beloved lady, to send, with full devotion, some word for my benefit. Thus the more abundantly your memory flourishes among us, the more your goodness will rejoice us. Farewell.

110r

Hildegard to the Abbess

Before 1173

In this short response to the abbess, Hildegard expounds the enigmatic biblical verse "Day to day uttereth speech, and night to night sheweth knowledge" [Ps 18.3], an explication which is itself, it must be admitted, somewhat less than clear.

Daughter of God, rise up in the nighttime through the four elements, which fulfill all works during the day. Night brings sadness through darkness, and day, joy through light. For it is written: "Day to day uttereth speech, and night to night sheweth knowledge" [Ps 18.3].

Here is the meaning of this Scripture: God is the day that never grows dark and never changes through the times and the seasons. And God chose the day for Himself, that is, the bright light from the light, because He made His creature, that is, man, whole with all things that were present to Him. But the serpent came and puffed up the woman through his eloquence, and she accepted it and inclined to the serpent. And what she tasted from the serpent she gave to the man [cf. Gen 3.1–6], and this has remained in the man, because man does all works fully. God did not command this to be done, but the serpent deceived the woman through his false and deceitful words. In this way the serpent passed on the taste of the flesh, and it is as slippery and fickle and false as the counsel of the serpent is. For the serpent, in his falseness, hid his evil will toward mankind, since man would never have consented to his counsel if he had known that perdition lay in store for him. And just as man has the knowledge of good and evil, so the serpent has a fraudulent and evil nature. But the swift hart and the strong lion in his den[1] had the means to cut the one off from the other. For God chose a virginal material in which He prepared humanity for His Word, because the Virgin knows no contamination of the taste of the flesh, and so the Word of God took on a foreign nature, that is, became man. So Christ the man lived on earth from day to day, and in this way He deceived the serpent that had cursed the man. For Christ the day conquered all poisonous things of the night, because, with amending penitence, He washed away the taste of the flesh that the serpent had put into man through his trickery. In this way He invests man with a foreign nature, when He gathers His own to Himself. Also, the serpent frequently harms many people through the fraudulence that conceals his malice, causing them to become doubtful, as if unaware that God exists, and thus he cuts them off without faith and without hope. Yet many people fight against this attitude, saying: My destruction will not come from my Creator, but from my own sins. This fight is like the torments endured by the martyrs and the pains suffered by the wounded Christ.

The first woman was the aforesaid night, and she showed knowledge to the night [cf. Ps 18.3], that is, to the man. But you, O daughter of God, make yourself beautiful with the martyrdom of good work, so that your soul may shine in God.

Note

1. That is, the Divinity.

Gottesthal

111

The Provost Frederick to Hildegard

Before 1173

The provost commends himself to Hildegard's prayers and asks her to send answers to the questions he had asked her—in a letter that has not come down to
us?—earlier.

Frederick, by grace of God provost in the Valley of God,[1] although unworthy,
to Hildegard, Christ's devoted servant, with a prayer that she receive "a blessing
from the Lord, and mercy from God the Saviour" [Ps 23.5].

We give thanks from the bottom of our heart to God, because you are strong
in Him, because you flourish in the beauty of virtues, and because with the entire affection of your heart you—along with the sisters committed to you—are
bound to your Beloved through love [cf. Cant 5.9]. Therefore, we have confidence in the Lord that you will keep us in memory before the Lord.

Weighed down as I have been by the great press of business, I have been
unable, as much as I had wished, to send a messenger to you. Yet I ask you not to
delay, beloved lady, to send an answer through the present messenger to the
questions I had asked you previously. Then you will receive a reward from God.
I implore that you, along with all your sisters, remember me to Christ.

Note

1. A literal translation, of course, of *Gottesthal.*

111r

Hildegard to the Provost Frederick

Before 1173

In her reply, Hildegard apparently addresses one of the questions the provost says
that he had asked her earlier. As so frequently in Hildegard's correspondence, this
writer too had apparently sought her advice about resigning his position to return
to a more individual moral life. Hildegard gives her usual advice: stay the course.

Now I say to you: A man who has a vineyard or a rocky field says to himself: It is
too difficult to work here. And so he leaves, for he is weary. But when harvest time

comes, his lord says to him: Go to the field and seek the fruit among the flowers, which sometimes flourish and sometimes dry up. But he finds nothing there.

Hear: The vineyard is the priestly office. He who holds the rod of correction over a recalcitrant people has a rocky field. And when he grows weary, he says to himself: This life doesn't suit me; that life is better for me. And so because he has such thoughts, he abandons his charge immediately, just like a flower that dries up. But if you were to act like this, you would have to be addressed in the same way as that steward who was criticized before his master for his stewardship. And when he considered that he was about to be discharged, he reduced the debt of everyone who owed his master. Therefore, his lord said to him: "The children of this world are wiser in their generation than the children of light" [Luke 16.8].

The first angel fell and refused to sigh in penitence, and would not permit the others to sigh either. But a priest should raise himself up and hasten to help others. Now, take the wise course: see to these things, and remain with the sons of this world, because if you act in accordance with the thoughts that are flying in you, you will be deficient in each part, and you will remember in penitence how you failed. But remain with your people and do not desert them, so that you may live in eternity.

Haina(?)

112

An Abbot to Hildegard

Before 1170

Threatened by ills of both body and soul, as he says, the abbot seeks to have the yoke of his duties removed, and thus seeks Hildegard's advice.

To Hildegard, beloved of God and venerable mistress of the sisters of St. Rupert in Bingen, W., administrator of the brothers in Haina, although unworthy, wishing her the gift of knowledge and wisdom, and the reward for perpetual chastity.

When I first heard of your fame, holy lady, I hastened to send a letter to you. But whether it ever arrived in your presence or not, I have no idea, and so I keep sending new ones until I am sure one gets through to you. And so now in this letter, poor and needy as I am, I rush to the riches of your prayers, because I do not know what gifts I have received from the Almighty other than the form of a man. My sight is cloudy, my hearing obstructed, my tongue afflicted by slowness of speech. I do not raise up divine praises as I should because, in my devotion, I am halting in both speech and mind. I am dull-witted and absentminded. My soul is puffed up with pride, set ablaze by ire, bound in by sadness, cast down by sloth, and is continually confounded by cowardice and shame.

On top of all these evils, I have been assailed by a grave and dangerous disease, which threatens my life unless I am cured by the mercy of God through you. But because "God is compassionate and merciful" [Ecclus 2.13] and "will do the will of them that fear him" [Ps 144.19], I ask that through your prayers I may evade all these evils in both body and soul, and that, with the yoke of the domination of my enemies lifted from me—for their yoke has been heavy upon me [cf. Is 47.6]—He will shower some small part of the multitude of His mercies [cf. Lam 3.32] upon me. Has He not reserved a blessing for me [cf. Gen 27.36]? I pray that He bless me. I ask also, saintly lady—if indeed I dare to ask—that you teach me about the future state of my life.

Presumption has caused me to seek all these things from you, for your great fame has shown that they are all possible to you through Christ, Who dwells in you [cf. Rom 8.9]. Farewell, lady, and may God make me worthy of both a response from you and the aid of your prayers. For I commit myself, living and dead, to your holy prayers.

112r(?)

Hildegard to the Abbot

Before 1170

Hildegard praises the abbot's choice of the high vocation of pastoral care, but advises him that if his flock will not obey him, he should resign from his position. Still, his present mood, she admonishes, is the result of weariness, and it would be better for him to retain his office.

The Living Light says: The first motivation, which you have kept in your heart, filled you like a river [cf. Ecclus 47.16]; the second showered you with light; but the third, which is pastoral care, is the best—if your sheep hear your voice. If they do not hear you, however, resign your office so that you can give a good account of the talent entrusted to you [cf. Matt 25.14ff]. For if you cannot serve well as a master over your brothers, then be in subjection like them.

But I say to you: You have been worn down by the vicissitudes of your holy vocation. But it is better for you to have anxiety for your other brothers than for you to force yourself, alone, into subjection. Live, therefore, in the fiery Giver, and do not be slack in vigilance.

113

The Monks to Hildegard

Before 1173

These monks ask Hildegard's help in settling down the dissension in their monastery.

To Hildegard, chaste dove hiding in the holes of the rock [cf. Cant 2.14], the brothers, troubled, alas, in Haina, with a prayer for the devotion of her prayers, because she looks to eternal salvation.

Because by the grace of God your light shines graciously before men, we glorify your Father [cf. Matt 5.16], Who makes you a lamp burning [cf. John 5.35] for the illumination of the Church, and, although sinners, we nevertheless rejoice greatly in your sanctity, through which you are singularly privileged to enjoy the embraces of your celestial Bridegroom. And we do not disregard your love, for day and night we desire to see you face-to-face, and pray for you assiduously, embracing you, though absent in body, as if present.

Therefore, we, poor beggars along the way, humbly pray your perfection to commend us to your Bridegroom, under Whose shadow you rest safely [cf. Cant 2.3]. We pray that the passing crowd will not drown out our cries, but that led by your prayers to the Lord, we may merit to have the blindness of our hearts illuminated.[1] We are bringing this matter up in the hope that you will concern yourself with settling down (or stamping out altogether) the dissension which, as you know, has arisen in our monastery. Indeed, led by the teaching of the Holy Spirit, you have already made some attempt. But we ask that you send a letter of advice to us right away, for if the dissension is not extinguished very quickly, we face grave danger to both body and soul.

May the grace of the Holy Spirit, which teaches you within and discloses many secrets to you, deign to reveal something concerning us. Farewell.

Note

1. Note the interesting use of Scripture here. The Bible is not being quoted, or even alluded to in the ordinary sense that we have noted in this work. Yet these two sentences are clearly influenced by Matt 20.29ff, where blind men cry out to Christ to illuminate their physical eyes as the passing crowd bids them to hold their tongues.

113r

Hildegard to the Monks

Before 1173

> Divine Wisdom established all things in proper measure, and in this way, Hildegard
> writes the troubled monks, He provided a pattern for the governance and appro-
> priate regulation of monasteries. Then providing specific examples from the Scrip-
> ture and working out a detailed allegorical description of the difficulties in their
> monastery, Hildegard implores the brothers to let the inextinguishable fire of life
> burn in them so that their community can return to the brilliance it had before.

Although burdened for a long time with a grave illness, I, a poor little form of a
woman, was forced by the true Wisdom to offer these words of His to the people
of this monastery. And these are the words that I heard: Since that same Wisdom had expounded His work to this people, that is, how He established heaven
and earth in proper measure, He had thereby given the pattern by which the
brothers of this monastery might know how their institution had been established
in the beginning, and how it has now degenerated.

   And Wisdom said: "I have compassed the circuit of heaven" [Ecclus 24.8],
establishing the height and depth in such a way that they would not exceed the
proper measure, and, moreover, I so ordained the width of the entire world that
it would not exceed its measure. I also made the sun so that it would give light in
the day and dispel the darkness, and I set the moon so that, along with the stars,
it would shine in the night [cf. Gen 1.1ff].

   For in that word when God said: "Let there be" [Gen 1.3], all these things
were made, and they still remain. Hence, O people, see yourselves reflected in
these things as in a mirror, so that you may continue that which you began. For
God breathed the breath of life into mankind [Gen 2.7], and so flesh and blood
was given life. Then He gave to mankind a host of angels to praise and minister
unto him, and He made the other creatures subject to him [cf. Gen 1.26ff]. For
God had given the light of eternity to mankind. But despite all this honor, mankind listened to the worm, and, by going astray, the light was extinguished, and
he became blind to the precepts of God. And the devil rejoiced within himself
and said: I was unable to conquer God in heaven, but in His work, that is, man
(who is another god), I have conquered Him. Note that the devil called man a
god, just as he himself wanted to be a god. But God, in the ancient plan that He
had in Himself before the ages, considered how He could so work out His ordering of things that nobody could stand out against Him with respect to it, and
He hid the knowledge of that plan from all creatures. Thus the devil did not know
it, and still does not, and will forever, until the last day, be ignorant of it.[1] But
then, then on that last day, in his great confusion, he will sense some parts of that
plan and will know how he will be utterly confounded through it. For the devil
thought that mankind was absolutely damned, just as he wished.

In forgetfulness of God and in great foolishness, people forgot that they would be restored as human beings. And so they lived as something less than human beings, until that ancient plan chose a certain sanctified people unto itself. And God foreshadowed sobriety and virginity in Abel, who became a martyr for the sake of justice [cf. Gen 4.8], doing what his father had neglected to do. That sanctified people knew themselves to be human beings, and they lived like humans. From these Noah arose, whom God preserved in the ark. But God, wishing to drown iniquity, opened up the mouth of the abyss, and covered most of creation with water. Then, He swore by His own Godhood that He would never again destroy all flesh by water [cf. Gen 9.11–17], for it was through water that mankind would be regenerated and saved.

After the flood the ancient plan disclosed many miracles by which the devil was confounded. After the murder of Abel, the devil rejoiced, saying: Behold, the work of God that I cast out of paradise lies destroyed on the earth. But sanctified by the Holy Spirit, Noah worked, and he built an altar to God, through which the ancient plan foreshadowed that altar which John saw in Apocalypse, from which the prayers of the saints ascended [cf. Apoc 8.3–5]. For when man prays in penitence for sin and when he seeks salvation from God, he is called saintly.

The ancient plan also brought forth many signs in Abraham. For Abraham, by his own will, left his homeland and his relations, and, in his sanctity, initiated that severe law through which death was confounded and the iniquity of the serpent was wounded with an incurable wound [cf. Gen 12.1ff]. Thus he fulfilled the precepts of God, as Adam failed to do when he deserted God's precept and followed his own will.

That plan also established, in Moses, the purification by law, and through the blood of goats and cattle [cf. Lev 16.15] foreshadowed that the innocent Lamb would be sacrificed for mankind. For the Son of God, coming forth from the heart of the Father, was born of the Virgin and fulfilled all these things in Himself. Virginity arose in the Son of God, and penetrated the heavens with banner raised, because that same Son of the Virgin was wholly untainted and fully holy, and through Him the great order of the virgins arose, an order that the Old Law had not known. But the Son of God was a priest when He sacrificed Himself for mankind on the altar of the cross.[a] Thus priests are joined in His priesthood, and they ought to imitate the angels, who are the messengers of God. The duty of angels is to show the works of mankind, as in written form, to God. And so it is with priests when they receive the sins of mankind through penitence and show them to God through indulgent mercy.

This is what the steward did who was accused before his master "that he had wasted his goods" [Luke 16.1] when he told all of his master's debtors to write less than they owed. For this steward is the synagogue, which could not have freedom through the blood of goats and cattle, but still prefigured the sacrifice of the innocent Lamb, by whom the steward feared that he would be deprived of his office. And he said to himself that he could not abide the hardness of the Law, which commanded: If a person do such and such, he shall die the death [cf. Lev 24.16]. Also, he was ashamed at being cast out so that he could not be reinstated by any petition for mercy. And yet it was through mercy that many were brought to indulgence in the Son of God, and so that mercy granted for one's deeds was almost praiseworthy, because when a servant gives recompense to his lord through penitence and confession, that lord praises him highly, because the servant loved him greatly, just as Mary Magdalene loved Christ. This Scripture about mercy is applicable to priests, and so it behooves them to imitate Christ, to love chastity, and to flee inchastity. For the Son of God suffered on the cross to make the unjust just, and He draws them to Himself, as was said of the steward.

Abel became a martyr for justice. After the Passion of the Son of God, however, a multitude of martyrs arose, who suffered for the faith and for the confession of His name. Other martyrs joined their ranks, that is, those who, by fighting against sin and vice, conquer themselves. These are the wings of the aforesaid martyrs. God's vengeance, however, will fall on those who persecute them unjustly. And those who persecute and torment virginity so that they bring tribulation upon it will not escape God's vengeance. And so it happens many times that, through God's justice, the noble become ignoble and the rich poor, and are, furthermore, subjected to many other dangers and calamities. Moreover, those who oppress and blaspheme the priesthood are as guilty as Cain, who killed his brother. Therefore, they should suffer Cain's own punishment [cf. Gen 4.8–16]. For the priestly office derives its authority from the Lord God.

Wisdom built a tower within the community of this monastery and adorned it with pearls and topaz and sapphire, and He stationed watchmen in that tower. And near the tower He constructed a winepress [cf. Is 5.2], which He entrusted to certain men so that they might use it to press out the wine. Moreover, He built a house in the vicinity, and ordered other men to live in it so that they might take care of all matters that pertained to His fields. But a terrible storm came, and a wave of insanity arose so that the men in charge of the winepress threw javelins at the tower, and the ones in the house threw stones at the tower, and then the men in the tower threw stones back at them.

This tower signifies the height of governance, which is decorated with pearls, that is, with those who have lived in innocence from childhood. And it is decorated with topaz, that is, with those who, having chosen the best part [cf. Luke 10.42], renounce the world. And it is decorated with sapphire, that is, with those who, on account of their love of God, have renounced themselves and the pomp of the world. In this tower are the watchmen, that is, those who are placed in governance over those subject to them. The winepress signifies the office of those who, joined through consecration, administer the sacrament of Christ's Passion at the altar, and cultivate and preserve the vineyard of the Lord of Sabaoth. The house stands for the management and regulation of those who are ignorant and who live in the world and yet have renounced the world and themselves for God. They labor for bodily necessities and still preserve the spiritual life. And the storm denotes the temerity of those in the winepress who hurl spears of pride at their prelates, and that same temerity makes those in the house defiantly disobedient to their prelates. At the same time, the prelates, provoked as they are, become harsh toward their subordinates, and take an angry tone with them.

But for all these things, Wisdom has established a healing truce, just as in the gospel the cultivator of the vineyard said to his lord concerning the fig: "Lord, let it alone this year also, until I dig about it, and dung it" [Luke 13.8]. For digging about it signifies that a person is to suppress his own will; otherwise, he will never be able to obey. But to spread dung means that he is subordinated to his prelate in humility and subjection. For when a person becomes obedient, he regards himself and all carnal desires as mud.

Now, I, a poor little weak form of a woman, say to you, the brothers of this monastery: Let the inextinguishable fire of life burn in you and so suffuse you with its light that you can remain in it, as you had begun. For when the fruitful "time of correction" [Heb 9.10] and emendation comes to you, the stones of your tower will return to the brilliance they had before.

Note

1. See Vol. 1, p. 65, n. 23.

Hameln

114

A Provisor to Hildegard

Before 1173

This writer implores Hildegard's help, with the hope that his illness will be cured by her prayers.

To Hildegard, gem of Bingen, true bride of Christ, grounded in the discipline of the Rule, H., unworthy provisor[1] of the Augustinian Rule in Hameln, with unstinting and devoted prayer for her.

In the long interval of our spiritual love, I have often wished to be in your presence, especially since I have been burdened down by a chronic illness. Once when I was in your presence, as you will remember, daughter of Christ, I was suffering a terrible affliction of body, which still torments me day and night. And just as human frailty is incapable of comprehending the vengeance of God, I do not know whether I have fallen victim to a bodily disease or a spiritual trial because of an increase in benefits.[a] Yet "by the grace of God, I am what I am" [I Cor 15.10], because I do not cease to show almighty God the weight of my meagre labor both in vigils and in prayers.

I implore you, saintly lady, to pray for an end to my suffering, if you please. Having faith in your piety, and your daughters', I beseech you to intercede with God for me. Asking your help, saintly lady, I pray that my disease will be rooted out through your prayers. Although "the continual prayer of a just man availeth much" [James 5.16], there is much that I cannot explain, immoderate sinner that I am, perilously overwhelmed by spiritual and physical weakness.

Please send me something in writing to inform me what the divine mysteries say I should do. Farewell, lady, and pray to your Bridegroom for me.

Note

1. Strictly speaking, a provisor was a kind of administrator who attended to the secular affairs of the monastery.

Heilsbronn

115
The Abbot Nicholas to Hildegard

Before 1170

The abbot beseeches Hildegard to provide him warning through her letters and protection from evil through her prayers.

To the venerable and much-beloved mother in Christ, the lady Hildegard of St. Rupert, brother Nicholas, unworthy abbot in Heilsbronn, with a prayer that she obtain her most felicitous and sublime desires.

Certain that you always take delight in foreseeing things that are universally beneficial, I pray earnestly that you console me with your customary affection. I am sure you know, saintly lady, why I have not visited you for a long time, although I have greatly desired to do so. Still, I perform in mind that which I cannot accomplish in deed. Whatever the case, I rely wholly on you.

Now, however, I ask, I beseech, I implore that divine consolation be given to me through you, that is, that through your letters I may be warned, and through your holy prayers I may be pulled from the grip of evil. For with God nothing is impossible [cf. Matt 19.26; Mark 10.27; Luke 18.27], and we know that this will not be denied to you. Farewell.

115r

Hildegard to the Abbot Nicholas

Before 1170

Hildegard praises the abbot for his service for Christ, but warns that he is allowing himself to be worn down by the trivialities of life. The Holy Spirit will help him, however, if he will have faith.

The True Light in the Light says through the mouth of Wisdom:[a] The Old Law provided indications of man's duty, but it grew weary of hearing the word and was unwilling to labor. And thus it was brought to an end. Then the Church arose under the banner of the King, and followed the Law with a pure eye, and did not grow weary, but labored gladly. Do the same, O tried and true knight.

And again: If while leading forth his army, a warrior allows his banner to fall because of some worthless soldier, another brave man takes it and carries it mightily. For this reason his lord loves that man very much, and rewards him generously. So will it be with you too if you toil mightily as Christ's representative.

Your mind shines brightly with honorable striving toward God. But you are caught up in a whirlwind of trivialities, and you are being worn down. Still, the Holy Spirit will cast this from you, and you will live forever.

116

Hildegard to the Abbot Nicholas(?)

Before 1173

Hildegard speaks of the evils of the time: the men of the Church are blind and astray. But soon a new light will shine, better than the one before. Then, Hildegard, the staunch Benedictine, launches into an attack on the scholastics, who, in their pride, seek to know everything, but have contempt for those who walk in the straight way, that is, the monks. Such men can be defeated only by humility and steadfastness in the faith.

The streets of certain cities are filled with mud, and the pathways of some men are filled with slime. Justice has grown dark with iniquity, and the precepts of the law are violated by abandonment of the laws of God. Therefore, let the shepherds wail and sprinkle themselves with ashes [cf. Jer 25.34], because although established as the "steps" of the Church, they do not seek to know what they are. For the head has no eyes, and the feet no paths, since the shameful deeds of man's iniquity have not yet been fully purged by the hand of God. But in not too long a time, those evils will come to an end, and a better light than before will shine.

Now, however, certain men are divided into two parts in their hearts. On the one hand, in high pride of mind they wish to know all things, and, on the other, they hate the success of those who walk in the straight path [cf. Prov 29.27]. This diabolical crowd, evil of heart, treat the others harshly and cruelly. Still, this generation of malignant spirits does not dare to contradict what God has established, but they make each cause a matter of disputation so that what they willfully choose to their own damnation they claim to be good and holy in God. In this way, they lead the people into great scorn. But how is this generation to be put to flight? It is destroyed by the humility and stability of the faithful.

Herkenrode(?)

117

An Abbess to Hildegard

Before 1173

In this brief letter, the abbess praises Hildegard highly for all the wonders God has worked through her and expresses a desire to see her in person, although she never expects to be able to do so because of the difficulties of travel. She commends herself and her community to Hildegard's prayers.

To the most beloved lady and dearest mother in Christ, N., unworthy abbess of the sisters of the N. church, with a prayer that she see the King of glory in all His beauty [cf. Is 33.17], and rejoice with Him forever.

Blessed be God, Who deigns through you to wondrously declare the mysteries of His secrets never before heard in our days to the world, and to confirm our faith through you, holy mother. Moreover, through you, He ineffably illuminates His Holy Church with the blazing virtues of His signs, as with the rays of a new sun. Who has ever heard the like? Who has ever seen such things [cf. Is 66.8]? Therefore, let us each, let us all say: Blessed be God.

I earnestly desire to see your face, holy lady, and to hear the divine words from your own mouth. But since on account of the difficulties of time and distance, I cannot fulfill my desire by seeing you in person, I will always see you in my heart and soul, and I will always love you. I also beseech your holiness, merciful mother, to deign to intercede with God—Who, without a doubt, will hear you—for me a sinner and for our community, which joins me in supplication to you. You may be assured also that your memory will always be blessed among us, and, through you, the name of the Lord will be magnified. Pray for us, merciful mother and lady.

Furthermore, for the mercy of God and of your maternal love, we ask you to send us a letter of consolation right away. May Christ our Lord deign to gather us along with you into His kingdom.

117r

Hildegard to the Abbess

Before 1173

Hildegard offers a general letter of admonition, warning especially against lack of stability.

Take care not to have a wandering, instable mind, in which the sapphire-colored cloud cannot be seen, for such instability frequently blocks out the light of the sun. Be zealous to stand steadfast, therefore, and do not foolishly inquire into useless matters, for those who do so often fall deceived from the love of Christ, just as the sapphire cloud is obscured by instability of mind. Keep your mind on the embraces of Christ, and seek all good things from Him. Offer up all your works to Him, and He will bless you, for, without Him, there is no salvation for mankind, since grace and salvation is obtained not through man, but through God. Also, Holy Scriptures, which flow from the divine fountain, are the breasts from which mankind sucks sustenance.

Learn, therefore, to flee the vanity that covers the light of the sun, that is to say, separates mankind from Christ. And you will live forever, and be crowned by Christ.

Himmerod(?)

118

Hildegard to an Abbot

About 1171(?)

Hildegard writes in answer to questions the abbot had addressed to her in a letter that has not come down to us. It is clear from the response, however, that the abbot had asked her to predict something about the state of a certain woman, and, apparently, also something about his own administrative situation. Hildegard answers that she can report only those things she sees in her visions, and does not ordinarily address the future lives of men and women. She does, however, instruct the abbot to rule his flock with discretion and mercy.

O gentle father, I am not accustomed to speak of the various events in the lives of men and what their future will be. For poor little untaught feminine form that I am, I can know only those things that I am taught in a true vision. Yet I will gladly include that woman you mentioned in my prayers, praying that the grace of God may rule in both her body and her soul, and that she may rejoice as a worthy heir of God.

I heard these words in a true vision of my soul: Beware, O man, lest you rise higher than your ability can reach, but in all cases embrace Discretion, sweet mother of the virtues, so that you may be guided by her in all things. Then you cannot fall. For a shepherd who holds the rod of correction but lacks discretion cannot please God, nor even be loved by his sheep. Rather, he is held in contempt.

Good father, rule your sheepfold with mercy, imitating God Who wishes mercy more than sacrifice [cf. Hos 6.6]. And take care that all your works are done in true humility. For it was through humility that the true Sun, that is, the Son of God, descended from the kingdom of the Father into the womb of the Virgin, so that you might live eternally with Him.

Hirsau

119

Hildegard to the Congregation of Monks

Before 1153

Hirsau was an old and famous monastery, having been founded in 830 A.D. It was a center of the Reform Movement, and was still flourishing in Hildegard's time. In this letter, Hildegard lashes out at the monks and the general evils of the world as a prelude to her plea for them to take a certain fugitive monk back into their community.

The Living Light says: O you who row your boat in the shipwreck of this world, why have you allowed the infirmities of the great dangers of fetid iniquity to debilitate you through your self-imposed blindness? Let no one disarm himself, for the world has entered an age of injustice, and has been cut off from the heights of glorious victory because of the storms of a black tyrant. Therefore, rise up and arm yourselves against the savage spears of the lust of the flesh and the spittle of the devil. Follow the footsteps of that One who carried His lost sheep back to the heights through the kiss of His humanity,[1] bearing it back in the arm of His power [cf. Matt 18.12f; Luke 15.4ff] through the sweet fragrance of His mercy [cf. Eph 5.2; Phil 4.18].

Therefore, mercifully take back that fugitive, for he laments his foolish behavior. Embrace him with full devotion, and, forgiving his guilt, lead him back into the stability of your community.

May God kindle His light in you, lest you be extinguished in the light of truth.

Note

1. Cf. St. Bernard on the opening words of Canticles. See Vol. 1, p. 142, n. 1.

120

The Congregation of Monks to Hildegard

1153–54

In distress of mind, the monks of Hirsau write Hildegard about the problems in their monastery—favoritism shown by their abbot, friction between the abbot and the prior, and (to them, most grievous) the disrepute that the community has fallen into among the laity because of these problems. They beseech Hildegard to intercede with God for them in their great need.

To the Lady Hildegard, chosen of God to build up the Church, a poor and fearful group of monks in Hirsau, with a prayer that she be so adorned with divine mercy that she will know how to console Christ's humble ones in their tribulation.

Blessed be the glory of the Lord, Who has looked down from His exalted throne in a wondrous and unheard-of way, for He wanted the great light of His grace to illumine the world through you. Therefore, all the sons of the Church rejoice, but we especially, who in our spiritual calling are steeped in a new light of exultation, although, at the same time, we endure great sorrow because of the failings of our community. We trust that you will be able to bring us the joy of divine consolation.

Please pay attention for a while to our problems, for we are in the utmost anxiety and great distress of mind. We would not, as God is our witness, detract from our abbot in any way. Still, we are forced to groan because he is so frequently deficient in paternal compassion toward us, while, at the same time, he is overly indulgent toward certain friends of his. Moreover, in all matters, he exercises unrestrained power recklessly. And if we grieve that our reputation is being torn apart by these insults and disgraces as a result of these matters, we weep even more for the lamentable discord that arose among us long ago and for the trouble that has recently arisen between that abbot of ours and our prior, which has brought our religious calling into great contempt among the seculars.

Therefore, uncertain what to do, we humbly pray that by your prayers the will of God will become a little clearer concerning these matters. But if we deserve to receive a letter of assurance from you about what is best to do in these matters, or what is pleasing to God, we will make it our goal, always, to pay back this kindness with our own prayers, for we know that this, our only possible course of action, will please you most, beloved lady.

120r

Hildegard to the Congregation of Monks

1153–54

Hildegard comforts the monks by assuring them that their monastery can regain its original luster, just as spring follows winter. The Living Eye, she assures them, knows the source of their difficulties, which she then lists in detail. Finally, she takes the opportunity—once again, as in her preceding letter—to beseech them to show mercy to those deserving of it.

The Serene Light says: O lamenting sheepfold adorned with the sign of obedience, be stable in your thoughts, and heave up your desires to the love of God. Take heed where prosperity lies—and where adversity. Consider the nature of the valleys. For a while they grow green and flourish from the dew of heaven and the warmth of the sun, but, with the change of the seasons, they dry up and fade away. Yet although they lose their beauty at the end of the season, I do not forget that they will flourish again.

So, too, I do not forget your monastery, for, through the grace of Wisdom, it retains the basic material of sanctity so that it can return to its pristine righteousness. Be, therefore, a bright, victorious sheepfold, trampling underfoot those vices which are troubling you in a difficult time. And do not blush to accuse yourselves of evil works, for God anoints all wounds, and, through penitence, cleanses.

The Living Eye has, nevertheless, taken note of the original cause of anguish that is troubling you, and knows too that it comes from the stubbornness of your higher prelates. For the sweetness of the anointing mother Mercy has been withheld from certain of the sheep among you, who were wrongly given penance out of all proportion to their fault. An unseasonable rain makes the land arid. Thus if a man sins and has no one to anoint him, he will flee and dry up, for the medicine administered to him is too harsh.

Now, dear sons, hear the voice of the Living Light. Reach out and grasp mercy, which comes not from you, but only from God; and so do not withhold it from those to whom it should be extended. Bring them back, therefore, and restore health to their souls.

121

Manegold to Hildegard

1156(?)

Manegold[1] was elected abbot of Hirsau on 25 March 1156 at the age of 60. Perhaps because of his advanced age, perhaps because of the general unrest in the monastery, he experienced many difficulties during the period of his administration. In his troubles, he turns to Hildegard for advice and assistance.

To his most holy lady and mother Hildegard, M., unworthy abbot of Hirsau, offers his prayers and obedience.

I have heard that there is a spring of water at Cyrene that flows with wine, just as among the Germans you, good mother, are a spring of waters rushing in and out, a bosom of spices, and, for visible things, sight to the eyes. For you, my lady, drink deep and pour forth into forms our minds can grasp, and, in practical matters, you are force and motion urging to the life of contemplation.[2 a] Therefore, I have long been impelled—and still am—to esteem, honor, and admire you, as well as to serve you and yours, and in all things, both in word and deed, to be yours and your sisters' in prayers and obedience to the extent that it is proper for me.

I beg you, my mother and lady, remember me in your most holy prayers, and love the one who most humbly loves you. May you take cognizance of the one who reveres you in Christ, and please, in God's name, write a letter back to me.

Notes

1. Despite Van Acker's unequivocal heading, there are problems with the attribution of this letter. The superscript in the MSS attributes it simply to the abbot of Hirsau, and the text of the letter supplies only the initial *M*. Van Acker's question mark after the date of 1156—the year of Manegold's election as abbot—is the only indication of the problem.

2. Our translation of this sentence represents our reasoned wrestling with an exceptionally obscure (perhaps corrupt?) text. See endnote for the Latin.

122

Hildegard to Manegold

Early 1156

It is difficult to determine the subject matter or the intent of this brief, enigmatic letter. The "vessel" (*ollam*) of the first sentence—as in the following letter—is apparently Hirsau itself.

The vessel I see now is much stronger than the one I saw earlier, and it will never fall or break. Your knowledge, which is the eye of your spirit, looks to God as a child looks to the father he loves. For you stand in the resplendent road, and you look to the east. A black cloud, however, is causing you to grow weary. Nevertheless, it will not destroy you.

A peaceful gift should have been given to you in the light, but those who are black in their ill will prevented it from being offered, and they gnash their teeth like a bear. I see that the spirit of your abbot[1] is somewhat less than courageous, but is still restless in the belly, breast, and brain.[a] After his death, I see that there will be a violent storm in that monastery—but, after that, a resplendent light.

Note

1. This sentence makes it clear that Manegold is not yet abbot. Therefore, if the preceding letter (where the correspondent is clearly identified as abbot) was indeed written by Manegold, it surely should be placed after this one.

123

Hildegard to the Abbot Manegold

1156–65

Hildegard seeks to comfort Manegold for the heavy burden of office that has fallen his lot. Then she advises him to keep a tight rein on his subordinates.

Sweetest father and brother in Christ's love, I saw a vessel bathed in such great brightness that I could scarcely tell whether it was a vessel at all. But I also see something somewhat bitter in taste, broken by great strife. Then, it is overtaken by a whirlwind. Still, it is predestined for God's reward.

Yet I saw that this heavy burden is not a sign of God's wrath.[1] Still, those with the character of bears and panthers will rush upon you, and you will be subjected to the poison of vipers [cf. Deut 32.33]. But the sword of God will cut them down, and you will arise among them like a noble knight.

Now I admonish you to rein in your subordinates, and not allow them to slander you. The True Light says to you, Why do you not strike those evil servants, who seize you like wolves, and lay secret ambushes for you like spiders. Keep a careful watch, for the morals of the people require it in this evil time.

O gentle father, the True Light does not reveal to me, poor little woman that I am, that you are to give up your office. Bear in mind that you are a human being on earth, and do not fear so greatly, because God does not always demand heavenly attributes from you.

Note

1. Probably in response to Manegold's own characterization of the new burden of office that has befallen him.

124

Hildegard to the Abbot Manegold

1156–65

Hildegard gives some general comments about the duties of office.

The Mysteries of God say: God wants the heavens to be upheld. Why do I say this? Heaven is that father who has the duty of providing sustenance for his sheepfold, for just as heaven reveals all the stars, so the father makes known to his sheepfold all the commandments of God. And the father should not become negligent and weary, lest his lord say to him: "Worthless servant" [Matt 18.32; Luke 19.22], why do you scatter my sheep [cf. John 10.12]? But let his lord say to him, "Well done, good servant" [Matt 25.21ff; Luke 19.17], and let him add, Mindful of me, you will lead the flocks to pasture, as long as the sheepfold does not say, "We will not have this man to reign over us" [Luke 19.14]. If the sheepfold says this, it is to be abandoned, just as Jesus left the unbelieving Jews behind.

As for you, O man, you will remain in God forever. Take care of all things faithfully.

125

Hildegard to the Abbot Manegold

1156–65

Hildegard seeks to comfort the abbot in his troubles, stressing to him that trouble and care are a necessary part of life.

Father, you supposed that there would be peace without anxiety in your days. Never will it happen! Such a thing is surely not possible in this age. The days that have been granted to you, however, are bright, for the night of incredulity, weariness, and horror is not overclouding your day. Bear in mind, therefore, that God chose David, and that David's kingdom did not perish with him, and that David did not lose his soul. For all that, however, he still endured great grief and toil. Still, God did not call David's days "dark." Bear in mind also that Elijah cried out, lamenting that almost no human being sees God in the dawn of faith. But remember too how God answered him [I Kings 19.9ff].[1] So it is in your case. For in your monastery there are many souls that shine like the bright dawn, because God loves them very much. This is the case in your own spirit. Adam was expelled from paradise [cf. Gen 3.24], and, thereafter, none of his children ever saw paradise again with physical eyes. But holy and blessed spirits make a paradise for themselves with the flowers of virtue, and they sigh for the things of heaven. And in the army of your people such heavenly things are a hundred, a thousand times more numerous than among others who are more changeable. But God said to the people of Israel that he would give them a land flowing with milk and honey [cf. Ex 3.8]. Nevertheless, the thunder and lightning of God's wrath still fell upon them.

Now, do not be incredulous about such things, for no one can have peace without anxiety in this present life, but only in life everlasting. But you are rather headstrong and dark in disposition. Still, there are some beautiful maidens knocking at the door of your mind, but you are not quick to answer them. Rather, you say, "I am so overburdened by trouble and worry that I cannot stay with you." The beautiful virtues then say to you, "We had no such trouble in forming you, and we have never failed to meet your needs. And so why do you answer us like this?"

Now gird yourself with holy Love, and she will, in purest humility, kiss your heart.

Note

1. The Lord's answer was that there were 7,000 left to Him whose knees had not bowed to Baal.

126

Hildegard to the Abbot Manegold

1156–65

A brief letter seeking to lift the abbot's mind from earthly worry to more spiritual concerns.

O father in your calling and brother in the love of God, eradicate the uneasiness of your mind from the eye of your heart, and remove every trace of sadness from yourself and your flock. Now is a time of war against the morals of mankind, for they have neither discipline nor consciousness of the fear of the Lord. As for you, however, do not be afraid because you are the vessel of the fiery Spirit. Sometimes you endure tribulation and affliction, but do not be afraid, because the Son of God endured the same things.

Now, live forever and the Holy Spirit will not abandon you.

127

Hildegard to the Abbot Manegold

1156–65

Another brief letter of praise and exhortation.

In the presence of God, you are like the smoke of myrrh and incense [cf. Cant 3.6], and, therefore, Mt. Sion asks that you be food in the house of Jacob [cf. Gen 42.1]. But if anyone cuts down the pillar that supports the entire house, he overthrows the house. Look out the seven windows, and consider what direction the hawk comes from, but take care that he does not carry you off.

Feed your sheep [cf. John 21.17] with mild chastisement, for the day of your salvation has not yet passed, and you will not yet become ashes. Also, be the mirror of life in the eyes of the dove.

128

Hildegard to the Abbot Manegold

1156–65

Hildegard senses that something is amiss with the abbot and the monastery, and she urges him to assert himself.

O father and gentle brother, I see that there is some matter that is causing you to become weary and forgetful. I see also that the fire is not blazing brightly in either your spirit or in your sheepfold. But you say to yourself, "I cannot stand against them." And so you settle your mind as if you were asleep.

But it cannot rest there. For the day of salvation shines forth in you because God helps you in everything you have undertaken with His guidance. For He brought forth all creatures, and He named them in Himself. Now, may He Who will gather all things unto Himself on the last day make the fire in you blaze brightly.

129

Hildegard to the Abbot Manegold

1156–65

Hildegard once again touches on the problems in the monastery—all of which seem to stem from Manegold's mild and gentle manner of governance.

O loving father, you are a son of the toils of this age, but still God draws you to Himself. The present age is a time of tribulation and grief, a time, among the sons of men, of going astray. And we, who are supposed to be spiritual people, have been overshadowed by the deceptions of the spirits of the air. And so even in your community I see malignity like lead. Still, God's light is with you.

Wisdom says to you: Withdraw and retire a short while and a short distance from your sons. Still, do not cast aside the rod of your authority, but hold it in your hand, just as a father sometimes withdraws from his son when that son has brought disgrace upon him. But when the son falters, he calls his father back, and begs him for forgiveness [cf. Luke 15.11ff].

This is now your situation. For your sons will be greatly embarrassed by the prelates and the other members of the community, who say to them that they refused to tolerate a good and upright man as their superior. Thus your sons, embarrassed and humbled, will call you back, beating their breasts, and your administrative relationship with them will be a lot better than before. This is one of the snares that He predicted to you, but, all the same, God will not abandon you.

Now, regain your strength and become a stalwart knight, and God will assist you.

130

Hildegard to the Abbot Manegold

1156–65

This obscure message, as Hildegard herself calls it, breaks off before it is finished.

In my vision your community is like a tower with two windows. One of these windows has the radiant splendor of the dawn, although it is overshadowed by a cloud. The other is as bright as daylight. Yet from its base up to the very middle, that tower is exceedingly black; and this blackness seeks to cover over those two windows. But it will be incapable of affecting them. Also, I see that your spirit is like that kind of day when the sun shines in the morning, although the day itself is full of storms. Still, those storms are not very dangerous, and from time to time the sun shines through them.

I am giving you this obscure message at this time, but, later, when God wills it, . . .[1]

Note

1. The letter breaks off at this point in the MS.

131

Hildegard to the Abbot Manegold

1156–65

Hildegard gives an allegorical account of the monastery, and answers specific questions that Manegold had directed to her about particular individuals.

I looked to Wisdom, and I heard and saw these words: There was a tree in Lebanon, and winter, as usual, came upon it. It is winter's nature to cause all things to wither and lose their moisture, but the root of that tree was so firmly planted in the ground that the winter was not able to destroy it. Still, the trunk of the tree was damaged somewhat by the weather. Its leaves, however, did not lose their viridity, and did not fall.

Now, father, understand that this imagery is directed to you. The monastery you ask about is like a valley set next to a field that is only slightly warm and fertile when the seed is planted, but which is yet magnificent in the part where the sun shines frequently. And the grace of God does not despise it, for it is caught up in the treadle winepress[1] that constantly churns until the people are cleansed from their present error. And the people will become better after not too long a time.

Also, concerning that soul you asked about, it now has great merit among the saints, but, earlier, it made a serious error in judgment, which it did not recognize as such. And so in attempting to justify itself, it sought out things that were none of its business. For this reason it suffered heavy punishments. When human beings who are predestined for sanctity do not do the good works they know and understand through divine grace, God does not show the signs of his saints to them.

The death of that individual about whom you asked is not yet at hand. Moreover, your own death is also not immediately imminent. And that person you ask about had a generosity that ascended to God, and God loved him.

These are the words of Wisdom that I, poor little woman that I am, have written to you. Now I admonish you not to greatly fear the gloom that appears on the trunk of that tree I mentioned earlier, the gloom that results from the filthy, vile character of human instability. And do not withdraw from your salutary way of life, nor from your good works. Then you will live forever, and your heavenly Father will receive you in joy.

Note

1. Cf. Isaiah 63.2–3: "Why then is thy apparel red, and thy garments like theirs that tread in the winepress? I have trodden the winepress alone, and of the Gentiles there is not a man with me; I have trampled on them in my indignation, and have trodden them down in my wrath, and their blood is sprinkled upon my garments, and I have stained all my apparel." For the Middle Ages, this verse is a figure of the crucifixion, and therefore of redemption.

132

Hildegard to the Abbot Manegold

1156–65

Hildegard advises Manegold to be more balanced in his governance, taking the good with the bad.

Oh, person, flee the storms and vices that incline to the vicissitudes of squalid morals, and do not regard the captain who steers his ship as a mere servant who is sometimes cherished and sometimes ignored. This is the way you look upon your garden: you rejoice when prosperity shines on it like the sun, and you grow angry when a cloud covers it over with excessive disturbance. But have patience in each instance, until God assists you.

Your worry was certainly understandable, for there was clearly too much heedless conviviality there, though I do not see this resulting in disastrous ship-wreck. And I do not see your monastery being totally disrupted. But let the Fiery Illuminator enkindle your heart.

133

Hildegard to the Abbot Manegold

1156–65

The details of this letter are quite enigmatic, though the imagery is familiar. Once again, Hildegard's point seems to be that Manegold should rule his community with more authority.

Loving father and beloved brother, the grace of God looks upon you with wide-open eyes. Yet your mind is caught up in a whirlwind, for you endure new losses over and again. Still, in the midst of this whirlwind, your mind shines like the dawn and sees a number of young men among your congregation, some of whom are black and filthy, but some a little purer. Nevertheless, in some sense, they are all like the whirlwind, and are of one mind. But, still, most of those in your congregation are bright as stars, and the others are like the dawn.

Therefore, sweet father, hold the iron rod in your hand vigorously [cf. Ps 2.9], and, with God's help, surrounded by the heavenly host, rule them as best you can. Then the grace of God will never desert you. Live forever.

134

Hildegard to the Abbot Manegold

1156–65

A brief letter of reiterated praise.

My father and the pastor chosen by God to rule over the blazing flock of your sheepfold, hear. I see you in a bright light and your community as a glowing radiance, as I told you before.

Now live, and be perfect [cf. Matt 5.48] in the viridity of the virtues of God.

135

Hildegard to Abbot Manegold(?)

1156–65

In this allegorical letter, Hildegard recommends patience to the abbot so that he might realize his full potential.

In your works and morals I see you as a tree that has great viridity in its leaves. One branch, however, is drying up. And the elements say: We have come to you on account of the blend of your viridity, but storms injure us. These storms are the doubts and the moral vacillation, which, on account of your tribulations, cause you to go in circles, like a mill wheel.

But let it not be so. Look to the farm land, which is tilled and plowed and fertilized so that it might bring forth much fruit. This is Patience, which produces humidity and viridity in all good works. Patience's house is harsh and bitter, but it gives great rewards and opens the gate of the heavenly kingdom.

And so draw Patience to you, and diligently avoid the jacinth and the beryl, which do not flash with brilliance; and keep yourself from those flowers that lack the viridity of virtues and therefore quickly wither, for these love you not for the love of penitence but for the discord of disobedience.

That monastery in which you live is pleasing to God. Therefore, embrace and kiss Patience, and do not put her aside, for you have the potential to wash clean the wounds of men, and thereby to set up a ladder into heaven. And you will live forever.

136

Hildegard to the
Abbot Manegold(?)

1156–65(?)

This brief letter is in answer to a query from the abbot about the relations between some unnamed man and woman.

Regarding the subject you ask me about: Victory does not drink deep of lust in
this matter. But, still, the bond of flesh, which you seek to know about, is stronger in that man than in the woman. Yet I would not want to see that sinful deed
consummated. But in you I see a whirlwind of heat that, having spent itself, will
disappear harmlessly.

Hördt

137

Hildegard to the Canon Lemphrid

1153–54

In answer to the canon, who had apparently asked her advice about changing
communities, Hildegard gives her usual advice: stay where you are; the pastures
only look greener over there.

He Who poured the good and sweet intelligence into mankind says these things:
Faithful men have the sweet odor of the gifts of the Holy Spirit. So in whatever
community holiness is, there man can be restored to life in the shipwreck of this
world. Therefore, O worthy knight of Christ, seek the salvation of your soul in
the community where you are, where the living fountain pours a sweet flood into
your soul, because those foreign monasteries that you have so firmly fixed in
your mind offer no security for you. Therefore, stay in your place, and, there,
love the first gift given to you from above [cf. James 1.17], when your soul was
renewed in righteousness. For it is not conducive to the safety of your soul to
seek out a different place. But flee this desire for change, lest your mind be confounded by fear.

   Now, be such that you become the friend of God, and do not flee the cer-
emonies of God [cf. Deut 8.11]. And God will save you.

138

A Provost to Hildegard

About 1160

The provost writes with lavish praise to Hildegard, thanking her for braving the difficulties and visiting his monastery, not just once but twice.

To Hildegard, his most blessed lady and, if he dares to say it, beloved mother, H., provost in Hördt (although unworthy) and your devoted servant, saintly lady, joins all his brothers in offering submission, prayer, and devoted service.

How can we ever sufficiently repay you, saintly lady and mother? For you, pious lady, would not let the great weakness of your body prevent you from visiting our monastery, nor did you, in the exceptional sweetness of your heart, shudder at the difficulties of the journey. Moreover, you even gladdened us with a second visit! The grace of the Holy Spirit is not slow to recognize great efforts.

Accordingly, you, beloved and foreordained bride of the mighty King, you who are worthy, by the mercy of the Bridegroom, to hear the proclamation of special praise—for He said, "Behold thou art fair, O my love, behold thou are fair, thy eyes are as those of doves" [Cant 1.14]—you, I say, are crowned with variegated garlands of virtues. You give forth a pleasing fragrance "as the lily among thorns" [Cant 2.2], for you are a good and pleasing aroma of Christ [cf. II Cor 2.15] among the daughters of Jerusalem. You are like a star of heaven and of sanctity amid the darkness of this world, and you bring the consolation of hope to us sinners by bringing us the joy of your maternal visit so frequently. For we are like the publican of the Gospel, not daring to lift our eyes to heaven [cf. Luke 18.13]. Yet we are consoled through the organ of your voice, and made worthy to hear the voice of the Lord Christ, Who dwells in you.

Therefore, we genuflect to Christ the Lord, and humbly give thanks that He deigns to console us, unworthy as we are, through you. With humble prayer, we beseech also, our lady and mother, that you pour forth your prayers for us poor sinners to Him Who has brought you into the chamber of His mysteries. So by the intercession of your merits, He may mercifully deign to rescue us from our sins and enemies, and from the grievous shipwreck of this world, bringing us through, with you, to the harbor of eternal blessing and security.

May the Lord go before you in the blessing of delight [cf. Ps 20.4], and may the Father of all consolation hear you praying for us. In all humility, we greet, through you, the convent of saintly ladies, who faithfully serve our Lord Jesus Christ with you and under your guidance, and we humbly commend ourselves to their prayers. With all devotion we desire you to write back to us.

139

An Abbot to Hildegard

Before 1173

The abbot complains that he has written Hildegard over and over again, but has never received a response. He begs for a letter and for her prayers.

To his lady and mistress, Hildegard, Brother N. in Ilbenstadt, helpless and poor, along with the flock entrusted to him, with a prayer that she be admitted to the eternal company of the virgins.

I have often importuned you with many letters, and I have petitioned you repeatedly, but I have never been able to get you to respond with a letter as you promised. Can it be—no, surely, that is not the case!—that my low birth and humble position has delayed your response, or perhaps—and this is more credible—my merits have had no weight with you? The Apostle says, "to the wise and to the unwise, I am a debtor" [Rom 1.14], and Truth itself says, "Suffer the little children to come unto me" [Mark 10.14]. Mother, the very idea that you show any partiality just cannot be so!

Now then, hear this wretch just once as I cry out to you [cf. Ps 26.7; 140.1], and pray our Lord on my behalf that He may deign to relieve me, the poor servant who trusts in Him, for I am surrounded by all manner of tribulations and distress.

140

A Prioress to Hildegard

Before 1173

The prioress asks for Hildegard's prayers that she might be assisted in the heavy duties of her administrative office.

To Hildegard, her mistress, N., unworthy overseer of the servants of Christ in Ilbenstadt, with a prayer that she attain to that loftiest, most sublime Good through that celestial gift which she has tasted to the full [cf. Heb 6.4].

Blessed be Jesus Christ Whose good odor unto God you are in every place [cf. II Cor 2.14–15], for not merely the fragrance of balsam but the very substance itself of the sacred unguent has flowed into you, and its fragrant scent has made your name sweet to the hearts and ears of all, so that everyone everywhere commends the signs of your humility and kindliness, and because of you, they "glorify your Father who is in heaven" [Matt 5.16].

Therefore, blessed mother, forgive me, and bear with my folly [cf. II Cor 11.1], nay, rather, my great foolishness, so that I may open up the grief of my heart to you. And when you have heard, console, I beseech, your humble servant. For I bear an intolerable burden, since it is my duty to correct the waywardness of my sisters—and this despite the fact that I can scarce fight off the dangers that surround me on every side.

When, therefore, you have gone forth to see King Solomon in his glory [cf. Cant 3.11], bear in mind those things I have asked of you with my whole heart.

Farewell.

140r

Hildegard to the Prioress

Before 1173

Hildegard offers consolation to the prioress, but, once again, as in previous letters, feels it necessary to advise against excessive flagellation of the body.

O daughter of God, as long as you have the ability, labor among the daughters of God, and let your labor cry out and pray to God. But, still, sigh in fear to God, and observe your oath.

When a person labors in the caverns of God's justice and in the narrow way, but still acknowledges the fall of Adam, and seeks the scourges of penitence for it, there is no doubt that, after the scourges of penitence, the gate of heaven will open for him.

A sudden premonition of death will not harm the one who afflicts the field of the body with proper discretion, for the symphony of the Holy Spirit and the joyous life will receive her. But one should beware lest she kill her body through excessive afflictions. Let her, rather, conquer sin through reasonable means.

Daughter, remember that you do not have the ability to create a person. Therefore, meekly pray God to give you a better life. For this is more acceptable to God than to beseech Him with too much sadness. May God make you the temple of life.

Indersdorf

141

Hildegard to the Provost Richard

Before 1170

Hildegard gives advice to the provost in the form of two allegorical images.

He Who Is [cf. Ex 3.14; Apoc 1.4] showed these things to me, saying: Say to that man, O man, in my sight, you are like a wooden tabernacle built by hand. And at the door of this building, two images are knocking. The one, filled with eyes [cf. Ezech 1.18], has black hair, and her name is Fear of the Lord. And she says to you: I wish to sanctify you with sacrifices. Therefore, yield to me, and I will enter your chamber, and I will bring forth a sweet odor of musk and spices in you. O knight, do not be slow to run with your sheepfold, and lead it to righteousness under the care of the Living Eye.

The other image is like a trumpet shining in a white cloud, and she wears a man's crown on her head, and her name is Fortitude. And she says the following to you: Ha, why do you sleep in your knowledge like a country bumpkin who gladly keeps still and will not fight with sword and spear in armor and helmet? Therefore, sound forth like a trumpet amidst many waters, and do not keep quiet, and my companions and I will help you. Stand on the wall of the temple, and do not be afraid of the violent winds, but know that you are a column in the palace of the King. Also, flee the double tongue, which is the wound of the soul, but speak truthfully everywhere, like the sun. And we will gladly make our habitation in you.

142

A Certain Provost to Hildegard

Before 1173

The provost gives thanks that, in these times, God has instilled a feminine breast with virile strength. Cutting his letter short because he knows that Hildegard is busy, he asks simply for her consoling prayers.

N., by the grace of God called provost in Indersdorf, to the sister Hildegard, mistress at Mount St. Rupert, may she abound in the spirit of fortitude.

The holiness of your religious belief has influenced many people, especially those in religious orders, and has filled them with the sweetness of your holy love. Therefore, for the grace divinely bestowed on you, we return thanks to the high Giver of all good things, Who has instilled a feminine breast with virile strength, not only to turn aside sin and shame but also to provide necessary counsel and help for the needy.

But because we know that you are busy, we do not dare to speak at length. We ask, therefore, that you mercifully offer the help of your consolation to us.

Justusberg

143

Hildegard to an Abbot

Before 1170

Hildegard advises the abbot to use moderation with his flock.

He Who gives gifts to givers and a track to runners says: Do not hinder your sheep from taking the right paths. What does this mean? Impose lighter burdens on those who cannot sustain the heavy labors of the journey. For a boy cannot be equal to a young man, nor a young man to an old one, nor can an old man be equated to any of them. Therefore, assign this man[1] a task that he can accomplish. May God so infuse your soul with this stability that you may avoid senseless fluctuations.

Note

1. Apparently in answer to the abbot's question about this person.

Kaisheim

144

The Abbot Conrad to Hildegard

1153

The abbot asks why Hildegard is so slow in answering his request. Also, as so frequently in these letters, he asks whether it would be acceptable to God if he resigned his administrative office.

Conrad, abbot of Kaisheim (although unworthy), to the holy lady Hildegard, prelate in the cloister of St. Rupert in Bingen, with devoted prayers and humble submission.

From the first time that I heard of your splendid virtues and the special gift bequeathed to you by God, holy mother, I loved you with the whole affection of my mind, although I was not known to you personally. I rejoice with you in your glory, because you have merited to find the Beloved Whom your soul sought, and you refuse to wander after the flocks of your companions [cf. Cant 1.6], for He Who feeds among the lilies [cf. Cant 4.5] has rested in your tabernacle [cf. Ecclus 24.12], and has filled your garden with a myriad of delights.

Beloved lady, since you are, as it were, a river springing from the fountain of Goodness, pouring forth your benevolence on all who desire to know and hear the great things of God [cf. Ex 14.13] through you, I marvel why you close up the bowels of mercy to me [cf. I John 3.17], a humble soul laboring in great anxiety of heart, and why you are so slow to send me the little gift that I desire more out of love than out of presumption.

I beseech you with full devotion, therefore, to intercede for me to the Bridegroom Who rests in the cubicle of your heart and gladly inclines the ear of His mercy to all your petitions. I ask also that you ask Him to make clear to you whether it would be best for me to lay aside my burden of pastoral care, for I am sorely oppressed by my duties, and am indeed wasting away. Or should I continue to bear my burden? If I get a response from you, I will know that He has heard you.

Farewell, lady dear to God.

144r

Hildegard to the Abbot Conrad

1153

Hildegard admonishes the abbot against sin, specifically the sin of homosexuality, and advises penitence.

The piercing Light sees and says: O man, you are pale and sickly because your mind has doubts, as if you lack the strength to stand. Why do I say this? I see your works, for they pertain to me. But you know how rebels think. Why, therefore, when you are before my altar, do you blush to look upon my sanctuary, and fail to adorn it like a temple endowed with living eyes?

O, what a burden for a good shepherd to lift his lambs up onto his shoulders [John 10.11ff; Luke 15.5]! When his sheep do not walk in the straight path, the gentle shepherd should lift them up through the solicitude of his soul, and should correct and anoint them, and teach them good works. For just as the hand works in conjunction with the arm, and the arm with the shoulder, so should the shepherd give examples to his sheep with the hand of good works, extend medicinal relief with the arm of assistance, and offer dissolution of sins through the bond of the cross, as with a mighty shoulder. For, truly, penitents should receive forgiveness for their sins. The devil, indeed, spews forth the might of his heart and the taste of his throat and the blazing flame of his serpentine mouth.

O man, listen to the wail of grief that is poured forth at the commission of that sin which is the contagion of the flesh that sullies the beautiful form of the human being. O virginity, weep at the loss of your primal sanctity! For the hand of the Great Artisan formed you, and set you in a garden of delight. But a flaming mind deceived mankind in the vain desire for its own will through pride and the sinful counsel of the deceiver. Thus mankind was cast out through the taste of disobedience. And so his belly went astray, even though, before, his side had been pierced by that most holy gift. But now his thigh is polluted with oozing poison. Thus man touched the taste of the serpent's throat when it burned in his poisoned veins. Then, later, he committed fornication in his viperish desire, which is the burning flame from the mouth of the devil. It was disobedience that produced this food. And because God made a person from a rib [Gen 2.22], the devil gave man the idea of homicide, so that he turned all His works aside, and brought about the unveiling of burning sin through the might of his heart.

O man, how great are the sins that you commit in imitation of the ancient destroyer. How is this so? The wicked accuser was cast behind [cf. Apoc 12.10] and cut off from all bliss. And because he was cast behind, he thought in the malignity of his heart that he might, in turn, lead mankind into that sin that was against his nature. Thus man abandons the form of the rib, and so, there, in that change, the formation of mankind perishes when he spills his seed.[a] Therefore, let the earth mourn, let the heavens tremble at these crimes. For when a man sins through the taste of his own work, though without having cast aside the creature formed from a rib, he still feels, at least to some little degree, that he is God's creation. But those crimes that take place behind are not a part of any creation, so that the man who commits them does not see himself as a man. O man, why do you reject the fact that you are God's creation. Ach, ach, O man, God formed you zealously, but you are entangled in many crimes. But, still, God is leading you back to him through His Son. Therefore, rise up through penitence and run to Me quickly.

Now, be a stalwart knight, arm yourself, go forth into the broad ways, and bring back viridity to the dry fields. Gird up the loins of those in your care, and force yourself to do good works. In this way, your heart may be illuminated by the sun, and you yourself will not grow weary on the straight path, fighting against your own self. Therefore, do not lay down your pastoral office, but let the perfumer,[1] who has a fragrant and well-watered garden [Is 58.11; Jer 31.12], see to it that His garden will bring forth good fruit that does not wither.

Note

1. *Pigmentarius*, Hildegard's usual term for prelates of the Church. See Introduction, Vol. 1, p. 8.

145

Hildegard to the Abbot Conrad

1153–65

Hildegard advises the abbot to put all his energies into caring for his flock, but that if he sees only flaws there, to give up his office.

Since your eye has sight and your knowledge is watchful, why do you sleep as if wearied by the obligation of looking after your sheepfold? Encircle them, therefore, and take good care of them, so that you do not, to your loss, hide your talent [cf. Matt 25.14ff]. For it is not profitable for you to cast aside the obligation by which you are bound while you have in your care two eyes, or even one, or any semblance of life. But if you see no eye of life among your subordinates, but see only their limping,[1] then flee and cast your office aside.

Note

1. Is Hildegard remembering here Matthew 18.8–9? All the individual elements are here—the casting aside, the limping, one eye, two eyes, etc.—although associated differently.

Kappenberg

146

A Prelate to Hildegard

1159–73

Fearful of coming to Hildegard in person, the writer sends a messenger to inquire about the present state of the Church.

To his revered lady, virgin, and bride of Christ, Hildegard, Brother N., prelate of the servants of God in Kappenberg, with a prayer that she attain the reward and everlasting crown of holy virginity and the religious life.

The fame of your devotion and your way of life, approved of God, has spread throughout the Church, and delights many people more than the fragrance of balsam and other spices. Even we in our cells, in the very caverns under the earth, as it were, have at last begun to get a whiff of it. Thus I, least of all men [cf. I Cor 15.9], desired to follow that fragrance, and so I decided to come to you. But impeded by the great storms and tempests that now shake the entire Church, and fearful of events and afraid for my person, I was detained and could not come.

Yet, still, I ask in the name of Christ, Who dwells within you [cf. Rom 8.9ff], that you listen to our beloved brother, the bearer of this letter, as if I were there in person. I sent him to you to consult the Spirit of God, Who dwells within you, about the present condition of our Church. Do not disdain to impart to us what comes of God, of love, of devotion, so that, consoled, we may breathe again through Him, Who consoles so many through you.

Sweet lady, we do not wish to exasperate you[1] with our uncouth language, but we earnestly implore you to give the present messenger, our brother, some indications, and to respond in a few words on the margin of this piece of paper.[a]

Farewell, in Christ's name, to you and all those entrusted to you by Christ. And, in His name, remember me to Him.

Note

1. The translation here does not adequately convey the wordplay that the writer indulges in. Translated literally, this part of the sentence would read, "we do not wish to bitter your sweetness . . ."

146r

Hildegard to the Prelate

1159–73

Hildegard admonishes the prelate to put aside all fears and doubts, and shoulder the responsibilities of his office, as God wishes.

I see that there is darkness in some part of you. Why do I say this? Because your heart is bound up in that sadness which is encircled by doubt, like a millstone, questioning, What is my purpose? What sort of purpose do I have?

Now, you should take note of the day which arises in the morning with a bright dawn, but which, afterward, is racked by shifting storms. Such is your life. For if you always had prosperity, you would be like the crab that cannot walk straight. This is the reason that God allows you to be worn down, for the father strikes the son whom he loves with a rod in this way [cf. Prov 13.24].

"Truth is sprung out of the earth: and justice hath looked down from heaven" [Ps 84.12]. Here is the meaning of this passage: God proves all truth through man, whom he formed from the slime of the earth. Hard and rocky farmland is plowed with great difficulty, but that which is good and yielding is cultivated with joy. Yet God is true in each: He breaks the hard and bitter man with labor, but He embraces the kind and compassionate man, the one who performs all good works gladly, with the kiss of love. The grace of God suffuses all things through the sun of justice [cf. Mal 4.2], both the harsh and the benevolent, and it hears all those who cry out to Him with the sighs of their hearts in order to know Him. For just as God established the sun to give light to the whole earth and to dispel darkness, so through His grace does He reject harshness so that He will not respond to the hard-hearted man who calls out to Him.

So do not fear those things that torment you, for I do not see that your monastery will be destroyed. God wishes you to fulfill the obligation of your burden. And so gather to you those sheep who run willingly to you, and, mercifully, tolerate those who will not, until they call out to you. And so, live forever!

Kaufungen

147

An Abbess to Hildegard

Before 1173

The abbess writes praising Hildegard for her prophetic gifts, and asks for a letter of consolation from her.

To the lady and sister Hildegard, N., a sinner, and abbess (in name only) in Kaufungen, with a prayer that she not hide the light of her knowledge under a bushel [cf. Matt 5.15; Mark 4.21; Luke 11.33].

Forestalled by the unexpected haste of this messenger, I was unable to write anything very polished to you, lady and mother, but could only manage very common language as to a beloved sister. So please receive it as such. It is widely reported that that flying scroll which was given to the prophet to eat [cf. Ezech 3.1ff; Zach 5.1f] now rests in your mouth, because of your wisdom. Oh, how precious is that treasure! Beware, therefore, not to foolishly gulp it down. But "run about, make haste, stir up" [Prov 6.3] the Church, or rather the leaders of the Church, to whom it is said as it was to Peter: Simon, "could you not watch one hour with me" [Matt 26.40]. We rejoice and tremble because you have seen the rod that keeps watch from the north over iniquity [cf. Jer 1.11ff]. Therefore, we desire to receive a letter of consolation from you.

Farewell in Christ. Remember me whenever you call upon Him so that I may merit to partake of the grace He has bestowed upon you.

147r

Hildegard to the Abbess

Before 1173

Hildegard advises the abbess to live virtuously and to continue in her zeal for good works, for her "days are not long."

In the Spirit, I tell you truthfully: Guard your spirit so that it will not be polluted with iniquity. Also, gird your body with the justice of God. Do this before the day of your death, because afterward there is no remedy, save what you find through God's grace and through the ornament of your works.

The hawk, your enemy, is circling around you, seeking to wound your spirit. Guard yourself from him by your zeal for good works and abstinence from sin, because your days are not long. Therefore, let the Holy Spirit kindle His fire in you, so that you will remember these words.

And so, again, I will tell you a parable: the trees wither in the winter, but in the summer they blossom luxuriantly. Now, in your spirit consider how long you have wandered astray in the winter of the spiritual life. And so run quickly to the viridity of the Holy Spirit, which is summer, by changing your morals. In this way, bring forth flowers of virtue, and gather your sheaves [cf. Ps 128.7] as fast as you can. Therefore, keep yourself from sin, for I tell you in truth that if you seek God's grace, it will not flee from you.

Kempten

148

An Abbot to Hildegard

About 1166 (?)

The abbot praises Hildegard for the gifts God has bestowed upon her, and asks her to communicate any revelation God has revealed to her about him or his church.

To Hildegard, bride and servant of Christ, acceptable to both God and man [cf. Tob 14.17], H., abbot, in name only, of the church at Kempten, sending his devoted service and continual prayer.

Blessed be God, Whose "Spirit breatheth where he will" [John 3.8], for He has so frequently filled and enriched the chambers of your heart with the delights of the heavenly music that he has made you an object of veneration and wonder to men and women alike. And so already, already, I say, the reputation of your sanctity has spread far and wide. Everyone can easily see that He that is mighty has done great things for you [cf. Luke 1.48f], and it is clear that He regards you as His humble handmaiden [cf. Luke 1.48f], for He takes care to disclose unheard-of things to you. Now, the heavenly King has taken you, His bride, nay rather His daughter, by the hand, and, by His will, He has brought you into His chamber [cf. Cant 2.4], and, there, leaning on your Beloved [cf. Cant 8.5], you have merited to hear His secrets, and to utter them gloriously to mortals. This is fitting, saintly lady, for, as it has been reported to us, you have heard this command from the very cradle: "Hearken, O daughter, and see" [Ps 44.11], etc. As for us, "What great things have we heard and known" [Ps 77.3], and again, "As we have heard, so have we seen" [Ps 47.9].

Therefore, with all our prayers we beseech Him to bring to perfection the mighty work He has begun in you [cf. Phil 1.6]. We also pray you to offer supplication for us for our sins, and we humbly beseech you to impart to us some revelation from heaven about ourselves and our church.

148r

Hildegard to the Abbot

About 1166(?)

A longish letter warning the abbot against the sin of doubt.

O man, "Decline from evil and do good" [Ps 36.27], because it is a natural inclination for a human being to go astray in his mind, and, besides, he sets the number one thousand[1] as his goal, which he can never achieve. Just so was it that Adam did not look at what he was doing when he desired to be like God, and did not consider it sinful to envy the honor and power of God.

O son of God, through faith dispel every storm. For Adam rejoiced to think that he was like to God in honor and power, which was great vanity, and yet he knew Him to be God. This is possible for every human being: to know that he has a God, whom he credits as his creator and liberator. And for this reason, flee to God, for, in faith, you know that He is God, as it is written: "All the nations thou hast made shall come and adore before thee, O Lord: and they shall glorify thy name" [Ps 85.9]. Here is the meaning of this verse: Man, who was made with the other creatures, knows that he has a God, and that, therefore, he should be faithful, and should zealously seek God, worship Him, and glorify His name. Therefore, let every man decline from that evil of doubting that there is a God Who created him. Rather, let him love the One Who created and liberated him, and in Him let him love his neighbor, who has done him a kindness [cf. Mark

12.30f], and not imitate the devil, who hated his creator, even though He had given him many good things.

By not loving God, the devil did not know Him, and, therefore, he does not seek liberation from Him. But he knows that God is mightier than he is. Adam, however, did not reject God out of hatred, but he vainly sought to be like Him. And so the devil did not find the same hatred for God in Adam that he himself has, but he deceived him, nevertheless, by his cunning. Thus he compassed Adam with a thousand machinations, seeking to find one who might doubt God. Just so the devil keeps man from good with a thousand machinations spewed from his belly,[a] so that when a person sighs to do good, he pierces him with his shafts; and when he desires to embrace God with his whole heart in love, he subjects him to poisonous tribulations, seeking to pervert good work before God. And when a person seeks the viridity of virtue, the devil tells him that he does not know what he is doing, and he teaches him that he can set his own law for himself.

The fight is against just this kind of thing, as it is written: "A thousand bucklers hang upon it, all the armour of valiant men" [Cant 4.4]. The meaning of that verse is this: The first shield is confession of sins, something not found in the Old Law, for the Old Law was blind. Penitence follows the confession of sins, as the good shepherd commands, and this is the covering of the nakedness of the Old Law. Thus "as the tower of David" [Cant 4.4], his neck was exalted in the humanity of the Savior, from which hangs "all the armour of valiant men" [Cant 4.4], that is, those who live well in accordance with the teaching of the law, the chaste and the virgins who "hang" from that tower. The Old Law foreshadowed all these things, and Christ revealed them through Himself by His incarnation, and after His ascension He will fulfill them through His disciples and all those who come after them until the last day. That is, they are the "thousand bucklers" which "hang upon it," with which the battle is waged against the ancient serpent, who seduced all mankind in the first man [cf. Apoc 12.9]. These stand as a defense, so that a man may defend himself when in the midst of his enemies, and fight them everywhere so that he will not be killed, just as the bridegroom says to the bride in Canticles: "My head is full of dew, and my locks of the drops of the nights" [Cant 5.2]. Here is the sense of this verse: like hairs on the head, mortal man is joined to Jesus Christ, the head of all [cf. Eph 4.15], but they are full of transgressions and sins because of man's delight in the flesh. But the Church regenerates and purifies these from the unclean stench and filth of sin by penitence and confession, just as hair is cleansed from dew and drops, and as dust is shaken out and cleansed from wool.

Go and do likewise, dear son of God, because you will live forever and will be a precious stone in the heavenly Jerusalem [cf. Apoc 21.10f]. This is why you need to be polished vigorously.

Note

1. That is, perfection, according to medieval number symbolism.

Kirchheim-Bolanden

149

Werner to Hildegard

1170

During one of her preaching tours, Hildegard made a stop at Kirchheim. In this
letter, the priest Werner requests a copy of the sermon preached there.

To Hildegard, immaculate in body and mind, and dedicated to God from the
cradle, Werner of Kirchheim and all his brothers who serve God, however un-
worthily, under the patronage of the blessed N., with a prayer that, by the example of Deborah, she crush the forces of the enemy with God as her guide [cf.
Judges 4.4–14; 5.1ff].

The fragrance of your virtues has spread widely over the earth, because the
grace of the Holy Spirit has illumined your pure heart not only to do good, but
also to prophesy things to come, and to contemplate heavenly matters.[a] And so
we have considered it worthy (although we are unworthy) to entrust ourselves
to you in the name of brotherhood, saintly lady. And, assuredly, because we are
the least of Christ's servants—though we will be, as we faithfully believe, members of Christ's body, along with you—we beseech you to fulfill whatever we
ask you in His name, whenever you can do so.

Mother and bride of the Lamb, kindly remember us abundantly in your
prayers. As for us, be assured that we will constantly make mention of you in
our prayers, for what worth they are before God.

We presume to put one further petition to you: We pray you to put into
writing those words you spoke through the guidance of the Holy Spirit to us and
to the many others present at Kircheim during your visit. Please send us this
sermon about the priests' negligence of the divine service so that we may keep it
ever before our eyes, lest we forget. For we gape after earthly and secular matters more than we should, and so many times carelessly cast transitory words
into the wind.

Farewell, beloved mother.

149r

Hildegard to Werner

1170

Under an allegorical image Hildegard condemns the sins and corruption of Church officials.

In the year 1170 lying for a long time in my sickbed, fully awake in body and soul, I saw an exceedingly beautiful image of a woman. She was so delightful and so beautiful that the mind of man could never comprehend it, and in stature she reached from the earth to the heavens. Her face shone with great brightness, and with her eyes she looked into heaven. She was clothed in a garment of dazzling white silk, over which was a cloak set with precious stones—with emeralds, sapphires, and pearls—and on her feet were shoes of onyx. But her face was smudged with dirt, and her dress was torn on the right side.[1] Moreover, her cloak had lost its exquisite beauty, and the tops of her shoes were soiled.

She cried out in a loud, mournful voice to the heights of heaven: Give heed, O heavens, because my face has been smudged, and mourn, O earth, because my garment has been torn, and tremble, O abyss, because my shoes have been soiled. "The foxes have holes, and the birds of the air nests" [Matt 8.20], but I have no one to help or console me, and no staff to lean on for support.

And again she said: I lay hidden in the heart of the Father until the Son of Man, who was virginally conceived and born, shed His blood. And I was betrothed to Him through that blood, and dowered, so that through a pure, unsullied regeneration of spirit and of water, I could give new life to those who had been diseased and contaminated by the venom of the serpent.

Those who nurtured me—the priests, that is to say—were supposed to make my face glow like the dawn, my clothes flash like lightning, my cloak gleam like precious stones, and my shoes to shine brightly. Instead, they have smeared my face with dirt, they have torn my garment, they have blackened my cloak, and they have soiled my shoes. The very ones who were supposed to beautify me with adornments have all failed miserably. This is the way they soil my face: They take up and handle the body and blood of my Bridegroom while defiled by the uncleanliness of their lustful morals, poisoned by the deadly venom of fornication and adultery, and corrupted by the avaricious rapine of buying and selling improper things.[2] They encompass His body and blood with filth, like someone putting a child in the mud among swine. For just as man became flesh and blood when God created him from the slime of the earth and breathed into him the breath of life [cf. Gen 2.7], so too at the words of the priest, when he invokes the divinity over the altar, that same power of God turns the offering of bread, wine, and water into the real flesh and blood of Christ, that is, of my Bridegroom. But man cannot see this phenomenon with his physical eyes because he was blinded at Adam's fall.

As long as the wounds of man's sins gape open, my Bridegroom's wounds remain fresh and open. And the priests, who are supposed to make me resplendent, and serve me in that resplendence, are contaminating these wounds of Christ by running from church to church in their great avarice. They are tearing my garment because they are perverters of the law and the gospel and their own priesthood. In this way they are blackening my cloak because they are completely neglecting the precepts established for them. Moreover, they do not fulfill those precepts with good will and perfect work through abstinence (that is, the emerald), nor through generous distribution of alms (that is, the sapphire), nor with other good and upright works that bring honor to God (that is, the other kinds of gems). And they soil the tops of my shoes by not following the straight paths of righteousness, that is, those difficult and arduous ways. Furthermore, they do not set good examples for their subordinates, despite the fact that I preserve the splendor of truth below in my shoes, as in my secret place. False priests are self-deceived, because they want to have the honor of the priesthood without its work. This cannot be, because no one will receive the reward unless he has completed the work [cf. I Cor 3.8]. But when the grace of God touches a person, it causes him to perform his task so that he may receive his reward.

And so let heaven rain down all kinds of calamities upon mankind in the vengeance of God, and let a cloud cover the whole earth, so that its viridity withers and its beauty fades. And let the abyss tremble because, along with heaven and earth, it will be whipped into a frenzy in vengeance and grief. O you priests! you who have neglected me thus far, the princes of the earth and the rash mob will rise up against you, cast you out, and put you to flight. They will take your riches away from you, because you have not attended to your priestly office. And they will say about you: "Let us cast these adulterers and robbers out of the Church, for they are full of every kind of wickedness." And in doing this, they believe that they have been obedient to God, for they say that the Church has been contaminated by you. This is why the Scripture says: "Why have the Gentiles raged, and the people devised vain things? The kings of the earth stood up, and the princes met together" [Ps 2.1–2]. For with God's permission many nations will begin to rage in their judgments against you, and many people will devise vain things against you, and will count your priestly office and your consecration as worthless. Then, the kings of the earth will aid them in casting you out, because they are greedy for earthly things, and the princes who will be your lords will agree in casting you out of their territory, for by your wicked deeds, you have put the innocent Lamb to flight.[3][a]

And I heard a voice from heaven saying: This figure represents the Church. Therefore, O man, you who see and hear these mournful words, convey them to the priests, who were established and ordained to rule and teach the people of God, for that which was said to the apostles applies also to them: "Go ye into the whole world, and preach the gospel to every creature" [Mark 16.15]. For when God created mankind, he sealed every creature in him, just as on a single small piece of parchment, one can mark the time and reckoning of an entire year. For this reason God named all creation "mankind."[b]

And again I, a poor little feminine form, saw an unsheathed sword hanging in the air, one edge of which was turned toward the heavens, the other toward the earth. And this sword was stretched out over the spiritual people, just as the prophet had long ago foreseen when he cried out in wonder: "Who are these, that fly as clouds, and as doves to their windows" [Is 60.8]? For these were those who were lifted up from the earth and separated from the common people, and they were expected to live saintly lives in simplicity of morals and works like the dove, but now they have become depraved in their morals and their works. And I saw that that sword was cutting off certain monasteries of spiritual men, just as Jerusalem was cut off after the Passion of the Lord. But still I saw that in that adversity God will preserve for Himself many priests who are devout, pure, and simple, just as He answered Elijah, saying that there remained to him "seven thousand men in Israel, whose knees have not been bowed before Baal" [I Kings 19.18].

Now, may the unquenchable fire of the Holy Spirit so infuse you that you will turn to the better part [cf. Luke 10.42].

Notes

1. See Letter 15r, n. 2.
2. That is, Church offices, the sin of simony.
3. Here, Hildegard echoes the biblical passage in greater detail than a translation can adequately render. See Latin passage in the endnote.

Kitzingen

150

The Abbess Sophia to Hildegard

Before 1153

Hildegard was on very friendly terms with Sophia, abbess of Kitzingen. In this letter of praise, the abbess announces that she is coming to meet with Hildegard, bringing along with her a close friend and praiseworthy nun. At the end, almost as an afterthought, she asks whether it would be proper for her to resign her administrative office.

To Hildegard, mistress of singular merit, unique with sapphires [cf. Cant 5.14] of spiritual virtues, Sophia, called abbess in Kitzingen but deficient in herself, with resolute prayer.

Because of your great sanctity, I am flying with swift wings to the bosom of your love, seeking, for the sake of light, to be commended to you, who, through the True Light, has merited to be revealed for the illumination of the people.

Who would not take delight in the home of the mother of wisdom?[1] Who would not willingly give ear to the symphony of heaven? Who would not long to hear the instrument of the Holy Spirit foreordained for the chimes of so many virtues, mystically embossed with so many miracles? Pleasing indeed was that sound that "hath gone forth into all the earth" [Ps 18.5], whose harmony the Spirit "who proceedeth from the Father" [John 15.26] made pleasant.

Therefore, cry out with fortitude, you who announce peace far and wide, and all the nations beyond the rivers of Ethiopia will come to you bringing gifts of praise. And I also, like the others, run to compete in the race, not expecting the prize [cf. I Cor 9.24], but still hoping, for, as the Apostle says: "It is not of him that willeth, nor of him that runneth, but of God that sheweth mercy" [Rom 9.16]. Thus it is with anyone who receives some part of your saintly prayers, which you offer for free to all as an obligation resulting from God's nearness to you and love of you.

Venerable mother, worthy of all praise, I am bringing with me a well-born peer of mine, a praiseworthy nun, a sister acceptable in every way, whom the heavenly Father has created as my spiritual sister. It is God's will that the two of us make your acquaintance.[a]

"Let thy voice sound in my ears" [Cant 2.14], and reveal God's will to me: Which would be more salutary for me—to lay down the burden I bear or to carry it longer?

Note

1. The word for *wisdom* here is *sophie*, in this letter from the abbess Sophia.

150r

Hildegard to the Abbess Sophia

Before 1153

In this brief reply to the Abbess Sophia, Hildegard, as might be expected, urges her to remain in her office.

O Sophia, I say this to you according to a mystic vision: Let your spirit be strengthened by God, touching God with appropriate sighs. The burden of your labor, which God has given you to bear, is good for you, as long as your sheep are willing to hear God's admonition through your governance. And if any spark still shines among them, do not abandon them, lest the devil[1] snatch them away.

Let your spirit shine in God, and your days burn bright in the Fiery Giver.

Note

1. Literally, the "snatcher."

151

Hildegard to the Abbess Sophia

About 1155(?)

In this second letter to the abbess, Hildegard once again urges her not to give up her administrative duties, while at the same time acknowledging that she understands the anguish she is going through.

In the True Light I saw a fiery sphere like a wheel turning inside you. You are walking on a narrow path, looking to the sun, but, for all that, the winds of a cloud's instability will overshadow you because your mind wanders. You cry out: When will God set me free? And He will answer you, I will not forsake you [cf. Josh 1.5; Heb 13.5], but I want you to seize the net so that it is not torn, for if you cast it aside, it will turn down another way,[1] and this would not be pleasing to God.

Now, rejoice in God [cf. Phil 3.1; 4.4] and live forever, because God loves you.

Note

1. The sense of this passage is not altogether clear. Is "seizing the net" an allusion to the gospels' "I will make you fishers of men," with the suggestion being that Sophia should govern her community effectively and not abdicate her administrative duties, lest her subordinates go astray?

152

Hildegard to Rumunda, a Lay Sister

Before 1170

A letter of comfort to a lay sister who is having problems and doubts.

The Secret Light says: You are worn out, like a person cut off from the household of the One Who created you. But you will be called back from among the foreigners. Therefore, cease from your sins, for God has not sold you into perdition [cf. Baruch 4.6], but He has found you like the lost sheep that has been called back to life [cf. Matt 18.12ff; Luke 15.4ff].

Why do you have doubts as if you did not have salvation? Seek God, therefore, in the anxiety and anguish of your spirit, and you will live [cf. Ps 68.33; Amos 5.4–6].

Knechsteden

153

A Provost to Hildegard

Before 1173

The provost expresses his great desire to speak with Hildegard face-to-face so that he could discuss with her all those matters that he could not possibly put into a letter. That being impossible, he beseeches Hildegard to pray to God for mercy for his great offenses.

H., by the grace of God provost (however insufficient) at Knechsteden, to Hildegard, venerable handmaiden of Christ. May you be strengthened by the grace of the Holy Spirit, and may you enjoy blessing at the end of your life.

How I long with all my might to be present with you and enjoy conversation with you. Then, I would tell you at length all the things that concern me, things that God alone knows, things that I could not tell you in a brief letter.

We have, beloved lady, heard of the grace that the Father of lights has bestowed upon you, from Whom "every best gift, and every perfect gift" [James 1.17] comes. Having great confidence in that grace, therefore, I felt it necessary to write this letter to the sweetness of your love, beseeching you not to cease imploring divine compassion for my wretched state in your devout prayers. For I know that I have offended that compassion in many things [cf. James 3.2], and I know that I cannot escape retribution for my indiscretion.

Therefore, because I have great hope in the grace that I know is yours, I felt the need to implore the aid of your prayers, for I know God hears them, and I hope thereby to receive some measure of consolation from you. I pray for Christ's sake that you not fail to write me, sending me instructions how I might placate the divine majesty I have offended.

Farewell in Christ always.

153r

Hildegard to the Provost

Before 1173

Hildegard answers the provost's petition, which she says she has examined in a mystic vision.

In a mystic vision I examined your petition, and I heard a voice say this to you: I compare you to a tree that puts forth thick foliage in the summertime, but whose fruit is somewhat damaged by whirlwinds and clouds. But then it is restored again by the dew of heaven and a cloudless sky. This is the state of your mind, because, although you have confidence when you are somewhat prosperous and, as it were, fruitful, you are still wearied by the instability of your character, as by a whirlwind, and, as by clouds, you are damaged by those you have charge over.

On those occasions, sigh to God, saying, "To thee, O Lord, have I lifted up my soul. In thee, O my God, I put my trust; let me not be ashamed" [Ps 24.1–2]. For in you is the breath that God gave life forever [cf. Job 33.4], and in you are the wings of rationality that He gave you. Therefore, fly to God on those wings through faith and good desire, lifting up your soul to Him. And know that He is your God, for He knew you, and you had your beginnings from Him. Therefore, ask Him to teach you His good things through the breath of His Holy Spirit, and to free you from adversity. Trust in Him so that you will not blush to set all your works before Him, and speak to Him, as a son speaks to his father who corrects him when he has gone astray, asking that He not forget His offspring.

As for me, I will gladly ask God to mercifully defend you through His grace, and free you from your unstable morals and other defects, and preserve you from the dangers that come upon you.

Koblenz

154

A Provost to Hildegard

Before 1173

The provost writes for consolation for all the troubles that have befallen him, because, as he notes, everything Hildegard has prophesied to him has come to pass.

To Hildegard, beloved in Christ, S., unworthy provost of the brothers in Koblenz, greetings in the Lord.

Because you have always refreshed me with your consolation in all my tribulations, and because all the things that you have foretold me have come to pass, I ask you to beseech the merciful Lord to console me now in the midst of the troubles that assail me within and without. And especially, beloved and loving lady, write back to inform me whether, from the merciful Jesus, I dare have hope for the life to come.

As for the rest, be aware that I pray the Lord from the bottom of my heart that before I die I may worthily repent from my sins.

Farewell.

Cologne (St. Martin)

155

Abbot Adalard to Hildegard

Before 1169

The writer pleads with Hildegard to beseech God to console him in his troubles, which are too dreadful and appalling to believe.

To the lady Hildegard, beloved of God, Adalard, unworthy servant of St. Martin in Cologne, with a prayer that she enjoy the paradise of eternal bliss after the course of this present life.

Lady, dear lady, beloved and blessed by God as it is truly believed, I know that all the things performed through you by God's might are indeed true and holy. And I am assured that you can obtain whatever you ask of God, as faithful men have asserted in all truth. Therefore, I am, as far as I dare, confident enough to ask you, saintly lady, to implore God to be merciful to me, a sinner, so that He might deign to give me some kind of consolation in my struggle with my problems. Beyond belief, "my spirit is in anguish within me" and "my heart within me is troubled" [Ps 142.4], because of the things that I have been suffering now, alas, for many years, and especially now, as a result of my sins. And no one can know except God unto whose eyes "all things are naked and open" [Heb 4.13]. I know that God alone is cognizant of the things that confront me, things that no mortal man could believe, since they are so unusual and unbelievable. Therefore, through the grace of the Holy Spirit, Who works with you and protects you, I pray that whatever hope He deigns to reveal to you concerning me, you will report in detail, just as it is, back to me in writing, through the good offices of this most reverend lord abbot, for he has promised to do this for me.

Venerable lady in Christ, how I wish that I had been able to come into your saintly presence and discuss these matters with you face-to-face. For I believe without doubt that you can fully expound these matters that I have kept completely secret until now. What do I say? Through the teaching of the Scriptures and the tenets of the Christian faith, I know that no one clothed in flesh should despair of God's mercy. Led by this hope and knowing that God is clearly with you, I have presumed to impart the causes of my grief to you in this letter. And I believe that I will be consoled by you in some way, and, if such is indeed possible, this is what I pray for most earnestly.

May Christ, your Bridegroom, hold you long in His embrace.

155r

Hildegard to the Abbot Adalard

Before 1169

Hildegard starts off by admonishing the abbot to be gentle to his subordinates, and then broadens out to discuss morality in general and man's inclination to sin through the devil's instigation.

I heard these words from the Living Light: You are like the potter who molds many vessels but who fails to fire them properly. Learn from this analogy that your works should not fail to possess the sheen of love. And you should dig around them with discernment, so that all your works may be reasonable. And they should be performed with abstinence and prayer, following the wholesome example of the saints who sprang forth like rivulets from the Living Fountain, and gave food to men which they could swallow with joy. For if they are given thorns instead of bread, they cannot eat them. Just so, if superiors use harsh words to their subordinates, they do not build them up, but lead them instead into error. For a superior must sift the words of his teaching with maternal sweetness so that his subordinates will gladly open their mouths and swallow them.

The millstone grinds grain and brings forth various kinds of meal. In the same way, the planters of the Church took legal precepts from the Old and the New Law. For the Old Law revealed by prophecy that Christ would be born God, and Christ Himself sent His word forth to be preached in every land [cf. Matt 28.19–20]. The millstone is the Old Law, which brought forth every grain of truth in Christ, and the pure wheat, sifted clean of all contamination, is virginity, which is the material of all spiritual life in the Church. And virginity brings forth the offspring of obedience, and these obedient children are the kiss of Christ's mouth [cf. Cant 1.1]. Therefore, let a superior always receive obedient subordinates with the embrace of love and not with the stumbling block of anger, because they are the kiss of God, and are to be fed on bread of fine wheat. But coarse meal, that is to say, severe chastisement, is to be fed to disobedient children. Bran is to be served to those who completely abandon obedience, for that is the food of brute beasts that lack understanding.

As for you, be provident and remember the sanctity of those who "ate manna" [John 6.31], drink from the streams of living water [cf. John 4.13–14], and be peaceable and devout in God, so that you may flourish in His garden with the viridity of other wholesome herbs. But flee the foolishness of those who forsake the sun they see to look for another sun that they neither see, nor can find. And flee also those new perfumers[1] who want to make the law their own personal province, for they will not prevail.

Now, therefore, make your beginning in Him Who Is, so that you may have your ending in Him Who Was and Who Is To Come [cf. Apoc 1.4]. You have been established by God in two ways: that He might call you into good knowledge and protect you from bad knowledge. When you raise yourself on the two wings of the knowledge of good and evil, resplendent works but also great suffering and misery lie on these ways. Therefore, pay heed to the three strengths with which God endowed mankind: understanding, the senses, and motion of the body—all of which man is aware of through their potential. In these three powers, and in the aforementioned two ways, God maintains you. For through the Spirit of the Lord, you see with understanding, and through the body you become aware of evil things by means of the senses. You know both good and evil, for you are both spiritual and corporeal. The grace of God calls you in admonition, and the Holy Spirit enkindles you with His fire to love God and rise up to Him by your good works.

But through his deception, the devil sometimes diverts you from God's admonitions, and prevents you from loving God. Through his evil instigation, he reminds you that you are a mere human being, and that it is, therefore, impossible for you to do anything unseen. Whenever a person denies God, the deception of the devil blows a black and evil instability upon him. Although the devil denies that God exists, he knows that he is mistaken, for, since he knows that he himself exists, he is, therefore, aware that God exists. He has some share in the sin of conceiving human beings, and through this share he lacerates many in the flesh. For whoever says in his heart that God does not exist [cf. Ps 52.1] is also saying that heaven and earth, and all things living in God and with God, do not exist, and is, moreover, denying his own existence. How very foolish it is for a person who sees himself and knows himself to say in his doubt, "I do not exist." For even a particle of dust has no existence apart from God. But when a person overcomes his body, even though he has some doubts, he cuts down the devil and his spiritual evils. Therefore, he will receive a reward and a crown in the presence of God and His angels and all the heavenly host.

The breath of the devil infuses man with many forbidden notions, which good knowledge blushes to name. It is his plan for mankind to be subject to the kind of vainglory that he himself displayed when he brought about that great ruin by which he caused the wheel of man's nativity to spin a fiery course [cf. James 3.6]. He also seeks to incite mankind to many forbidden actions, mankind whom he knows to have been created in the image of God [cf. Gen 1.26f]. Therefore, he shows him many things that are impossible for any created being. But he has no power over them, and it is for this reason that he implants his evil ideas in mankind, so that man might, by his own choice, bring his malice to fruition. In this way, he brings God's law into derision, so that every man, as a god unto himself, might establish a law for himself out of his own will. And the devil delights in this, because he doesn't want anyone—neither himself nor anyone else—to be subordinate to God.

As for you, O son of God, the God who created you wishes to receive you through the victory of His army, so that you might come into the eye of His knowledge, for He will never abandon you [cf. Deut 31.6ff]. Through faith, therefore, look to the sun, so that you may become a faithful servant. And look to the moon in the night, whenever vices oppress you, so that through the fear of the

Lord, you may overcome all these things. And you will not be wounded, but will live forever.

Note

1. That is, other administrators. See Letter 144r, n. 1. Hildegard's point here seems to be, as throughout the letter, that an administrator should govern with discernment and with mercy.

Cologne (St. Agatha?) / Bonn

156

An Abbess to Hildegard

1163(?)–73

The abbess beseeches Hildegard to send her the advice and admonition that she sees in her visions. She also reminds Hildegard of the letter she had promised on her recent visit to her community.

To Hildegard, mistress of St. Rupert, illumined by the grace of the divine light, N., abbess (although unworthy) of Didenkirch near Bonn. Insignificant and unworthy though I am, I send an earnest request for prayer, along with the perseverance of service owed to you, great and worthy lady.

Trusting in your great sanctity and humility, I have sent this messenger to you with a letter, in the hope, holy lady, that if it does not offend your eyes, you will send me a brief response with some words of admonition, loving mother, to edify my spirit and bring confidence in God to me. Indeed, when you were here with us, you promised that, when you could find the time, you would write to offer me support and strength.

Moreover (if I dare to ask more), I will employ the prayers of the Canaanite woman who in the Gospel responded to the Lord by saying, "the whelps also eat of the crumbs that fall from the table of their masters" [Matt 15.27]. With that same devoted faith, therefore, I ask you to set before me briefly some of those crumbs from your table, that is to say, from that vision in which you often see many miracles, for I greatly desire them.

Indeed, as you will recall, I recently sent you the parchment to be used for this very purpose.[a]

To our utmost ability, we implore that God, by His everlasting goodness freely given, complete the good that He began in you [cf. Phil 1.6].

156r

Hildegard to the Abbess

1163(?)–73

Hildegard advises the abbess to use moderation in her administrative duties, and,
by use of a parable, teaches her to set an example of labor for her subordinates.

Your mind is unsettled because of muddy places and because of anxiety over
many waters that run dry. "Muddy places" means those who are unstable in character, and "waters that run dry" means those who are hard and rocky in disposition, and who are not softened by the streams of doctrine flowing from the Holy
Scripture. But you say in your heart, "Who, or what, am I? How can I endure
such things?"

Listen now to a wise man's parable: A certain man wanted to dig a cave, but
while he was working with wood and iron, fire burst forth from a rock he had
dug into. And the result was that this place could in no way be penetrated. Nevertheless, he took note of the location of the place, and with great exertion he dug
other tunnels into it. And then the man said in his heart: "I have toiled strenuously, but he who comes after me will have easier labor, because he will find
everything already prepared for him." Surely, this man will be praised by his lord,
because in length and breadth his work is much more useful than work done in
arable land that is turned by the plow. And so his master will consider him a
mighty knight competent to be in charge of his army, and so he puts him in charge
of the other farmers who present him fruit in their due season. For whoever has
labored first is preeminent over the one who succeeds him. Indeed, the Maker
of the world undertook creation first, and thus set the example for His servants
to labor after His fashion.

O daughter of God, keep a close watch over the plot of land within you so
that it will not wither, deprived of fruitful utility for your children. Also, be firm
of purpose, and avoid the intemperance of unsettled morals, for otherwise you
will cause your daughters to flee from you. Be like fertile earth that is watered
often with seasonable rain, so that you may produce good and delectable herbs.
How can you do this? When a person feeds his flesh moderately, he has a mild
and gentle character, but when he lives on an overabundance of food and high
living, he causes all kinds of noxious vices to sprout in himself. On the other hand,
a person who afflicts his body with immoderate abstinence always walks in anger.
In all these matters, be fertile soil so that you may console your daughters when
they weep, and reproach them when they rise up in wrath. And when they become savage, you may lead them to submit to the discipline of the Rule. Moreover, summon into your presence, and the presence of two others, those who
have thoughtlessly turned away from you, and call them back with lessons drawn
from history and lessons from the Gospel. And then if they still are disobedient

to you, be obedient to the High Judge, and remember Jacob who switched his blessing from the one son of Joseph to the other [cf. Gen 48.15ff].

Now, look to the beginning of your good desire so that you may finish in faith, and receive eternal rewards from the High Judge.

Cologne (St. Ursula)

157

An Abbess to Hildegard

Before 1173

The abbess beseeches Hildegard to send her some consolation for her overwhelming grief.

To her lady and mother Hildegard, who dwells in the tower of Jerusalem, N., abbess (in name only) of the monastery of the holy virgins of the church at Cologne,[1] with her most devoted prayer and due service.

I cannot express in words how much I rejoice in your blessedness. Although I am physically separated from you, I am all the same bound to you by a deep feeling of love. I long to see you and to unfold to you the grief I bear in my heart, a grief that finds no human consolation, and I desire to regard you, who are full of all love, as my mother. I place all my hope in you, after God, and I desire to be consoled and made joyous by you from this point forward. Therefore, let the tears and sighs of a grieving daughter move you. Be mindful of me and ask God, Who became poor for our sake, to deign to free me from everlasting poverty, and to gather me to the final abode of eternal bliss.

Farewell, and greet all your congregation for me.

Note

1. The abbess's monastery was dedicated to St. Ursula and the 11,000 virgins, who, according to legend, were martyred at Cologne. Hildegard was especially devoted to St. Ursula, for whom she wrote a number of musical compositions.

Cologne (The Holy Apostles)

158

A Dean to Hildegard

1169

The dean writes on behalf of himself and his brothers to offer praise and thanks-
giving to Hildegard and her nuns for taking in Sigewize, the lady possessed of a
devil.[1] They have heard, he writes, that the devil has been cast out, and he requests details about the exorcism.

T., by the grace of God, dean (that is, schoolmaster), though in name only, of the
Church of the Holy Apostles at Cologne, joins with all his brothers to offer de-
voted prayer in the Lord and greetings in the name of true salvation to the lady
Hildegard and all those who fight for Christ at Mount St. Rupert.

Ever since we learned that you had brought our sister—rather, our beloved
daughter—the lady Sigewize, into your order, blessed lady, we, and indeed the
entire city of Cologne, have been enkindled to the love of spirituality by the will
of God. For this reason everyone throughout our region proclaims, Behold, "the
aroma" of the ladies of St. Rupert "is as the smell of a plentiful field, which the
Lord hath blessed" [Gen 27.27]. May the Lord bless all of you who, on your
modest and humble mount, sing praises to His works of love, which all our lofty
mountains and all our broad valleys—I cannot say "have been unable," but rather
"have failed" to celebrate.

We have recently heard that the ancient enemy has been cast out by your
prayers, at least according to rumor. If this is true, we beseech you to inform us
in a return letter the manner and rite of his expulsion so that we may rejoice with
you and join you in praising the Lord with ceaseless devotion.

Because the lady Sigewize is a very good friend of ours, we send her special
greetings, renewing our devout prayers in Christ and awaiting the same from
her. Farewell.

Note

1. See Letters 68, 68r, and 69, Vol. 1, pp.147–52.

158r

Hildegard to the Dean

1169

In the beginning of her letter, Hildegard answers the question about Sigewize in large, allegorical terms, and, then, in more specific detail, with the emphasis, however, on the prayers and alms of others, with no particulars about her own efforts.

God created His work, but He did not establish it in one set way.[a] Adam perished, and did not complete his full cycle, but fell asleep after noon. Then, God sent His breath into the prophets so that they might utter the truth, and thus Wisdom spoke through the mouths of those she had established, so that they might produce miracles. Next, the apostles, through the guidance of the Holy Spirit, brought God's work to completion by faith; and their martyrdom, and the martyrdom of others, revealed the existence of God. Nowadays, the Holy Spirit has filled spiritual people, who bring the age to completion among themselves, and cultivate the angelic order.[b]

Thus God's work is like the day. All have spoken in unison, but have clamored as individuals. At daybreak, dawn precedes the sun, and in the morning the sun's rays shine forth. At the third hour it begins to blaze with heat, and at noon it is fully ablaze. Then, about the ninth hour, its heat decreases, and toward evening the heat it had during the day comes to an end, and, finally, is hidden in the night. Thus the day is completed and rests from all its works, and if these works were completed in one set way, mankind would be greatly displeased. Whence it is that God is called "Sabaoth," because each person is obliged to fulfill a course of this kind. In just this way God acts in all His works.

This has been the case in the woman you inquire about. On her behalf, the exalted, and the even more exalted, the lowly, and even more lowly, have spoken as one with their labors and prayers, and have clamored as individuals, in accordance with the instructions of the Holy Spirit. For some individuals have labored on her behalf through sighs of compassion; others, by prayers and vigils; and others, by fasts and scourgings. Moreover, many have given alms for her sake, and a large number of others have taken her part by helping her with all the good in their power. Others have brought this duty to completion with their great and persistent zeal. Thus, just as the day completes its cycle, all were looking to God at the same time for her sake.

Now, let us all together say: Glory to you, O Lord.

The blessing of God's grace be upon you and upon all those who have been moved to compassion for her, for, as the Lord Himself says, "I will have mercy and not sacrifice" [Matt 9.13; 12.7; cf. Hos 6.6].

Krauftal

159

The Abbess Hazzecha to Hildegard

1160–61

During her preaching tour of 1160, Hildegard visited Krauftal, and, in this letter, the abbess recalls that time with joy. In addition, she asks for further words of chastisement and correction from the Living Light.

To Hildegard, the provident steward of the house of the great Father of the family [cf. Luke 12.42], Hazzecha, humble and unworthy abbess of Krauftal, with maternal veneration and daughterly devotion, through the love by which we are joined together in Christ.

After your friendly visit, which I had desired such a long time, I merited, God helping, to be relieved from my weakness of spirit and my earlier tribulations [cf. Ps 54.9], and managed to rest a little. And because I have no doubt that your words do not come from any human imagination but from the True Light itself, which has illumined you more than any other human being, I have followed your advice and postponed what I originally proposed to do.

I want you to know, my lady and dearest sister, that just as I greatly desired to see you—and still do—I always cling to you in my heart, even though I cannot be with you in person. Now, since I am sure that you abide in love and love abides in you [cf. I John 4.16], I beseech you in the name of that love not to delay writing to inform me of the fitting chastisement or correction the Living Light reveals to you through His Spirit concerning me.

159r

Hildegard to the Abbess Hazzecha

1160–61

Hildegard criticizes the abbess for not performing her administrative duties to the best of her ability, and warns her to give up her plans to seek out a solitary life.

He Who sees all things says: You have eyes to see and look all around yourself. Where you see mud, wash it away, and where you see aridity, make it green. And make those spices which you have give forth a sweet odor. If you had no eyes, you could excuse yourself, but since you do have them, why do you not use them to look all about yourself. You use high-sounding words in your sophistry, for frequently you judge others for the very things you yourself would not want to be judged for. But then, sometimes, you do speak with wisdom.

Take care to carry your burden properly, and gather good work in the sack of your heart, lest you fall by the wayside. For you could not find quiet in the solitary life that you ask about because of your unstable character. And then your last days would be worse than the first [cf. Luke 11.26], and as heavy as a stone. But emulate the chastity of the turtledove, and diligently watch over the choice vineyard, so that you might look to God with a pure and righteous face.

160

The Abbess Hazzecha to Hildegard

About 1161(?)

The abbess pleads with Hildegard for consolation and advice, for she is terrified at the burden of her office.

To the most loving lady Hildegard, effulgent with the sacred gift of divine and true visions, Hazzecha of Krauftal, abbess (in name only), with a prayer that she receive the overflowing gift of perfect love.

My lady, the eloquence of your most holy soul flows down from the height of your contemplation as from the tops of the eternal hills, down into the deepest valley of other souls. And like "a shower upon the herb, and as drops upon the grass" [Deut 32.2], it permeates them, and causes them to bring forth flowers without thorns, and to put forth living shoots of celestial desire bursting forth with a wondrous aroma that reaches to the very throne of the glory of almighty God.

Therefore, I, your handmaiden, hope to see a letter from you, saintly lady, and to be refreshed by your sweet words of consolation as if by a light breeze. For, my mother and lady, all my hope and security, all my refuge and safety depends, after God, on you. And so I run back to you alone, and, after Christ, I entrust myself to your advice and aid.

Therefore, I humbly entreat you again, and implore you, in your compassion, to pray to God on my behalf. May you please also let me know what I must do for my many excesses, for because of them and because of other transgressions, as I mentioned earlier, I am remiss in the burden of the title that has been imposed on me. For I am afraid—indeed terrified—that I am incurring God's wrath. Farewell.

160r

Hildegard to the Abbess Hazzecha

About 1161(?)

In large allegorical terms, Hildegard advises the abbess about her administrative duties.

In a true vision I heard these words that with burning desire you sought from me because of your great need. Faithful governance is exceedingly praiseworthy when it has these two edges of a sword: one which, along with shields, breastplates, and other armament, is used to guard the tower, and fight those who would destroy it; the other which defends its city with brave knights so that its walls are not captured by the enemy, its gates opened to treacherous spies, and the knights killed. Under such governance, men are blessed.

Those who lack such governance are worse than peasants who shrewdly and selfishly manage their farms thinking only of their herds and their fodder. About such it cannot be said: "Who is she that goeth up by the desert, as a pillar of smoke of aromatical spices, of myrrh, and frankincense, and of all the powders of the perfumer" [Cant 3.6]. Nor can the following be said: "How beautiful are thy steps in shoes, O prince's daughter" [Cant 7.1]. Here is the meaning of the verse: He who denies his own will in the exile of this world (which is what "the desert" signifies) rises up to God, through all his works, by sighing to Him, for, as it is written, the perfume of aromatic spices rises in the sight of the Lord [cf. Cant 3.6]. For he chooses to mortify his flesh, and so from the perfume of the spices and the mortification of the flesh, all the virtues grow in him, and he is never satiated. That passage concerning the celestial citizens of angels and saints is addressed to the one who does this: "How beautiful are thy steps," that is to say, the zeal in which you walk by mortifying the flesh, "O prince's daughter." But, according to the prophet, he who is neither hot nor cold will be spewed out of the mouth [cf. Apoc 3.15–16], because he puts forth no effort in either earthly or heavenly things. I compare such a one to locusts, which do not fly with the birds, nor walk with the animals on the earth. Rather, they drift uselessly, like a whirlwind, which quickly dissipates.

O daughter of the Sacred Name, open your ears, and with diligent heart hear the meaning of this allegorical message: What glorious praise there is for the towers of that well-established city, for they are love and harmony joined. And why do I use the term "tower"? Because the fountain that springs [cf. John 4.14] from the most high God flowed forth, encircling the whole earth, for God Himself so established all of creation in His absolute love that they lacked for nothing. Learn from this, therefore, that holy persons, in whom love dwells, lack for nothing, because their hearts are surrounded with gentleness and peace, as by the flowing aroma of balsam. It is for this reason that the ancient serpent is not able to destroy them, because just as a noisome stench is dispersed by the scent of balsam, so does the devil flee from love and hide away in a cave. But wherever holy persons, in whom love does not dwell, are gathered together in the name of the Lord, they are like a city that has no tower or like beautiful houses that have no loftiness. Therefore, in this disorder they are despoiled of the money of justice and of the Rule, because they do not have well-built houses and so, frequently, they are destroyed, because just as a tower both adorns and sustains a city, so love adorns and sustains all the virtues. The knights of Love—Obedience, Faith, and Hope—are stationed in the tower. Obedience is girt with a shield, because it is always subordinate. Faith is clad in a breastplate, because it approves all good things which are in God, but which it has never seen with its eyes. And, through Faith, Hope embraces heaven with all its adornments. For Faith always looks to God through Obedience, and thus carries out what has been commanded.

Indeed, "God is love" [I John 4.8], because all His work is holy. But in humility He came down from heaven in order to free His prisoners who abandoned love when they did not know Him. He did this through His humanity, and thereby set an example for us. How? When we have given up our own will in performing the duties of this world, we follow His footsteps. And when we are gathered together in His name, just as all other birds gather to the eagle, we imitate Abraham, who left his people and his native country [cf. Gen 12.1ff], and, in accordance with God's command, performed the circumcision [cf. Gen 17.23–24], which was foreign to him. And when we are obedient to God's commands, through the Man who is like to us, we are multiplied in blessings like the stars of heaven, just as God promised Abraham through His angel [cf. Gen 22.15ff], for we too are searching for something foreign to us according to His incarnation, and thus we regard ourselves as nothing, and labor in the spiritual life. When we do this, we fortify our tower on all sides with stalwart knights through humility. And we too are stalwart knights when we overcome the desires of this world, subdue the madness of wrath, endure our poverty for the sake of Christ's love, reject the murderous thoughts of envy and hate, spurn not other sinners like ourselves or judge them unjustly, and do not seek false testimony against the upright and innocent.

These stalwart knights are those who guard our city on all sides, so that the wall of the holy Rule and our calling will not be breached by our enemies, that is, by hateful, spiteful morals, nor the door of peace repudiated by contradiction, for if that happens, the bolts of our door will be opened, and our enemies will come unhindered into our city. Let us not join with those who say in their ever-erring heart: We reject that which man's reason chooses and imposes upon us, because the things we choose and set for ourselves are more useful and just. Those treacherous people are the ones who destroy our city through their treachery, because they repudiate those things which have been passed down to us from our ancient, holy, and learned doctors concerning fasting, vigils, prayer, and other virtuous activities. But they choose, instead, their own will in place of the God Who created them.

Listen, O holy daughter: No stalwart knights are protecting your tower, and the guardians of your city are asleep. And so they have been led into the desert, through their own will. Thus your tower and city are so arid that they can scarcely stand. So rise up from your sleep, because the cables of your ship (that is, the

custom of your holy calling) have not yet been broken. Yet in the great foolishness of your character, you enjoy gossip and seek it out. This does you no good
at all. For just as in deserted homes there are mice—big ones, small ones, blind
ones—that gnaw up men's clothing, so also every holy custom is destroyed by
such attitudes. The larger mice are disquieted minds of impiety, the small mice
represent stupidity which, being nocturnal in nature, turns from the way of truth,
and the blind mice stand for the vanity of this world which is blind to the light of
justice. And so it is written in the Gospel: "Every kingdom divided against itself,
shall be brought to desolation" [Luke 11.17]. Consider what great ardor of the
Holy Spirit you are planted in, for He is not willing for you to fail in serving
Him. Regard first the Rule of St. Benedict and other great masters with diligent
heart, so that you will not perish but will live forever.

As for you, all you superiors, take care not to be like foolish farmers who
take great delight in seeing the plow moving properly by itself, but when it goes
off the path, do not take the trouble to turn it back to the right way. And take
care lest the mighty Father of the household say to you: You are useless to me
because you are bad stewards [cf. Luke 16.1ff]. Rather, consider carefully the
needs of your subordinates and their adversities. Then protect them with all
proper concern.

161

Hildegard to the Abbess Hazzecha

Before 1160(?)
or 1171–73(?)

In her usual manner, Hildegard exhorts the abbess to remain in her present office. She also demurs from answering questions about persons that the abbess had
apparently inquired about.

My dearest daughter, I do not see that it is profitable for you and those two close
friends of yours to seek out a hermitage in the forest, or even the shrines of saints,
since you have been sealed with the seal of Christ, by which you make your way
to the heavenly Jerusalem [cf. Heb 12.22].[1] For if you undertake greater toil than
you can endure, you will fall, as I foretold, deceived by the devil.

Also, in the love of Christ I tell you that I do not usually speak about the
end of life of individuals, nor of their works, nor of the things that lie in store for
them, but, rather, although I am untaught, I speak and write only those things I
am shown by the Holy Spirit in the vision of my spirit.

In my prayers I will gladly commend to God's grace those you have commended to me. I will also willingly pray God to free you from all that does not
avail you, and to protect you from all future troubles. I will also pray that you

will so perfectly complete the labors of holy works with pious discernment that, strengthened by the splendor of unsullied holiness and enkindled by the ardor of God's true love, you will achieve the perfect bliss in which you will live forever.

Note

1. On stability versus pilgrimage, see Letter 92, n. 1.

162

Hildegard to the Congregation of Nuns

1161–70

A long allegorical exhortation for the nuns to cultivate obedience and denial of the world, and return to the pristine purity of their community.

The first plant, which flourished in the first root of Jesse [cf. Is 11.1ff], says to this assembly: "A certain man had a fig tree planted in his vineyard" [Luke 13.6]. And just as a blessing multiplied the blessings of a noble seed, so God with great zeal and with His blessing planted a spiritual seed in the vineyard of Sabaoth [cf. Rom 9.29]. And that plant was pleasant and delectable through the beginning of sanctity, and it grew in good reputation like the leaf of the fig tree. But good reputation without fruit will not be profitable unless it appears sweet as an apple in the taste of obedience. A fig tree must be cultivated with great care, lest it wither, for its fruit is bitter at first, but, later, becomes sweet.

So it is with the spiritual life: it must be cultivated with great care, lest the winter of tedium cause it to wither in a person's mind. In the beginning the labor is bitter, because it prohibits the desire of the flesh, the individuality of the will, and other such matters, but contempt for the world is very pleasant and sweet when the spirit, sanctified, envelops itself in sanctity. Still, care must be taken, lest it wither.

Now, that man who had the tree also had a fountain from which many streams flowed. But some horribly black and evil beasts came and tried to keep that fountain from flowing. Some of them picked up weeds with their mouths, and others reeds, and still others took up bellows, and they fanned a fire against the fountain.

O assembly, the Ancient Man brought you forth, a fountain, from which flow streams of sanctity. But terrible beasts of spiritual vices, horrible in their perversity and exceedingly black because they shun the brightness of innocence, come in their malevolence, seeking to influence you so that sanctity will not come forth from you. And some of them pick up weeds of filthy morals in the mouth of their endeavor, and others reeds of vain weariness of good works, and still others take up bellows to puff up arrogance. And they all fan a fire against you, as their minds swell up with great iniquity, so that they regard life in God as punishment. These are the horrible beasts, O daughters of Jerusalem [cf. Cant 1.4], that are seeking to dry you up, and cause you to despair of life.

But the Ancient Man, who planted the fig tree, regards the fruit of His tree in its various works, and He holds the rod in His hand. For through the merits of sanctified spirits that frequently embraced God, He wishes to remove vice from you, and hold you in His hand. But when those precepts of the holy Rule and obedience and good custom established by the saints of old dry up in you, that Man says to the cultivator of the vineyard (that is, to the precepts of discipline), "Behold, for these three years I come seeking fruit on this fig tree, and I find none" [Luke 13.7] in this tree when I look for the works of love and obedience and perseverance. For it merely gives forth the sound of fame, but does not eat the food of the life of perfection. And it does not bring forth apple blossoms of virtues, nor green leaves of holy works, nor works perfect in the chaste chastisement of the body. And He says with the rod of His correction: "Cut it down therefore: why cumbereth it the ground?" [Luke 13.7], as He chastises it with His scourge. For your convent was sanctified when it was first established, but, later, it became an exile, for it was unwilling to suckle its mother's breasts in sanctity and election. Therefore, it is strangled by tribulations and afflictions.

Yet it will not be cut down. For God remembers that He greatly loved it when it was first planted, and that within it He built up holy works within holy spirits. Therefore, in the admonition of the Holy Spirit, He will not abandon it, since the precepts of discipline say: "Lord, let it alone this year also, until I dig about it, and dung it" [Luke 13.8]. For God has regard for the blood of His Son, as it is written, "Ask of me, and I will give thee the Gentiles for thy inheritance" [Ps 2.8], because I was well pleased with you [cf. Matt 3.17]. And thus He is gathering this assembly in its tribulation and affliction and poverty to Himself, as it is written: O Jerusalem, "return to the Lord thy God" [Hosea 14.2], and again, "Arise and stand on high" [Baruch 5.5], and "behold the joy that will come to you from your God" [Baruch 4.36], and be adorned with virtues, because God seeks a sacrifice of praise from you [cf. Ps 49.14;.23], and wishes to keep you as He saw you when you were first planted. The gifts of the Holy Spirit will not desert you, and you will remain in your sanctification.

Lubolzberg(?)

163

An Abbess to Hildegard

Before 1173

Having learned that Hildegard has consoled many others through her letters, the
abbess writes for help in her own time of trouble.

To Hildegard, bride of Christ in Mount St. Rupert, N., humble superior of the
sisters in Lubolzberg, with a devout prayer in Christ.

God, Who searches the heart and reins [cf. Ps 7.10], knows how much I have
longed, and still long, to see your face and to enjoy conversation with you. But
because my sins stand in my way, I have never been able to achieve my desire.
Still, since I have often heard that many have been consoled by your writings
(although it has not been granted them to see your face), with the same hope, I,
sinner that I am, have dared to seek your advice through the present missive, if
by chance God's mercy will grant that my affliction be consoled by your goodness. Complex indeed is the sorrow of my heart, but I hope with all my being
that it can be relieved by you.

163r

Hildegard to the Abbess

Before 1173

A letter of encouragement to the abbess, stressing that God still loves the person
who wanders astray.

Day brightens light, and night darkens darkness. Even if the night wishes to fight
against the day, however, it cannot extinguish it. But if the day wishes to overcome the night, it has the ability to vanquish it. May the true light, which God
foresaw for man on the first day, be with you. For a father loves his son even
when he leaves home, because he is aware that the son is not looking for an opportunity to sin as if there were no God. Just so, God sees that your spirit is
wandering, but still your mind mocks sin's forbidden fruits, which destroy the
spirit.

Therefore, I see you like the radiance of the sun glowing through the inspiration of the Holy Spirit, totally avoiding the exile of perdition. For, through

penitence our sweet mother, you look to the sun like the eagle. And, therefore, God loves you very much.

Now, live forever.

Lutter

164

A Certain Priest to Hildegard

Before 1173

The writer praises God for giving a manly spirit to one of the "frail sex," and asks for advice about the state of his soul and of those who live with him.

To the lady Hildegard, radiant with the radiance of the divine light, N., unworthy priest and instructor of the poor in Lutter, that is, in the hospice here, with a prayer that when the glory of the Lord appears, she will be satisfied, along with the elect [cf. Ps 16.15].

Frequently recalling your grace and kindness which many have experienced, we give thanks to God almighty, who deigned to confer a manly spirit (and so many virtues) on so frail a sex, especially on a woman who has lacked bodily strength from childhood. May the Lord increase His grace in you and all who dwell with you. And in His benevolence may He cause you to be mindful of us (and of the many who have put their hope in you) before the Lord.

We hope to hear wholesome examples of your sanctity, and to learn the state of our lives from you. And so whatever God reveals to you concerning this matter, please deign to send it to us in writing, resting assured that we have determined to obey your advice and admonitions to the best of our ability. For we have been enjoined to serve the poor—a task we cannot complete without our spirits being troubled and burdened down by a heavy weight.

Therefore, we desire to know from you whether it would be better for us to lock ourselves away in our cloister, or to persevere in this turmoil. May God reveal to you which course of action pleases Him better in this matter.

164r

Hildegard to the Priest

Before 1173

Writing back to provide the requested advice, Hildegard gives a long allegorical
and moral interpretation of the parable of the good Samaritan.

In a true vision, with eyes fully awake, I heard these words in my spirit: My son,
you who are the image of God, listen to this parable, which the Son of God spoke
to those who decided among themselves what they had chosen for themselves:
"A certain man went down from Jerusalem to Jericho" [Luke 10.30]. This is what
the Son of God said about the first man, who learned that he could sin through
the report of the serpent which he heard from the woman [cf. Gen 3.1ff]. And he
himself made that choice for himself which he had heard through the report. For
the mind is, as it were, male, and the choice, as it were, female. For when a person chooses some matter for himself, and has drawn it to himself through his own
choice, he loves that thing very much, just as Adam loved his choice which he
heard from the woman, because the woman was an integral part of him, just as a
choice is an integral part of the mind. And when Adam had done this, he went
down from "the vision of peace,"[1] and became like the moon which wanes. Yet
although he was an outcast, he still knew his Creator, and in that knowledge he
was like the moon which sometimes waxes.

"And he fell among robbers" [Luke 10.30], because his will deceived him, just
as a robber deceives people with his crafty whispers until he captures them. "Who
also stripped him" [Luke 10.30], that is, his will stripped him of all the glory he
had in paradise, just as robbers strip people and divide up their property. Therefore, every person who wishes to be happy should avoid what his will chooses, for
it is harmful to him (like Adam's listening to the woman), and it wounds him so
deeply that with great sighs he must seek a physician if he wishes to be healed. For
Adam's transgression made him an exile so that he was scarcely alive to the knowledge of good and evil, and he could be relieved neither by Abel's sacrifice [cf. Gen
4.4], which Noah perfected in building the altar [cf. Gen 8.20], nor by Abraham's
obedience [cf. Gen 22.9ff], which Moses fulfilled through the law [cf. Ex 24].

But the Samaritan raised him up. For the Samaritan is the Son of God, made
incarnate in the shrine of the Holy Spirit, that is, in the immaculate Virgin, without
any of the blindness of Adam, which human nature has as a result of sin. And He
raised Adam and all his race from the pit of hell. He also poured oil and wine on
his wounds [cf. Luke 10.34]: oil when, moved to pity for him [cf. Luke 10.33],
He revealed Himself in His incarnation; wine when he commanded penitence
for his sins, as it is written, "Do penance: for the kingdom of heaven is at hand"
[Matt 3.2; 4.17].

"And setting him upon his own beast, he brought him to an inn" [Luke 10.34].
His body is like a beast, because it carried a man on its shoulders onto the wood

of the cross. This also shows that when He made man, He created beasts along with him, just as He also saw His own incarnation when He formed man. And when He became incarnate as He willed, man, along with all creation, looked upon Him and recognized Him as both God and man. And He gave the whole world to man for a tabernacle, an inn, as it were, and He brought him into that inn when He freed him through His Passion and cured him by mercy and penitence.

"And the next day he took out two pence, and gave them to the host" [Luke 10.35]. On the next day, after His resurrection, He left the man[2] to his representatives, that is, to the apostles and all those who have followed their example, commanding them to do just as He had done [cf. Luke 10.37]. And He gave them two covenants: one that the New Law had made and one that He Himself had created. For just as God created the beasts when He made man, so too men under the Old Law sacrificed creatures, that is, birds and beasts, to God, but afterward they made unseen sacrifice in the Holy Spirit through the sacrificial offering of Christ's incarnation, because we recognize His incarnation through our selves,[3] but are unable to gaze on His divinity. Yet we embrace that divinity through faith, just as we know this world but look to eternal life through faith. We see our bodies but we can in no way see our spirits, save that we know that we cannot live without our spirits. So it is with all our works—some seen, some unseen—and so it is too that we regard the Creator of all things in His humanity and His divinity.

It was in such a way that God left the man to His representatives in the two covenants, so that they might do with him as He had shown them, that is, by anointing his wounds with mercy, and cleansing them by penitence, and to continue this until the last day. Then, when He returns, He will give a mansion of "eternal inheritance" [Heb 9.15] to all those who have done with goodwill what He has shown them.[4]

Now, you, O steward of God, do likewise, and beware lest your mind become darkened—without sun or moon or stars. Take care, that is, not to choose one thing or another according to your own will and pleasure, saying that this is good and that is good, because, in that case, your mind becomes a dark cloud. But look to the true Samaritan, and in the service to which you have been appointed by your superior, do as He did, because it pleases God that mercy is shown to the poor, and that sinners are brought to penitence. Do this to the best of your ability, giving aid to the one who gives alms for his sins, so that you may live forever.

Notes

1. That is, from Jerusalem. *Visio pacis* is the usual medieval etymological/symbolical interpretation of the name *Jerusalem*. Hildegard is engaged in working out her explication of the parable of the Good Samaritan.
2. That is, His humanity.
3. That is, through our humanity.
4. Hildegard's extended interpretation of the parable may seem uncommonly strained, atypical, even original. It is not. St. Caesarius—and others—explicated the parable in a similar fashion. All such readings go back at least to Origen, who interpreted the Samaritan as Christ, the wounds as disobedience, the ass as the body of Christ, etc.

Mainz (St. Victor)

165

A Provost to Hildegard

Before 1173

In shame and confusion on account of his many abominable iniquities, the provost writes seeking Hildegard's intercession with the Lord. He wants to know
whether he is predestined for life or eternal death.

To Hildegard, mirror of divine contemplation, G., "outcast of the people" [Ps 21.7]
and provost of St. Victor in Mainz, if the sighs of a contrite, humbled heart are
efficacious.

Attracted by the good aroma of your reputation and animated to the hope
of salvation from the depths of sin, I request that you allow me, nurturing mother,
to approach you, and lay bare my wretchedness with tears of compunction. Perhaps it is presumptuous of me—but presumptuous, I think, for the right reasons—
to seek your aid and advice. I can scarcely find the words to express my misery,
my confusion and shame, my tears of distress. And no wonder! For my body and
spirit were sinfully polluted—worthy, it grieves me to confess, of divine chastisement by the just and merciful judgment of God, although even worse pas-
sions followed. For I have often fallen into abominable iniquity, both in thought
and deed—which, however, you know well through the revelation of the Holy
Spirit. Therefore, it is hardly necessary for me to write that things are not well
with my soul, for the Spirit teaches you everything.

So, saintly lady, I cast myself at your feet, since "I am dust and ashes" [Gen
18.27], and with humble devotion beseech you to pray for me to the Consoler
and Liberator of our souls. And please inform me whether I have any hope for
salvation: am I predestined for life or foreknown for death. Please do not regard
my presumption as foolishness. May the Holy Spirit, who dwells in you, grant
you to respond to all these things, in answer to my prayers, according to my faith
and humility. Farewell.

Mainz (Altmünster)

166

An Abbess to Hildegard

1167–70(?)

A brief letter asking Hildegard to intercede with the Lord for her sinful soul and to write a letter of admonition back to her.

To her lady, Hildegard, virgin dedicated to God, N., abbess (in name only) of the sisters of Altmünster in Mainz, with a prayer that she enjoy the blessing of life in heaven after so long an illness.

If you have recovered to any degree from your illness, my lady, I rejoice. If not, I grieve with my whole heart. Lo, I write to you, making presumption on our friendship, and I ask you to heed my devotion for you, and to work diligently to placate the Lord for my sins. I pray you also through the bond of love to admonish me through the bearer of this letter, and gladden me with a written response, according to the revelation granted you by the Holy Spirit.

Mainz (St. Martin)

167

A Dean to Hildegard

Before 1173

The dean asks for Hildegard's prayers and consolation. He also expresses his desire to come to see her, if opportunity arises, so that he can ask her what he cannot ask in writing.

To Hildegard, reverend lady and beloved mother, N., unworthy dean of St. Martin in Mainz church, with a prayer, modest as it is.

It is not necessary for me to write how greatly I venerate you, saintly lady, how sincerely I love you, and how prepared I am to serve you if you will but deign to employ our service, such as it is. How I long to be frequently consoled by your writings, because the splendor of divine wisdom, which illuminates you within, reveals these things to you. I had determined once to see you myself and be consoled by your words, but I have been hampered by a bodily affliction, and cannot come at the present time. When an opportunity arises, however, God willing, I will see you, and will ask in person what I cannot ask you in writing.

In the meantime, beloved mother, please pray to our Creator and Redeemer on my behalf to so order our life to His will that He may be pleased with us. I ask further that if you have need of our service, you will instruct us as seems best to you. I also long to be consoled again by your writings, brought to me by the present messenger.

May God deign to preserve you and to always illumine you with His Holy Spirit, O blessed mother worthy to be revered with all my devotion.

167r

Hildegard to the Dean

Before 1173

The dean, Hildegard writes, suffers the weariness of sin on account of his previous licentious life. Now, her advice is to do good works, and emulate the prodigal son.

As a result of excessive eating and wine-drinking, excessive vices grow unchecked, and a man's flesh sometimes languishes so much that it can barely live. Afterwards, it is weighed down by the weariness of sins, as if by a heavy sleep. But the devil once more arouses him to sin, and persuades him to put off the time of penance. And from that lethargy, he awakes to sin, with the devil vehemently urging him to continue in his sin. Thus it is that many men put off penitence through the deception of the devil, and wind up in perdition.

When a person sighs for his sins, however, he joins the angels in hymns of praise, and when he performs good works, he shines like the sun. But when he adorns himself in this way, the devil, who had previously roused him to sin through his wicked machinations, attacks him in a furious storm of desperation. Let that man take heed from the publicans and sinners [cf. Matt 9.10–11; Mark 2.15–16; Luke 5.30]: However much they had sinned, they rose again through penitence, and, afterward, became pillars of heaven. Let him put on the breastplate of faith and the helmet of hope [cf. I Thess 5.8], and he will vanquish his enemies.

O servant of God, you lived luxuriously in your childhood, as you know, and you sinfully enjoyed the taste of the flesh in your youth. For this reason you now endure the weariness of sin. Therefore, begin now to do good works before the shadow of this life departs from you, so that in the future you will be able to give a joyous response to the voice that is saying to you now: You were to be a garden on which I could feast my eyes, but you are not, because unwholesome weeds, thorns, and thistles have grown there and choked off the wholesome herbs [cf. Matt 13.7]. Cut down those weeds with the sharp sickle of penitence, and emulate the son in the Gospel, who, having come to his senses, ran to his father, and his father received him joyfully and kissed him in his humanity [cf. Luke 15.11ff]. Plant the seed of fruitful virtue in your garden, and be like the woman who sought her lost drachma, so that heaven will rejoice over you [cf. Luke 15.8ff], and you will become a gem in celestial life. And you will live forever.

168

A Provost to Hildegard

Before 1173 (1152–58?)

After words of high praise for Hildegard, and a wish that it had been his lot to remain constantly by her side, the provost[1] seeks a letter of advice from her on how to amend his life.

To Hildegard, lady worthy of all glory and honor, H., provost of the house in Mainz, though a filthy sinner, offers whatever a servant or son may to his beloved lady and mother.

My spirit burns and is awed. Burns to speak, but is awed by the magnitude of your wisdom and eloquence. With blessed felicity, it has been granted to you to perceive wisely, and to offer us the fruits of your wisdom. The authority of the abounding Scriptures has found an abode in you, and remains with you, making you its repository. Moreover, favored with the dowry of learning, you have become the adornment of the Church, and an example for the people.

I wish that it had been granted to me from above to cling to you constantly, to hear you always, to be restored by associating with you without interruption. Then, I would not be cheated of my desire, for I have always longed to hear you. Therefore, please deign, I beseech you, if the Lord our God so grants, to convey to me in a sealed letter whatever in me is displeasing to Him, and how I might rid myself of it.

Flourish forever, saintly lady, and may all your faithful daughters be well, and always remain my beloved sisters.

Note

1. The provost is variously identified in the MSS. Hence Van Acker's double set of dates. In agreement with H. Lindeman ("S. Hildegard en hare Nederlandsche vrienden," *Ons Geestelijk Erf* 2 [1928], 128–60), however, Van Acker thinks it most likely that the recipient was Baldwin of Utrecht, who was later to serve as bishop of Utrecht from 1178 to 1196.

Mainz(?)

169

A Community of Brothers
to Hildegard

1163

The brothers have heard that Hildegard has written against the heresy of the Cathars, and they write to request a copy of her treatise.

To the dear lady and most holy mother, Hildegard, servant of Christ and mistress of the sisters in the monastery of the blessed Rupert in Bingen, from the whole community of the brothers of St. N., with a prayer that she be granted to walk with consent in the house of God [cf. Ps 54.15], and be pleasing to the Bridegroom of virgins in this valley of tears [cf. Ps 83.17].

Because it is proper that we look to God's will in matters that concern us, we flee to the refuge of your compassion, pious lady. For God has regarded you and has marvellously endowed you with a divine gift—a gift unheard of in our time—and, in accordance with God's bidding, you employ that gift not for yourself alone, but for the benefit of many others. Indeed, having seen and heard the miracles that the Lord works through you, we offer to God our resounding praise, unworthy as it is. But because we frequently neglect God, we are crushed by numerous tribulations, afflicted by countless disasters, and subjected to anxieties without number. And so lest despairing, we perish, it is proper—as it is necessary—for us to flee to those who devoutly love God, and who, with Mary, have chosen the best part [cf. Luke 10.42], so that we may seek their counsel and help. We have heard from truthful persons that you have written against the heresy of the Cathars, just as you learned to do through a vision of the secrets of God. We devoutly ask that you send this writing to us, for we have greater faith in revelations and responses from God than from man. And so we commend ourselves to your saintly prayers, asking you to kindly send to us whatever your Bridegroom, the Lord Jesus, deigns to reveal to you concerning these matters.

Farewell.

169r

Hildegard on the Cathars

1163

This is Hildegard's treatise against the Cathars,[1] in which she cites liberally from
the apocalyptic biblical books of Daniel, Isaiah, and Apocalypse.

In the month of July of the present year, which is one thousand one hundred and
sixty-three from the Incarnation of our Lord, I looked from afar and, in the shadow
of a true vision, I gazed under the altar [cf. Apoc 6.9] which is before the eyes of
God [cf. Apoc 9.13], and I gazed also under the throne of God.

And I saw that the twenty-four elders, who sit around the throne [cf. Apoc
4.4ff], moved the glass sea, which is before the throne [cf. Apoc 4.6], and they
said: Let us move the vain foundations of mockery laid down by those who seek
to substitute their injustice for justice; and let us move the sparks of burning injustice kindled by those who say that they govern the people, but do not really
govern them; and let us move the weeds of various squalid morals and the gilt
cords of illusions and the schisms of schisms.

For the ancient lion roars, longing to fly into the midst of the aforesaid sparks
of burning injustice. But the time has not come for this. Let us call upon the
Ancient One, in Whom all species of growing things and all creatures are enumerated; and let us look upon the sword that appeared in the mouth of the speaker
[cf. Apoc 1.16; 19.15]; and let us consider the cost of two pounds of wheat and
barley [cf. Apoc 6.6]; and let us contemplate the trumpet that sounds before the
first woe; and through the oath of those and through the power of the One Who
sits on the throne [cf. Apoc 7.10; 21.5], let us bind the neck of the ancient lion,
and restrain him with the bridle, lest before the time of times and the half time
[cf. Apoc 12.14], and before the forty months, he send the sea forth after the
woman fleeing in the desert [cf. Apoc 12.6].

For it has now been twenty-three years and four months since the four winds
brought about great ruin through the permission of the four angels at the corners of the earth, and this came about because of the perverse works of mankind,
which are blown forth from the mouth of the black beast. For their own works
rose up over them so that the instability of filthy morals was blown forth in the
East, and in the West blasphemy and forgetfulness of God came upon His saints
through the ill-repute of the calf and through the worship of idols which per-
verts the holy sacrifice [cf. Ex 32.4ff], and in the South the filth of hateful vices,
and in the North widened phylacteries of vestments [cf. Matt 23.5] in accordance
with the will of the coiled serpent, and these are contaminated by the sudden
arrival of all the aforementioned evils.

Yet it has been sixty years and twenty-four months since the ancient serpent began to delude the people with the phylacteries of vestments. Now, however, the innumerable saints of God, who are under the altar, lift up their voices,

crying out that the sprinkling of their corporal ashes is violated by the iniquity of the people [cf. Apoc 6.9f]. Thus from the sound of these saints, a wind is beginning to blow, which is now working miracles. Still, the one who sits upon the black horse [cf. Apoc 6.5] is sending forth the noise of a contrary wind to dissipate those miracles. But it will not prevail.

And, again, the ancient dragon roars in anger against the saints of God, and lifting himself up on the wings of the winds [cf. Ps 103.3], says: What is this? I will destroy what these, and those like them, have established. And they answer him: "Who hath measured the waters in the hollow of his hand, and weighed the heavens with his palm? Who hath poised with three fingers the bulk of the earth, and weighed the mountains in scales, and the hills in a balance" [Is 40.12]? For we have weighed by God's scales, by Whom we do all things through the fiery spark that blazes before His face. You, however, have eyes that flash forth a destructive fire, and you will send forth a flame almost to the place where you were first established, and you will do this against God and against the heavens and against all those who are in heaven. But you will not be able to accomplish that. For when God has weighed the heavens in his palm, then a burning mountain will fall upon your neck, and all your strength will be utterly destroyed. But at that time a new canticle [cf. Ps 39.4] will be given to us from the throne, and to us also will be given eyes that look around on all sides, seeing and understanding all things. You, however, no longer have the time for devouring with your voracious throat. Therefore, in the name of God's throne and all His garments, give up this madness!

But, O you people, hear the Spirit of God saying to you: Within your midst, the ancient serpent is building towers in their ears, that is, those who are like the Sadducees and like those who call Baal God, and do not know the just God, so that by the cunning of a deceitful spirit, he sometimes appears to them like a spark, either black or stormy, or bright and local, and which soon vanishes. And this is a diabolical and deceptive thing, for deceptive spirits sometimes disguise themselves as the four elements and all their powers, because they conquered the first man. This, however, is by the permission of God, the source of wisdom and prophecy, but the revelation of matters that do not pertain to man remain hidden, because God is incomprehensible.

These men in whose ears the devil is building towers are like a crab, which moves forward and backward, and they are like scorpions, which furtively sting you with fiery tails and kill you with the terrible poison of cruel unbelief. These men the devil at times inspires with seemingly divine precepts, which they themselves seek by their own will, since they are, after all, the image of God. And the devil does this so that he may the more easily deceive them.

They are also like those large birds that cast aside their own eggs. And they say: Let us get rid of this, because it is poisonous. These are the people who deny first principles, that is, that God created all things, and commanded them to wax and multiply. These are the people who deny the sovereign principle, that is, that it was clear even before the ancient days that the Word of God was bound to become man. These people should be considered worse than the Jews, who are too blind to see the fiery form that now shines as man in holy divinity. After a long time, these Jews will think that they have seen the just one, until God strikes the one that they believe in with a fiery scourge.

These Cathars are also fiery, sulfurous mountains, along with that evil beast who will open his mouth against God, and against heaven, and against all those who are in heaven [cf. Apoc 13.6]. And they are the very bowels of that unnatural beast, which coughs up and spits out the most disgusting impurity. And just as the prophets preceded the Lord and prophesied the way of salvation, demonstrating that He was filled with all the virtues of justice, so too do these precede the beast, embracing the filth and wickedness of all evils, going the way of the errant. For these prophets were inspired and taught by the finger of God, just as the devil fills these people with blasphemy, wickedness, and the falseness of all evil. For in the beginning of his ruin, the ancient serpent lost the key that he thought he had, but now he thinks in himself that this wicked beast is his key, and that he will be able to fulfill all his will through him. But in that beast, all his strength will be utterly destroyed.

Now, you, O people who hold the purest faith, looking to God, hear the voice of the one "who was and who is and who is about to come" [Apoc 1.4]: Hear the words of the priests who hold and preserve My justice. For these My words will sound in their ears, and they will speak these words to you in My name. Then with clamoring voices cast this impure and profane people out of your midst, and torment them with harsh and cruel words. Send them into exile, and put them to flight into the unhappy caverns and caves, for they want to seduce you. And do this immediately, lest you be cursed by God and peace flee from you. For you cannot be called teachers, and priests, kings, leaders, and princes of the people before God while you allow these people to live among you, for your cities and villas will be destroyed, and your estates will be plundered while these wicked people remain among you.

Now, praise be to God, Who sits on the throne and looks into the abyss [cf. Dan 3.55], and Who governs all of heaven. And the Spirit of God says: Whoever will neglect to hear and understand these words, and refuses to believe them—this one the sword of God's word [cf. Eph 6.17] will strike with great tribulation.

And soon in that same vision, I heard a resounding voice saying to me: Write these things which you have seen and heard, and send them quickly to those priests of the Church [cf. Apoc 1.11] who worship God with the purest faith, so that they may preach them everywhere to the people in their parish, and thus protect them from these devilish treacheries, lest those evil people put down roots among them, and they perish.

I, a poor little form of a woman, languished for many days oppressed by sickness so that I could scarcely walk until I had committed these things to writing.

Note

1. On the Cathars, see Introduction, Vol. 1, pp. 11–14. See also Letter 15r.

170

Certain Priests to Hildegard

Before 1153

The priests ask for a letter of general admonition and advice because they feel that they fall short in their duty and their lives.

To Hildegard, venerable and beloved lady and mother of the monastery of the blessed Rupert, the priests (alas, in name only) N., A., H., and E., along with other brothers of their community under the protection of St. Martin, with a devout prayer that she receive the blessing of both saints.

O elect and beloved servant of sanctity and dearest mother of many who follow sanctity, because we have heard many things about you that bring the "odour of life" [II Cor 2.16] to many people, we flee to your protection, seeking with thirsty hearts those things which are of God. For we were consecrated to the service of God from childhood so that we might faithfully serve our Creator in the holy orders of divine office. Yet although we have achieved the priesthood, and therefore ought to live worthily and irreproachably, we nevertheless frequently neglect the things that are of the spirit and do the things that are of the flesh [cf. Rom 8.5]. For although we ought to be the eye of contemplation, the ear of obedience, the nose of discernment, the mouth of truth, the hand of just work, the foot of the way of righteousness, and an example of virtue for God's people, we are more the "odour of death" [II Cor 2.16] and a stumbling block than a true rock of solidity. Therefore, we are guilty of many evils, for we have, so to speak, fallen from the sanctuary of the Lord to the filth of the slime.

Now, you, O pious mother, knowledgeable of the secrets of God, hear us earnestly and humbly beseeching you to offer us words of divine admonition, and to correct and advise us, because, although we have a modest knowledge of Scripture, we greatly desire to hear you who have received true and marvellous knowledge from the great Teacher Himself, and not from man. Now, may God pour into you that which you can then pour out to us who thirst.

Farewell.

170r

Hildegard to the Priests

Before 1153

A letter of general admonition and advice to the priests with a special emphasis on chastity.

The voice of living wings [cf. Ezech 3.13; Apoc 9.9] says: O you who support the stones, and gird the members of diverse people, hear what I say to you: Run through the level streets to perform the sacrifices prescribed by the law. And gird your loins and restrain your limbs, as this figure shows through the mystical gift of God: "Gird thy sword upon thy thigh, O thou most mighty" [Ps 44.4]. For divinity looked upon the simple character of a humble girl, and rested there in sweetest chastity, which was not touched by earthly viridity, but by supernal heat in its secret.ᵃ Then, True Man arose as if from dry earth, which the plow did not break. And the fruit of this earth was not inseminated, but produced a flower from the heat of the sun. Therefore, this Most Powerful One was girded with a sword, that is, with pure and piercing true justice, for the heat of the flesh and sin were not in Him. But as the son is from the father, the noble from the noble, the king from the king, and each from its own kind, so priests were established by Me, just as the father bequeaths his substance to his son, as it is written: "Israel is my inheritance" [Is 19.25], because it is imparted to the highest priesthood by mercy and grace and truth.

This testament is transmitted from Me to you, just "as a man of war" [Is 42.13] who has a large army passes it on to his son. So let priests imitate their Father and Lord, and just as He walked, let them walk in restraint of their bodies. Yet if a priest commits sin in the putridity of the flesh or in the wantonness of pride and lasciviousness, let him rise up, seek out a physician, and vomit up that sin as if it were poison, certainly not hold onto it longer, as if it were his close friend.

Therefore, hear: A lord had two regions: one, humid; the other, dry. In the humid region, all sorts of business transactions were being carried on, as in Tarsus, Tyre, Macedonia, and Ethiopia. In Tarsus, understand those who were running quickly and growing in everything, but still struggling with difficulty; in Tyre, those laboring in straitened circumstances and sometimes suffering want in their great need; in Macedonia, those burning in dryness, like the fruit that at one time flourishes, at another fades, or like a wolf, which at times devours, at times desists, at times carries off, at times kills; in Ethiopia, those feasting furtively and rejoicing in venomous tyranny and burning in shamelessness. In the arid region, on the other hand, there were opulent men, who had the beauty of herbs and flowers not planted by human hand. These remained in quiet contemplation of their Lord, where there was the sweetest odor and the most delightful sound, just as was prefigured in Abel, who was the first to act properly [cf. Gen 4.4], and in Abraham, who revealed obedience [cf. Gen 22.9ff], and in Moses, who gave instruction to souls by establishing the precepts of sacrifice [cf. Ex 29], and in the Son of God, Who fulfilled all good things. This parable denotes the world, which grows among secular people because they bring forth children, but which decreases among spiritual people because they do not sow their seed. But God established chief teachers over the common people for the instruction of their souls. And also the Son of God came as the supernal teacher, as it is written: Behold the Lord will appear on a white cloud [cf. Apoc 14.14], "and with him thousands of saints" [Deut 33.2], "and he hath on his garment, and on his thigh written: King of kings, and Lord of lords" [Apoc 19.16]. For the Son of God appeared in the innocence of a simple girl as in a cloud, "and he hath set His tabernacle in the sun" [Ps 18.6] when He marvellously illuminated the mind of that Virgin, when she said: "Behold the handmaid of the Lord; be it done to me according to thy word" [Luke 1.38]. And there arose in her a great column towering over all those who are born after the flesh when the Son of God came forth "as a bridegroom out of his bride chamber" [Ps 18.6], born of that sweetest Virgin, as if in a delightful dream and in the sweetest desire, as a bridegroom sweetly joins his spouse to himself in his mind. Therefore, many admirable virtues appeared with Him, far exceeding in good works the institutes of the Old Law. And so on His vestment and on His thigh was written: "King of kings, and Lord of lords," for His flesh sweetly sweated forth from the Virgin, and not from the thigh of a man.[b] Therefore, He rose up over all creatures, like a king who rules men, because sin did not bring Him forth, but the mighty power of divine might that foreknew all creatures before they came forth in the world. Thus He administered all the institutes of the law to His members, like a good steward who shows the people subject to him what is necessary for them, and what is not, as it is written: "Thou shalt rule them with a rod of iron, and shalt break them in pieces like a potter's vessel" [Ps 2.9]. For in the strongest might of divinity, the Living Fountain sprang forth, Who, through Himself, shows the purest and most constant precepts of the law, thus commanding justice to the righteous with an iron rod, both breaking and establishing all things according to what was just, as a potter breaks one vessel and makes another.

Now, hear, O you who would emulate Me [cf. I Cor 4.16; Phil 3.17]: From the beginning of the world, My people had predecessors and teachers. Why, therefore, do you display indignation and audaciousness and instability of character in your garrulous pride, as if you could create new heavens or a lofty mountain of ivory? For the wind easily disperses these things, and men trample them underfoot. In this way, you bear away in your souls the ten pounds and that penny which is the payment of the heavenly kingdom among righteous men [cf. Luke 19.12ff; Matt 20.1ff].

Rather, "Embrace discipline" [Ps 2.12], that is to say, the precepts established by the Law for your members, and be as pure in your thoughts, your words, and your works as the burnt sacrifice offered up by a priest, avoiding venomous words in the vanity of this world, because transgression of the Law is not expedient to you. But bear the light of faith in your hands so that all the people will run to you. These are the precepts of the Law, like a great mountain upon which a light cannot be hidden. And embrace discipline in the girding of your loins, shining as a good example to other people, for you hold the rod of governance over them.

Also, "take heed" [Josh 23.6], "lest at any time the Lord be angry, and you perish from the just way" [Ps 2.12], for you ought to walk according to the example of the Son of God on the path of good works. For these attributes of your office were anciently prefigured in the sacrifice of calves and lambs. In the Old Testament, the priests were not restrained in their loins, because no one girded in his loins had preceded them. Now, however, the "sun of justice" [Mal 4.2] has shone forth. Therefore, walk in that sun and preserve your chastity, for neither a calf nor a goat nor a lamb was hanged on the wood of the cross for you, but the great and good Shepherd was given to the Passion of the cross for you. Imitate Him in your works.

Against injustice, however, "be ye angry, and sin not" [Ps 4.5], that is, do not have hatred, or envy, or harshness in the derision of your heart when you see people fall on account of the foolishness of their way of life, but anoint them with compassion, and correct them with gentleness [cf. Ps 140.5]. And do not be puffed up in your own self-esteem as if you are holy on account of the tonsure of your flesh so that you say in your hearts: The Lord chose us in sanctity, and nobody can exceed us in virtue. And why do you scorn the bright face of those who have embraced My garment through circumcision of their minds [cf. Rom 2.29], those who according to my ordination imitate the angels (who are the mirror of My face), and in contempt of the temporal world follow them. For an angel announced salvation to all people [cf. Luke 1.26ff]. And also in Abraham and in Jacob and in the rod of Aaron, angels announced salvation to the people beforehand [cf. Gen 22.15ff; 32.1ff; Num 17.2ff]. Why, therefore, should not these imitators of angels and of My garment not be able to, or even be obliged to, foresee the salvation of the people "for the present necessity" [I Cor 7.26] of those in need?

Therefore, enlist in the army of sanctity and "be sorry upon your beds" [Ps 4.5], so that humility may build a tower in you, a tower with windows of the virtues of good works, and with vaults of holy medicine, to each according to his measure [cf. Eph 4.7]. And let them see your interior mysteries, which are your good works. Therefore, be solicitous to see to it that your sanctity is gold, and not lead, because Jacob was upright in the height of felicity, but Esau was straitened and laid low in his conceit. Likewise, your mind is moved in the two parts of the spiritual life. Now, therefore, be vigorous and strengthen yourselves in all good things so that you do not fail.

171

Hildegard to the Abbot Dieter

1153–54

A letter of general advice to the abbot.

The Wise Man of the bold light says: O man, hear these words: a person who desires to achieve eternal life must make a reflective inspection of his spirit with living eyes, because God is vigilant in such matters. When fleshly desires seek to overwhelm a man, spewing forth all sorts of nasty vices, then let a man rein in the appetite of his mind so that he grows weary of the intolerable deed. Then he will be able to rise up to the Dawn of Light, that is, to Mercy, Who laid death low and crushed the filthy bowels of hell, and cleansed the sins of mankind. Thus a person ought to have windows in the soul through which he may reorient himself to the good.

But, O you who are noble in your will, take note that many rivers run in you, rushing in great uproar. O strong bond, turn aside the breasts of burgeoning desire for vice. Model yourself on the turtledove, bending your knees when you conquer yourself. O living figure, open the closed door of your mind in that beautiful face of yours, because that befits you in the sight of the high King. Beware, too, not to be leaden in the harshness of your mouth, failing to anoint the wounds of the wounded. Therefore, kiss God in your mind, and do not let your desires be embarrassed in their good desire to do good and just works.

Now, take refreshment in your toil, rein in your secular concerns, and make the face of your soul as beautiful as the dove [cf. Cant 2.14], so that the windows of celestial Jerusalem [cf. Heb 12.22] will welcome you. God will not abandon you [cf. Deut 31.6ff], but will give you the refection of salvation.

172

An Abbot to Hildegard

Before 1173

Worried about the duties of his office, the abbot writes to Hildegard for her prayers and consolation.

To Hildegard, spiritual mother and venerable sister, H., abbot of Maulbronn (would that I deserved to be!), with a prayer that she receive perpetual salvation from the Lord.

We have heard good things about you, O servant of Christ, have heard, and give thanks to the Giver of all good. Therefore, since I have some hope that I will be heard, whatever my condition, I send this letter to you, and request the singular support of your prayers. For I have an arduous and worrisome duty, that is, the governance of souls, and so I request, I beseech, I implore help from the Lord, through you, for a happy outcome.

I trust that it will not be too burdensome or trivial for you to write back to me so that my body and soul might be instructed, comforted, and consoled.

Farewell.

173

The Monk Heinrich to Hildegard

Before 1170

Heinrich praises Hildegard highly, and asks for her prayers.

To Hildegard, the beautiful olive tree [cf. Ecclus 24.19] and pearl of great price [cf. Matt 13.46], Heinrich, unworthy monk in Maulbronn, with a prayer that she go out to meet the celestial Bridegroom with burning lamp [cf. Matt 25.1ff].

"O how beautiful is the chaste generation with glory: for the memory thereof is immortal: because it is known both with God and with men" [Wisdom 4.1]. From that beautiful, blessed generation, it is clear that you have arisen as the daughter of the mighty King, adorned with blazing proofs of virtue, for you bear in the outward appearance of your notable work the beauty of your inner person. The resemblance to your mother is reflected by the great beauty of your virtue, for, following her example, you have sought wool and flax [cf. Prov 31.13], and you have woven "clothing of tapestry" [cf. Prov 31.22] as the covering of your spirit. Indeed, each faithful soul puts on clothing of tapestry when it is clothed with the virtue of love, into whose fabric is woven many various images. In clothing such as this, regal Humility, Obedience, Piety, Restraint, Chastity, and Saintliness stand resplendent, along with many thousand qualities like those I have just named. Garbed in this variety of virtues you stand at times at the right hand of the mighty King, like that queen named in prophecy [cf. Ps 44.10], since you have found the priceless treasure of wisdom [cf. Ecclus 1.26ff; Col 2.3], from which you have shown to mankind, as if from the abyss, the brightness of eternal light [cf. Wisdom 7.26].

"Hearken, O daughter, and see, and incline thy ear" to me [Ps 44.11] so that with the salvific aid of your prayers (for love consists in esteem for one's neighbor) I may find perfected in me what I now perceive to be less than perfect. I am absolutely convinced that His special attention is on you and that it has fallen to you to be forever in His gaze. Sister and lady, I also ask that you graciously send me some admonition from heaven, so that through it I may have ever before the eyes of my heart a memorial of your saintliness.

What more? Though absent in body, I greet you in spirit [cf. I Cor 5.3], earnestly beseeching that you be mindful of me, a sinner, for with the Apostle you always direct the course of your mind to the things that are to come [cf. Phil 3.13].

Farewell.

173r

Hildegard to the Monk Heinrich

Before 1170

Hildegard relates a parable about proper penitence, and applies its moral to Heinrich.

The Shadow of God's mysteries says: The wind blows, the air shifts, and clouds become so intermingled that sometimes they are stormy, sometimes black, sometimes white, and sometimes luminous. And you are just like that, O knight of God. For sometimes you have worldly sadness like the blowing wind, and sometimes you are caught up in the pleasure that the devil lays down as a trap like the shifting air, and sometimes you are morally astray like the mingling clouds, so that sometimes your morals are squalid in storms, sometimes terrified in darkness, sometimes sweet in whiteness, sometimes wholesome in luminosity.

Therefore, listen. A certain lord stood on a high mountain, and called his servants, saying: Pay your debt [cf. Matt 18.34]. One of those servants was standing before him, and the other was seated. And the one who was standing answered: Lord, I have come as an exile from a far distant land, where I acquired an unstable character through my many vices and sins. O woe that I have broken all your precepts! Therefore, for fear of losing your love, I swear that I will repent with my whole heart. Moreover, I have always loved and honored your sun, moon, and stars. And his lord answered him: Good servant, I—an ever-turning wheel—accept your answer, saying: I, who live without beginning or end, will give you great honors above all that you have loved before, and I will not condemn you, because you have called out to me in penitence. But the servant who was sitting answered with disdain: Your sun has burned me, your moon has oppressed me, your stars have beaten me down, your dew has drenched the hairs of my head, and your rains have inundated me. And so impeded by all of these, I could not look to you. Therefore, I do not know what I can say. And his lord answered him: Iniquitous servant [cf. Matt 18.32], when I established the sun, moon, and stars, did I need your help? And why do you not blush to respond to me so rashly? For such temerity you deserve to be bound hand and foot, and cast into outer darkness [cf. Matt 22.13] until you pay back everything.

Now, you, O knight of Christ, heed this parable. This lord is your God, Who keeps watch from the heights, because God ought to be invoked by all things. And God exhorts men with this admonition: You must be judged by your works. But some men labor in honor to the Divine, while others dawdle in the doldrums of tedium. Yet those who honor God say: By the instigation of the devil, we fell when Adam went astray, and we have contracted many vices in our works. But we tearfully lament that transgression, and for the glory of Your name, we promise that we desire to abstain from our sins. And in great love, we have venerated Your honor, Your justice, and the Scriptures that You have given us. And the Lord, Who is inscrutable, praises them, and gives them charge over many good things [cf. Matt 25.21ff], and He does not condemn them, because they invoked Him in penitence. But those who slumber in disregard of divine fear say: Your glory has afflicted us, Your justice has wounded us, the multitude of Your Scriptures has suffocated us, the viridity of Your Spirit has turned aside the desire of our mind, and the outpouring of Your zeal has tired us out so that we cannot look to You in joy, and we cannot excuse ourselves. And the Lord calls them iniquitous servants, declaring that He had no need of their aid in administering His justice. Moreover, He asks why they do not blush to assail Him with the temerity of their words. Therefore, they ought to be bound and punished until they get rid of all their vices.

Now, you, O knight of Christ, understand that all these things pertain to you. Indeed, the servant who was standing denotes you. For you did few good things when you were in secular life. But the admonition of the Holy Spirit struck you, and turned you to good. Yet beware lest you be like the sitting servant, that is, lest you say that you are burned by the Rule as by the sun, or lest you have contempt for governance as for the moon, or lest you grow tired of the communion of your brothers as of the stars, or lest you bring derision upon the admonition of the Holy Spirit as the dew, or lest you disdain correction as the rain. But always embrace God in good will and desire, and, by embracing, persevere in Him. Then you will live.

Metz (St. Glodesindis)

174

An Abbess to Hildegard

Before 1173

Greatly concerned about her ability to perform the duties of her office, the abbess asks advice of Hildegard.

To the lady Hildegard, sister dearest to her in Christ, N., abbess (although unworthy) of St. Glodesindis in Metz, with a prayer for salvation in the true Savior.

Because we greatly presume on your grace and your benevolence, we do not wish to hide from you that we are placed in great danger, since we are forced to govern the souls of many although we are not sufficient to the task. Thus we ask you, saintly lady, and earnestly beseech you by our Lord Jesus to strengthen our shaky ignorance, and take care to advise us in a letter what we ought to do: whether we should remain in our office or cede our place to another who might do better. Please inform us if the Lord Jesus deigns to reveal something to you about this matter.

Farewell, and for God's sake pray to God for me, and, if it please you, write back again to me quickly.

174r

Hildegard to the Abbess

Before 1173

Predictably, Hildegard argues that an administrator should not lightly set aside the duties of office, and continues to discuss the "plagues" of sin that mankind inherited from Adam.

Mt. Sion is high, and its shadow, stretching into the valleys, shows its great height. There are other mountains in the pilgrimage of this world, through which Mt. Sion is made strong, and which are beautiful for the people to look upon. Prelates and teachers, who are the firmament of the Church, are signified by the height of Sion and the other mountains, and their disciples are called the "daughters of Sion" [Cant 3.11; Is 3.16]. It would be a great shame if this mountain should fall, or if the others destroyed it.

Therefore, let anyone who holds the reins of governance beware of casting off his yoke, or allowing others to depose him. For just as the mountains serve as a defense for many against their enemies, so also administrators, through their learning and the power to command obedience that God grants them, defend many from the treachery of their enemies. Therefore, as long as he can offer words of doctrine, let no administrator cast aside the rod of correction that he has received from the hand of God, for often mud is cast off by mud, just as an administrator is cleansed by his subordinates, and the subordinates by the administrator.[a] For out of fear for his subordinates, he will afflict himself, and he is punished by the tormentors of his unruly subordinates, and in this way he imitates the Great Master who preceded him.[b] Then, he will say, I showed them your precepts, et cetera [Ex 18.16], and also: "He that hath ears to hear, let him hear" [Matt 11.15]. Therefore, learn from these things lest you flee because of the cloud of instability among your subordinates,[1] or because of the tedium of your labor. For many flee from the tedium of the labor, more than from the fact that they cannot control their subordinates.

A clear day that is not overshadowed by a storm is full of joy. That is what Adam had before the Fall, but the first great deceiver overshadowed that day of his through temptation. From this come the seven plagues [cf. Apoc 15.1ff] that wound the spirit.

The first plague is vainglory, which gathers to itself what it neither sowed nor merited, and takes to itself what was never granted to it by God. The first deceiver taught this, for he acted in just this way. And so vainglory does not seek God.

The second plague is a person's awareness that he has the power to sin, and thus treasures the delight of the flesh, and, once he has tasted it, embraces and kisses it.

The third plague brings on great disaster[2] and grief through filthy morals, so that a person lives as if he were dead to God and scarcely hopes that God knows him.

The fourth plague is that deceit through which a person excuses himself of the aforementioned sins, and defends himself, saying that those sins are not so perilous as he has been told. Thus he becomes so hateful toward his fellow man that he trusts no one.

The fifth plague is pride, which says that since a person cannot abstain from sin because of the flesh of his humanity, he should not have to deny his carnal desires. In its temerity, this is the law that pride adopts for itself, and so shows no respect to God.

The sixth plague manifests itself when a person seeks his salvation from another created thing, and demands it to show him everything, despising his Creator and seeking nothing from Him, as if He were unable to help him.

The seventh plague is enslavement to idolatry, which worships the devil and despises God.

These seven plagues have, as it were, an army under their control more numerous than the branches on a tree, because they all lay hidden in the transgression of the bite that Adam took. For God said to him: In the hour that "thou shalt eat of it, thou shalt die the death" [Gen 2.17]. God set this precept for him lest he should do as the devil did, that is, that he should not be free from His precepts, as the devil wanted to be. Thus no person can be secure in this life on account of the first temptation of the devil to which Adam succumbed.

Therefore, O daughter of God, gird yourself with the mighty armor of the seven gifts of the Holy Spirit, through which you can conquer these seven vices. Gird yourself lest, bewailing, you are wounded by them; and rise up and conquer them by strenuous war like a stalwart knight, so that you may live in eternity.

And so, O daughter, may God see you in the mirror of salvation.

Notes

1. Here Hildegard uses the feminine form *discipularum*, unlike the masculine *discipulorum* that she uses a number of times above.

2. Reading *tertia ruinam* with the *Patrologia*, rather than Van Acker's *tertiam ruinam*, which makes nonsense of the passage. Van Acker does indicate in the textual notes that the *Patrologia* reading is "perhaps correct."

Metz

175

Hildegard to a Certain Priest

Before 1170

A brief letter of admonition to the priest.

The Light of Visitation says to you: O son of salvation, you should flee the castles of the enemy that throw out flames toward you to wound your soul. Now, take heed to perform your stewardship properly lest you be found guilty in the eyes of the Lord. First, "decline from evil and do good" [Ps 36.27]. Then, perform your priestly duty and observe your oath of obedience. Take care to guard your soul vigilantly, and you will live in eternity.

Neuenburg

176

An Abbot to Hildegard

Before 1173

Fearful of the turmoil of war, the abbot had postponed an intended visit to Hildegard, and writes this letter instead, seeking her consolation and advice.

To Hildegard, blessed and saintly woman, E., abbot (in name only) of the brothers of Neuenburg, may we both attain our mutual desire.

The widespread fame of your sanctity has greatly stimulated our spirit to see your face. Therefore, this past summer I prepared to make the trip to see you, but terrified by the storms of war threatening at that time, I did not dare to start out. Nevertheless, I sent a messenger to you with a letter, but he has not yet returned with an answer. And since this letter may be lost through the negligence of the messenger, I will repeat the contents of that letter.

First, I give thanks from the bottom of my heart that you met with a delegation of our brothers. Then, I beseech that through your prayers the Lord help me in these threatening dangers, for placed in a position of authority, I am buffeted by the storms of secular matters. Therefore, I flee to the harbor of your saintliness and prayer so that, no matter what, I will not give in to sin in these matters. And since I ask this in all earnestness, I beg especially that through your prayers I may merit salvation from the Lord, body and soul, when the course of my life has been completed. Amid all these pressures, one stands out above all the others, for which I beseech you to pray to the Lord. Through the present messenger, please send some token of salvation through which I may prosper and have a remembrance of you. My desire to visit with you will never leave me until—"if life accompany" [II Kings 4.16]—I have been able to do so.

Farewell.

176r

Hildegard to the Abbot

Before 1173

Hildegard exhorts the abbot to persevere in his office.

Your mind is like the sphere of the fixed stars, which moves those stars here and there. But frequently a cloud is stirred up by a whirlwind and by the darkness of fire and water until the sun penetrates all things with its fiery sphere.

In your doubt, you are weary, and you are unwilling to labor because of the multifarious wars of mankind's morals. Now, if a young knight, who rejoices to be called a knight in his youthful strength, should say when his enemies attack him, "I cannot conquer my enemies," and throws down his arms, he would be derided and called a fool because his weapons did not flash honorably in battle. Similarly, O master, you say that you are naked as a snake lying in its hole, because you do not strive to vanquish the storms assailing mankind with your armament.

This is not the way it will be. For in the first age the Lord established stewards and caretakers over all His possessions who were to render an account to Him [cf. Matt 25.14ff; Luke 16.1ff]. When a steward receives gifts, let him gather up his spears and arrows—spears to infuse the savage with Scriptures, arrows to infuse the impious, the crafty, and the furtive with the lessons from other writings. But if a great storm should arise with whirlwinds and black fire and water, with wrath and transgression or neglect of God's precepts, let him give way until the storm abates. Then let him offer medicine [cf. Ecclus 18.20] with the sun of Scriptures, as it is written, "I will have mercy and not sacrifice" [Matt 9.13; cf. Hos 6.6].

Mercy demands prayer, which God loves. May the Holy Spirit make that prayer fiery between us, so that He may bring us into the heavenly Jerusalem [cf. Heb 12.22]. Amen.

Neuss (St. Quirin)

177

An Abbess to Hildegard

Before 1173

Recognizing that her community has fallen away from its pristine ideals, the abbess asks for Hildegard's advice and prayers.

To Hildegard, beloved lady and mother, N., abbess (although unworthy) of the sisters at Neuss. Please accept this trifling prayer and service offered with complete devotion.

Because we have no doubt, blessed lady, that you have heard it noised abroad concerning our condition, how we have fallen back into our early state and, alas, abandoned our aspirations, we are all the more earnestly and insistently beseeching your prayers, so that we may be made aware for God's sake why our erratic spirit has been so burdened that we are buffeted here and there by various impulses and are forced to endure such distress.

We are fully aware that God is "terrible in his counsels over the sons of men" [Ps 65.5], and so, fearing the inscrutable (though not unjust) judgments of His chastisement, we commit fully the matter of our soul to you, whom we trust more than any other human being, and to your venerable sisters. We also long with our whole heart to receive a written response from you.

Farewell.

177r(?)

Hildegard to the Abbess

Before 1173

If this letter is indeed in answer to the preceding, Hildegard offers the general advice of penitence and compassion.

O servant of God, run in the circle of the sun in the zeal of your heart, and sigh to God for your sins. Also, do good works before your day sets when you can no longer work [cf. John 9.4]. Heed that steward who was accused before his master and who lowered the amounts in his account book of those who were in debt to his master [cf. Luke 16.1ff].

Do likewise. For since you have not performed your duties well, help your daughters now with sound advice and be compassionate toward them, just as seasonable rain falls on the grass and brings forth luxuriant vegetation. In this way, through penitence and compassion you will be wiser than the sons of light [cf. Luke 16.8], that is, the fallen angels, who were unwilling to behave thus.

For when you do good works, those works will receive you "into everlasting dwellings" [Luke 16.9] after your death. For if you had plowed the earth properly and had seasonable rain, you would be fertile soil. But the dew that should have caused you to bring forth is lacking in you, and you are turning on the wheel which you call your salvation, but which is, in fact, full of ashes.

Now plow in your heart with the knowledge of sacred Scripture, receive the rain through sighs of earnest zeal, and in your felicitous way of life keep the dew of blessing through good works. Do this before the day of your death, and you will live forever.

Otterberg

178

A Certain Brother to Hildegard

Before 1173

The brother asks Hildegard to appease God's wrath against him for his many offenses.

To the lady Hildegard, his spiritual mother, Brother S., least of the brothers of the church at Otterberg and darkened with the filth of sin beyond all others, with a prayer that she serve the spiritual banquet with Martha, and sigh with Mary for the joys of life in heaven [cf. Luke 10.38ff].

I rejoice with joy [cf. Is 66.10; Matt 2.10], spiritual mother, that you have found grace in the sight of our Lord God, and that you have kept the lamp of your blessed soul kindled so far with the fire of the Holy Spirit in anticipation of His coming, and have not grown weary [cf. Matt 25.1ff].

O friend of God, because with the wise virgins you are strong in the integrity of chastity, and because you keep the eye of contemplation firmly fixed upon the divine brightness, my puny devotion prays that with your righteous prayers you will take pains on my behalf to appease the face of the Lord [cf. I Sam 13.12], which I have greatly offended with the fiery brand of my perversity. I am certain that our God, our refuge and strength, will gladly deign to hear your petition on my behalf [cf. Ps 6.10], and, for your sake, will not cause me, justified because of you, to founder forever [cf. Ps 54.23]. Surely, because He is righteous,

He will not, once the spirit of blasphemy, which has for too long assailed my unhappy spirit, has been put to rout.

I also request this of your abundant goodness: Please, saintly lady, send me, puny creature that I am, a written response through the present messenger. And offer to your nuns, who follow the monastic way of life, as many greetings and prayers from me as there are dwellings in the eternal mansions of the Lord [cf. John 14.2].

Farewell.

178r

Hildegard to the Brother

Before 1173

Hildegard offers penitence as the only remedy for the brother's sins.

Your mind wheels like a bird, arranging and categorizing everything it encounters. Your beginning was consecrated because you have been so imbued with God's grace that you are able to lay hold of virtue and many other noble attributes.

Some people, however, have winds in their disposition, and because of the viridity and humidity of the earth, and the air and the waters, their minds are subject to sensuality.[a] For God was pleased to say, "Let there be" [cf. Gen 1.3ff], at which word all creation came forth according to its kind, as it is written: "God hath spoken once, these two things have I heard, that power belongeth to God, and mercy to thee, O Lord; for thou wilt render to every man according to his works" [Ps 61.12–13]. For with his command God created all things, and He did this once for all time when He said, "Let there be." In this, two things are to be understood: that His power was great in giving man the law, and that He Who rules all things by mercy paid the ancient debt through His Incarnation, for He forgives the sin of all who see and understand these things through penitence. But He casts off those who will not see or learn, and He exacts righteous retribution from them according to their works.

God cast the first angel into the lake of misery because he had unrighteously exalted himself, and He cast the first man into the prison of this world because of his foolish vainglory. For God has established nothing in vain. The first angel had great knowledge and wisdom, but out of his great malice he would not render God His due honor, and thus he fell and has remained fallen. Man, however, fell because he tasted food, and for this reason the Son of God offered Himself as a sacrifice for his sin. Thus when a man recalls that he has greatly sinned through his knowledge of good and evil and sighs out to God, he is reborn in God through penitence [cf. John 3.3].

As for you, O son, keep learning day and night so that you may live forever.

Park

179

Hildegard to the Abbot Philip

1170–73

Hildegard exhorts the abbot[1] to treat his subordinates with mercy, and informs him that she is sending to him a woman named Ida, so that he might anoint her with the "medicine of penitence."

O father, neglectful though you are, you fear God and love Him so that you sigh to Him in all your distress. Now, run to the fountain of living water [cf. Num 20.6; Jer 2.13] to wash yourself, and not only yourself but also others that you see weak and wounded. Never cease pouring the wine of penitence upon them and anointing them with the oil of mercy [cf. Luke 10.33–34].

In this way, you imitate the Living Fountain and Unbroken Wheel, Who receives sinners that run to Him for the aid of His mercy, and Who judges harshly the impious that gainsay Him. No mountain can match the circumference of this wheel, because its shadow towers over all things, nor can it be overshadowed by the depths, for it is exalted over all. God has life from nothing but Himself, and so He has neither beginning nor end. Therefore, whosoever runs to the aid of His grace will never fall from the bliss of eternal life, but the spark of salvation vitalizes him anew through the living God. For God does not wish the death of a sinner, but, rather, to have life through Him [cf. Ezech 18.23; 33.11].

Now, mild father, you who serve as Christ's representative, receive this woman Ida, who has not yet completely shown her hidden wounds, and diligently treat her, and all others running to you, with the medicine of penitence, so that you will live forever in the wheel of the true Trinity.

Note

1. Philip was a learned and diligent abbot, noted in his time for his emphasis on the copying of MSS. Thus it is perhaps not surprising that an important early MS of the *Scivias* was copied in the scriptorium at Park.

179r

The Abbot Philip to Hildegard

1170–73

The abbot prefaces his letter with high praise for Hildegard, reminding her of the wearisome journey he made just to see her face-to-face. He has, he reports, received the penitent Ida, but asks for further revelations from Hildegard with respect to the lady.

Philip, by God's grace abbot of St. Mary's in Park in the diocese of Louvain, to Hildegard of Bingen, venerable mistress of God's maidservants, with a prayer that she attain the blessing of eternal salvation.

Believe me, venerable mother, believe me, lady beloved of God: I have loved you ever since I got word of your virtues, with which divine goodness has exalted you, his handmaiden. You are all I have talked about, always singing your praises, for you have been the whole meditation of my heart [cf. Ps 18.15; 48.4]. Witness, for example, the wearisome journey I undertook so that I could see your venerable face—that is, the mirror of your illuminated mind—and to speak with you face-to-face. Thank God I was granted the sweetness of your presence that I sought and had long hoped for so very much. And thanks to Him too that you did not refuse to speak with me, unworthy though I was.

But I grieve that I gave in to the brothers who had come with me and did not permit me to linger there as I wished. But I hope that I may yet "enjoy thee in the Lord" [Philemon 1.20], either in this present life or afterward when, by your prayers, I have been brought into the pleasant places of paradise. Pray for me, therefore, venerable mother, pray for the one who loves and venerates the grace of God in you, and pray for the congregation of brothers and sisters which I must govern, so that the Lord may grant us peace and harmony, forgive our sins, and cause us to persevere in His service.

Now, regarding the penitent Ida. I have obeyed your will in the belief that it comes of God, and I have enjoined penitence for the sin which, by God's revelation, you have laid bare to be cleansed. But because she is weak with age, and has for a long time been worn down by the conditions of penitence, I request that you reveal to her whatever you perceive in your wisdom that would be useful to her soul, so that she may be relieved.

Farewell.

180

Hildegard to the Abbot Philip

1170–73

Uncharacteristically, Hildegard refers to a specific event in her life, noting that the abbot came to hear her speak (apparently on her fourth preaching tour, which she undertook in 1170). She asks for his prayers, and exhorts him to govern his subordinates with mercy.

The faith that one has before God in his blazing heart through the inspiration of the Holy Spirit is very glorious when he embraces with the embrace of true love the things he cannot see as if they were the visible things he prizes [cf. Heb 11.1]. And so it is a praiseworthy thing in you that, out of your love of God, you deigned to come and hear me, a weak and uneducated woman. For a wind blew down from a lofty mountain, and with its breath sent a small feather into the presence of the people and towers in all their finery, a feather which has no ability to fly save by the wind. Assuredly, God almighty took care to do this so that He could reveal what He could do through a thing which would not presume anything of itself.

You, however, who stand manfully in the office of the prophets, to whom the care of the apostolic order has been assigned, please extend the petition of your prayers to me, whom you have seen prostrate for a long time upon the bed of my infirmity. Pray for me that I may remain in God's grace, because, having no security in myself, I have set all my hope and confidence in the mercy of God alone.

Now, O father, you who are Christ's representative, tend the sheep of His flock with the rod of God's precepts by which you chastise and guide them, lest they are puffed up with pride. For pride is like a city that is not founded on rock: it collapses and falls because it did not have a strong foundation [cf. Matt 7.24ff]. Frequently anoint with the oil of mercy those wounded with sin, whatever kind it may be, lest they stink from the evil habit of their sins like the four-day-dead Lazarus [cf. John 11.39]. And lift up over all your subordinates the horn of salvation [Luke 1.69], that is, the horn of true humility, a virtue that is like a sapphire-colored cloud through which the sun shines brightly. In this way, you will imitate the true sun, that is, the Son of the Virgin, Who descended to earth in utmost humility, and also in humility ascended to the right hand of His Father. Cut off the evil habit of their sins from them, and in this way be zealous to adorn them like a necklace set with precious stones, so that you may come with them, and they with you, to eternal joy.

Now may the grace of the Holy Spirit make you the lamp of true love for God almighty. May He deign to grant you eternal reward for the help you render me, in both spirit and body.

181

Hildegard to the Abbot Philip

1170–73(?)

The abbot, one gathers from Hildegard's remarks, has written Hildegard seeking the meaning of some trouble that has recently befallen him.

O good and faithful servant of God, you are fearfully examining the cause or the meaning of the sign that God recently revealed. Yet that is known only to the Spirit of God, Who has no beginning and to Whom no creature can be compared. Nevertheless, hear my response to your query.

I see that what has befallen you is like a bough divided into many branches, because it occurred not only for your sake but also for the sake of your subordinates and many others, so that the hearts of those who hear this may fear, and correct their negligence, and so that they may celebrate the divine offices only with fear and reverence, lest they fall under the judgment of God or be mocked by demons with God's own permission. For I saw that this happened through the scorn of airy spirits, with God's permission, for the reasons already enumerated.

Do not be disturbed, dear, gentle father, but thank God if some of those who hear this are amended for your sake, and do not put off your priestly office any further for this reason, but, cleansed by confession and penitence, serve God zealously with celebrations of the Mass.

Now, therefore, servant of God, rejoice without fear and exult in the Lord [cf. Ps 32.1], because God loves you and will receive your spirit.

Pfalzel(?)

182

An Abbot to Hildegard

Before 1173

The abbot wishes to know whether he has merited salvation through the performance of his duties, or whether it would be better for him to resign his office.

To his lady Hildegard, the refulgent glory of sacred religion, H., unworthy abbot of St. Maria, offers the duty of his prayers, whatever it is worth, and his devoted service.

We would rather speak to you in person than write from a distance, if the time were available, or the distance not so great an obstacle. We did once, in fact, have the opportunity to speak with you, saintly lady, though all too briefly, and therefore we would like to hear you often, because we were pleased with the things you said on that occasion. We have now taken the courage to write you because the bearer of this letter, beloved to both of us in Christ, has, during his visit with us, commended you to our poor prayers—as he has done in several other monasteries—and he has asserted that you beseech this of us. Therefore—although we ourselves are nothing—we do remember you in our prayers, and will continue to do so, and, with body and humbled heart [cf. Ps 50.19], we pray that we and all our brothers may be worthy to be named in your intercessions.

Through Him for Whom you live devoutly and from Whom you have received the pledge of the Spirit [cf. II Cor 1.22; 5.5], we request this singular and secret gift, since you are accustomed to have your requests answered: that you beg the Lord to deign to impart to you, among the other revelations to you, something about the state of our humble condition. Have I, that is to say, merited my soul's salvation in bearing this duty of mine, fraught as it is with both honor and burden, with authority and peril, or would it be better for me to resign my position? If you receive any revelation concerning this matter, please do not hesitate, beloved lady, to console my sorrow with a written response through this present messenger.

We thirst, in turn, for your salvation, as we have said, and we trust that the Lord will augment your humility to the magnitude of your revelations, so that you may keep the lighted lamp which you received from heaven so bright before men that you may go out to meet Christ in glory, the unfailing oil you await [cf. Matt 25.1ff].

Regensburg (St. Emmeram)

183

A Provisor to Hildegard

Before 1170

In this instance, the messenger *is* the message. The provisor[1] sends a messenger, who is despairing of his salvation, to Hildegard so that she can minister to his needs.

To the devout handmaid of Christ, Hildegard, A., unworthy provisor of the monastery of St. Emmeram in Regensburg, offers his prayer that she may continue in all the good things bestowed by the Father of lights [cf. James 1.17].

We thank our Lord God that he has wondrously adorned His Church by giving you to it. Through you, all the righteous rejoice mightily, and those who were once despairing exult because they now have hope to be reconciled to Christ through you. It is for this reason indeed that the bearer of this letter, who confesses that he is despairing of his salvation, recently bewailed his wretchedness to me, and begged me to send him to you, blessed lady, with a letter of recommendation.

Therefore, O servant of Christ, I commend him to your devout compassion, humbly beseeching you for the love of God almighty to labor with all your might, in concert with those you govern, for his salvation. Furthermore, O beloved of God, I ask you of your maternal goodness to deign to continually pray to Christ for me and those in my care—to Christ, the recompense and recompenser of the labors of His saints. Amen.

Farewell.

Note

1. Strictly speaking, a provisor was a kind of administrator who attended to the secular affairs of the monastery. Designating administrative duties as it did, however, the term tended to be ambiguous, sometimes specifying the office of abbot itself. Thus note that what Van Acker takes as the response to this letter has "abbot" in the heading, while at least one MS supplies the heading "Letter of St. Hildegard to that same provisor."

183r

Hildegard to the Abbot

Before 1170

Hildegard exhorts the correspondent to watch over his sheep, for clouds of unbelief are settling among spiritual people.

"He Who Is" [Ex 3.14; Apoc 1.4] says: Look all around you, O man, and drive off those who lie in wait for your sheep. Take care also to examine their wounds, because multitudinous clouds, filled with vice, are drifting among spiritual people. And when the devil sees these clouds upon some person, he quickly subjects him to persuasive suggestions insidiously, causing him to run in all directions impelled by his flying shafts.

These clouds are the vexation and disbelief resulting from sin, which bring penalties rather than banquets, because misery is found wherever these are. Victory is rare, and the veins of these people are arid when they examine their sins in their unsettled minds, for they always seek out infelicity, believing that they cannot be saved, denying even the glory of God, not, to be sure, as if God did not exist, but as if a kind of cloud overshadowed their knowledge, suggesting these things to them with deceptive words. But if a person staunchly resists these suggestions, he understands that this is not reality but only his perception, just as a person's auditory sense picks up foul words but knows them to be wicked. Therefore, if a person refuses to translate vicious thoughts into actions, these penalties often lead to martyrdom.

Now, as for you, O man, whose duty it is to watch over your sheep, look with the eye of your knowledge where these clouds are in your sheepfold, and anoint those who are struggling under these penalties with mercy and consolation. But correct these gluttonous sins with the rod of discipline [cf. Prov 22.15], lest your subordinates fall into the lake [cf. Ps 27.1; 29.4]. For the refulgent sword flashes in your consciousness, but your character is beset by whirlwinds. Look, however, to the true light [cf. John 1.9], and you will live.

Regensburg (Niedermünster)

184

Hildegard to an Abbess

About 1162(?)

The one who gives aid to those who suffer in His name, Hildegard assures the abbess, will herself be aided.

The will of God had laid me low, as it were, in the seal of death, as if my soul had sighed its last in this world, but now His grace has raised me up a little with His new gift.

As I see in a true vision, the mysteries of God say to you: Whoever, for my sake, gives aid to someone who suffers in My name will himself be aided—this is the reward of praise. Your mind is ablaze as if sprinkled with flaming oil, and for this reason you sometimes grow weary with grieving, as if you were unaware what your potential is.

Now live in God and devoutly bear your burden as far as your strength will allow, and God will grant that you continue in His service.

185

An Abbess to Hildegard

Before 1173

The abbess asks for the consolation of a letter from Hildegard.

R., through God's grace humble steward of those serving the blessed Mary at Niedermünster in Regensburg, to her intimate friend Hildegard, offering whatever ceaseless prayer and the devotion of appropriate service can achieve.

If a place or means of serving you is denied me, my affection for you still has a remedy: letters between the two of us will quickly assure me of your well-being.[a] Know, dearest lady, that although steep mountains, chasms, and floods keep me from your presence, my heart is fully joined to you in the benevolence of perfect faith and love. Acquaintance with you is greatly to be desired, and I ascribe the granting of this desire—which has led to the salvation of the one desiring—not to my own merits, but to God's gracious mercy, for He deals mercifully with His faithful.[1]

Yet please do not think that I am abusing your friendship merely because I enjoy it so fully when, by the grace of God called to the sweetness of internal delight, I dare—or am able—to confer with Him intimately. In the name of the consolation of that love, I ask you to let me know by letter in accordance with my petition whether you will bear me in your memory.

By your gracious leave, I greet our sisters faithfully and lovingly with the obedience of the service I owe them, for they have stood firmly by me in the spirit of God's might and strength, and, if I may say so, by the example of your good deeds, they kept me safe and sound when I was falling into the jaws of death.

Farewell.

Note

1. The English here can scarcely aspire to the emphasis on longing and gratitude in this passage with its employment of varying forms of the Latin for "hope" (*Optandam* uestri notitiam et in salutem *optantis* feliciter *exoptatam*) and for "mercy" (sed gratuite *pietati* Dei qui *pius pie* cum suis operatur fidelibus).

185r

Hildegard to the Abbess

Before 1173

Hildegard exhorts the abbess to be merciful and patient.

O you who are a daughter of God because God fashioned the first human being, approach your Father, and look to Him so that you may do His will, for He created you. Recently, He admonished you by chastising you, and for a reason which I see in you, He will continue to admonish you about your bad habits, which you must correct.

Look to Him, make manifest all your ways to Him, and imitate the dove of mercy. For the dove acknowledges every good work, and banishes the sorrow of toil. Learn thereby to keep your mind pure, and when your mind becomes unstable and totters by seizing upon many things that you cannot hope to bring to completion, stand firm and learn moderation, for the dove is moderate and stable. Thus when vehement anger wearies you, look into the clear fountain of patience, and your anger will soon come to an end, and the storm and billowing waters will abate, because the dove is patient. But when you are so weary that day-to-day existence beats you down, remember that this life is a time of exile, and that you sigh in expectation of another life.[a] Act, therefore, in accordance with the sorrow of the dove. Gather together all the useful examples of other good people, and live after the example of the dove so that you may have eternal life.

Regensburg (Obermünster)

186

An Abbess to Hildegard

Before 1173

The abbess asks for Hildegard's assistance on a matter (for which she supplies no specifics) that is a source of worry to her. Moreover, she wants to know whether it is possible for her to be relieved of the burden of her office.

To the venerable and estimable mother in Christ, Hildegard, E., by God's grace, if so it was, abbess (although unworthy) in Obermünster at Regensburg, offers whatever prayers she can in conjunction with sincere faith and esteem.

Beloved lady, my spirit greatly longs to see your face, and my ears have long desired to hear the words of your mouth. Because of my great desire, I have on occasion greeted you in a letter, saintly lady, but I have never received a response.

Humbly cast down at your feet, therefore, I beseech you to deign to respond to two questions of mine through the present messenger. Is there a real danger in the matter that is now greatly afflicting my heart, or should I simply rely on the mercy of God? I long to know your advice concerning the office entrusted to me: how and when can I be relieved of this burden?

Humbly, repeatedly, imploring your love, I entreat you, if you possess the bowels of mercy [cf. Luke 1.78], please take the trouble to send a letter to relieve the great anxiety threatening my heart.

186r

Hildegard to the Abbess

Before 1173

Hildegard condemns idle curiosity, and praises penitence. Then, she advises the abbess to persevere in her office, and exhorts her to do good works.

O daughter of Adam, God is that rationality which has neither beginning nor end, through which man himself is a rational being. That rationality is vivified life in him, and it will never fail.[a]

But now look into and heed the Scriptures, which are rooted in the Holy Spirit and which were written from the rationality which is God. The Scriptures are a mirror in which we see God by faith, for our adversary is ever vigilant and does not sleep. We must, therefore, fight him with the Scriptures, and we must not tempt God [cf. Deut 6.16; Matt 4.7; Luke 4.12], but, rather, adore Him with all devotion. For the devil is fully aware that man is inconstant and, in his morals, unstable; and, therefore, he does not allow him to remain quiet in the stable morals of peace. Frequently, as if impelled by God, a person wants to know something that it is not permitted to know, and, for this reason, leaves off serving God. Therefore, the devil is greatly delighted, because he sees that that man has failed in two ways. This desire to search into forbidden things is foolish, such as one might expect from a false prophet. In all these things, God is not to be tempted but to be worshiped. For in his raging wickedness, the devil frequently hurls his shafts into man's heart, with the result that that man seeks to thwart God.

Blessed, however, is the man who will neither do these things nor consent to them, but lives as if suffering death by them. It is human nature to sin as a result of original sin, but when a person subsequently repents and gives up that sin for the sake of God's glory, he resists the devil by faith. God will never destroy the person who offers his more grievous sins up to Him, and He also forgives the lesser ones.[b]

Now, sweet daughter, armed with this truth, see to it that you do not lay aside the office entrusted to you because of the exertion or the weariness of the task. And take note, too, whether your thoughts are good or evil about the church of that monastery, because you commit great sin if you do not properly attend to this. For the tree that is full of flowers is beautiful to look upon, but it is far more useful when its fruit has ripened. The desire to do good works gives joy to the mind like those flowers, but the zeal for good works—that is, when the fruit begins to grow—is far better. When a person has done good works, his fruits have ripened, and his good works offer him the food of life in eternal pastures after he has departed from this life.

Therefore, good daughter of God, perfect your wholesome desires with good works, and when your soul departs your body, God's beautiful gift will spring forth for you. May God's grace teach you this.

Reutlingen

187

The Priest Bertolf to Hildegard

1151–53

The priest consults Hildegard about his sin of doubt, and his fears that his friends are leading him astray. He also requests a copy of her book.

To Hildegard, worthy mistress of the brides of Christ, Bertolf, by the grace of God priest (though unworthy) and a sinner, offers the absolutely certain devotion of his great esteem and obedience.

Full of bitterness, I am weary of my life [cf. Job 10.1]. Until now, I have put off that task that you are aware of, saintly virgin, awaiting certain faithful friends of mine, and, therefore, my path is, to use the words of the prophet, hedged in on all sides with thorns and a wall [cf. Hos 2.6]. Still, I do not wholly reject the scourges that in all things instruct Israel [cf. Judges 3.1], but because those friends do not provide a way out of temptation [cf. I Cor 10.13], I am terribly afraid that I will give in to temptation and fail to complete my assigned task. My heart, however, still rejoices amidst my sins and tribulations, for I derive great confidence from your consolation, to which I frequently have recourse.

Therefore, O virgin devoted to God, all of us sigh to you (after God), entreating you, begging you, knocking at your door with all our might: Please do not desist from your accustomed prayers until merciful God deigns to impart to you, on our behalf, a specific place for our dwelling. Or, if that seems to you to be tempting God, pray that He will at least reveal a separate order of religious life for us. We firmly believe that God has already ordained these things through you. You know this full well from experience, since "nothing upon earth is done without a cause" [Job 5.6].

And, therefore, just as by your insight into God's mysteries you liberated my spirit in part from its distress, so you ought to pray for us and, by the means entrusted to you by God, help to deliver us from the sin of doubt. I greatly desire a letter from you about this matter, and others as well.

Finally, I would like very much to make a copy of your book.

187r

Hildegard to the Priest Bertolf

1151–53

Hildegard exhorts the priest to be about his duty, and not to concern himself with his companions who remain idly behind.

It is a praiseworthy and marvelous thing when a pilgrim hastens to his homeland. How great then is the mourning and sorrow among his acquaintances and fellow citizens, who feasted and enjoyed life with him, and how those wanton fellows blush when their companion has abandoned the vessel he used to carry with them.

Bear in mind that you were foreseen by the eye of the Living One to be a man of great zeal, just as the gentle Father requires of His sheep.[a] Those companions who sit idle have peace among themselves, but the valiant knight finds himself amid violent storms. Therefore, stand on the path of righteousness, and prepare your soul to fight along with those who continually serve with the King's mandate.

Take note that if a hornet leaves the swarm, and flies high, looking up to the sun, the entire swarm will rush upon it to crush it, but the sun covers it with its light so that it can no longer be seen, and it thus escapes. Then the whole swarm is thrown into confusion, but that one becomes, as it were, a valiant knight.

May God stretch out His hand to you, and may you live forever in those regions where the sun does not grow dark.

188

The Priests Conrad and Bertolf to Hildegard

Before 1153

The priests ask Hildegard to intercede with God for them.

To Hildegard, friend of God, and virgin to be admired beyond all other persons of this age, Conrad and Bertolf, unworthy priests in Reutlingen, with their prayer that she continue, as she has begun, in the fear and love of God, and that she illumine the darkness [cf. II Sam 22.29; Ps 17.29] of the world through the Living Light at which she gazes ceaselessly.

We rejoiced and were gladdened by the report that a delegation would come to us to console us. And we waited with expectation, but you have not yet directed that company to us. We were saddened, therefore, but are still awaiting the grace of God, "who hath not forsaken them that hope in him" [Judith 13.17].

Now, however, because you have commanded that a messenger be sent to you, we are consoled. But, beloved of God, please remember that although we have steadfast hope, we are at the mercy of the fragility of our mortal bodies (in which we long to remain, like weak, untrained soldiers), and, therefore, we humbly pray you, holy mother and "helper in due time in tribulation" [Ps 9.10], to intercede diligently for us so that He may direct our paths [cf. I Thess 3.11], for we put all our faith in you, after God.[a]

We do not say these things as if, oppressed beyond measure [cf. II Cor 1.8], we had excessive grief over this fact. Rather, we say them so that you, saintly lady, may obtain for us who are weak some consolation from God's mercy—a consolation that our sins obstruct—lest we falter. We do not dare to suggest anything further about this matter, but still we wish to commit this our petition to the Judge of your heart, Who knows what is best for each. For He Himself says that your heavenly Father "knoweth what is needful for you, before you ask him" [Matt 6.8], and He knows what medications are appropriate for each, and He does not cease to supply them at His own fitting time. This alone should be our outcry: Woe, woe for this earthly matter. When, do you think, will it hide itself in the presence of the Living Eye?

Finally, we greet in the Lord your provost,[1] your sisters, and all those who dwell with you. We devoutly ask in turn that you be mindful of us, His poor ones.

Note

1. That is, Volmar, who remained Hildegard's provost and secretary until his death in 1173.

188r

Hildegard to the Priests Conrad and Bertolf

Before 1153

Hildegard praises the priests as pilgrims in the exile of this world, and urges them to continue in the battle.

The Living Light says: O you valiant knights who argue against the contradictions uttered by the double-tongued, listen: O who are these who seek life in pilgrimage, and are exiles for God's sake? The hands of those who labor always lay up riches for themselves. Oh, how great is that sanctity which in the midst of mortal plague crushes the poison underfoot! Therefore, a beautiful flower arises from the destruction of sin, and this flower joins company with the angels.

Therefore, O sons of pilgrimage, hastily run to Me, and store up great riches for yourselves, because you are seen by the Living Eye, which ever gazes into the mirror of the dove. Labor, and do not grow weary out of the fatigue of deceptive, wicked works, for the sun has stored up for you the eternal life of light. Run hastily to God because His day is coming [cf. Ps 36.13; Is 13.9; Joel 2.1].

Suffer the man who has been filled with doubt and vacillates like water swelling amid great storms; suffer him as if he were a tree that cannot be bent like a reed because he is too caught up in his own concerns. Let him consider himself in this light, and if no guilt is found in him, then let him look to his concerns.

But you, My lovers, run to Me, because I see your groaning like gold, bright and powerful, and I see your mind joyous and benevolent. Enter the battle, therefore, like valiant servants. Those who are in exile cannot win a sure victory as long as they remain in the body. And so they must flee the disastrous shipwreck of this world and shore up the columns of their mind with the Cornerstone [cf. Ps 117.22; Matt 21.42].

Therefore, brave knights, do not grow weary on account of the instability of the body, because God seeks his lambs among wolves [cf. Luke 10.3].

Reutlingen(?)

189

Hildegard to the Priest Conrad

Before 1153

Hildegard advises Conrad on his duties as a priest.

In His mystic gift, the Spirit of Truth [cf. John 14.17] says: A physician should frequently anoint the wounded man with mercy, the wounded man who has sprinkled oil into his wounds but cannot bear wine poured over them [cf. Luke 10.33–34]; and he should not allow that man's bruises to fester, because the Great Physician cleanses leprosy away when a person shows himself to a priest [cf. Matt 8.4; Luke 5.14; Mark 1.44].

Many come to Me with their minds overclouded, not wishing to see with their eyes how their wounds can be cured, but wishing instead to touch Me with a tongue oozing all sorts of words. For their inner mind cannot comprehend Me, but rather brings them to a way of life that absorbs them in their intoxication with their long-standing vices. But they say: We have drunk the bitterness of chastisement, and we have wiped away our iniquity, and so they are unwilling to abandon their wicked ways.

Because they are unwilling to give up their iniquities, such men surely should be restricted, so that they cannot move along worldly paths. But the person who gives up his sins in sorrowful penitence, and is no longer willing to be sunk in sordid vices, should not be restrained in this manner, but, in his sorrows, should be anointed wherever he goes. For the Great Physician rouses those who are watchful, chastises those who are sleeping [cf. Matt 26.40ff; Mark 14.37ff], and cuts down those who continue to live wicked lives. Therefore, you, O physician, consider what is most necessary in both these matters.

Rome (*St. Anastasius*)

190

The Abbot Eberhard to Hildegard

1166–73

The abbot[1] requests Hildegard's prayers for himself and those in his care, and inquires also whether he might be relieved of his duties. He also requests a copy of her book.

To the beloved in the Lord and devout sister, Hildegard, by the grace of God, mistress of the community at St. Rupert, brother Eberhard, abbot (in name only) of St. Anastasius, greetings and prayers.

Glory be to God, because you are "the good odour of Christ" [II Cor 2.15] both to your people and to ours. The great name of Christ is blessed, praised, and sanctified in you. Indeed, you glorify and bear Christ in your body [cf. I Cor 6.20], worthily making yourself worthy of the calling to which you have been called [cf. Eph 4.1]. And by the grace granted to you in the Lord's house, you show yourself to all as a "vessel unto honour" [Rom 9.21].

And because you are the beloved instrument of Christ and the vessel of His Holy Spirit, we humbly beseech you to pray in spirit and truth [cf. John 4.23] for me and for those who have been entrusted to our care, so that He may perfect that which He began in us—"to will and to accomplish, according to His good will" [Phil 2.13]—so that we may finish the race and the good fight [cf. II Tim 4.7], and, at the same time, glory in His praise [cf. Ps 105.47].

Furthermore, I ask that the Spirit, Who reveals the secret mysteries of His wisdom, impart to you what is best for me in bearing the burden of obedience to Christ, whether, that is, it is better for me to persevere or to rest so that I may have leisure to contemplate Him. Do not conceal from me whatever is revealed to you concerning this matter, because "my heart is ready, O God, my heart is ready" [Ps 56.8, 107.2] "to do thy will" [Heb 10.9].

We request that a copy of your book be made for us, for we have need of your advice and aid, and your goodwill. We desire with our whole heart to have that book so that we can see the miracles of God [cf. Job 37.14] in it.

In addition, I earnestly ask that you send us a written response and console us with the breasts of the consolation [cf. Is 66.11] of Christ in our toil and endurance for Christ.

Farewell. Greet your sisters. Pray for us.

Note

1. Eberhard was formerly abbot of Eberbach, but was forced to flee the ire of Frederick Barbarossa because he stood with the papal party in opposition to the antipope established by the emperor. In 1166, the same year of his flight, Eberhard became abbot of St. Anastasius, the monastery where Pope Eugenius had formerly served as abbot.

190r

Hildegard to the Abbot Eberhard

1166–73

Hildegard advises the abbot to persevere in his office, providing instruction and correction to his sheep.

"He Who Is" [Ex 3.14; Apoc 1.4] says to you, O man: Your mind rises so eagerly through your reputation for good works that you exalt yourself on high in your desire to do more good works than you can possibly accomplish. But sometimes your mind deceives you by sifting your affairs, saying: These are the best things. But because you are not doing those things at the moment, you let go of the matter that you have undertaken to do.

Therefore, support your sheepfold without fail, and give it instruction, that is, by using the rod of your position, and then by furnishing the unguent of the physician. For it is better for you to be vigilant in your toils while others are doing service under your tutelage than to exercise your own will. For if you give up, weariness will wall you in so that your mind grows dry. Therefore, keep watch over your flock, offering it the good examples your mind longs for, lest your mind be brought into derision. For the one who stands on the height and shouts down into the valley frequently does not know whether he is on the heights or walking in the vale.

Therefore, stand firm so that with God's help you can do the good works you have begun, and walk in Christ's footsteps lest you deceive yourself. Then, you will live forever.

Rothenkirchen(?)

191

An Abbot to Hildegard

Before 1173

The abbot praises Hildegard highly, citing examples of holy women from the Bible, whom she exceeds because of the holy virtue of chastity.

An administrator vowed to poverty sends greetings to his lady and mother, Hildegard of St. Rupert in Bingen, with his abiding love and prayers.

As a multitude of the faithful proclaim, it is no wonder that you have sought and found God [cf. Matt 7.7; Luke 11.9], for He shows Himself to you because your faith in Him is unfeigned [cf. I Tim 1.5; II Tim 1.5]. And, more importantly, by His favor and grace, you consecrated your childhood to Him, and, from that time forward, have lived in saintliness and justice as a vessel of election [cf. Acts 9.15] before Him. It is beyond all doubt that He Who appointed you to such a life deems you worthy to be heard for whatsoever you ask in His name [cf. John 14.13; 15.16; 16.23], and this can be seen especially in the fact that He makes His secret mysteries known through you.

Further, I believe that the gifts bestowed upon you—which I have myself witnessed in some measure—are assuredly divine and holy, and I can have no doubts at all concerning them, since I know that nothing is impossible with God [cf. Matt 19.26; Luke 1.37]. For just as God used male prophets, so too did He employ holy women to open up the secrets of His divinity, as Joel witnesses: "I will," He said, "pour out my spirit upon all flesh: and your sons and your daughters shall prophesy. . . . Moreover upon my servants and handmaids I will pour forth my spirit" [Joel 2.28–29]. Indeed, we read that Deborah [cf. Judges 4.4–5.32], Holda [cf. II Kings 22.14–20], Hannah, the mother of Samuel [cf. I Sam 2.1–10], Elizabeth, the mother of St. John the Baptist [cf. Luke 1.41–45], and other women devoted to God, had the spirit of prophecy—and this despite the fact that they were married women. How much more so you, who have had no part in the weakness of the flesh, and have from your earliest years preserved your chastity for God!

Dear lady, I render boundless thanks to almighty Mercy that I have merited to achieve a modest acquaintance with your blessedness. Therefore, I humbly beseech you of your maternal goodness to direct some written words of consolation to me. As you have frequently done in person, please lift me up now with a written response so that my memory of you may be strengthened, for I am floundering amid great storms.

191r

Hildegard to the Abbot

Before 1173

A letter of general exhortation.

Your mind is like a snow cloud, which rises above an airy cloud in which the sun radiates, and sometimes it is like a windy cloud that brings storms. The snow cloud is the weariness of an unstable mind. The airy cloud, however, indicates unsullied knowledge acquired with the patience of faith. But the windy cloud brings the disturbance of great distress found in unquiet minds.

Now, learn that the snow cloud is full of air that is neither cold nor hot: wholesome herbs cannot grow from it. The pure air, on the other hand, bestows dew, stable temperature, and rain: vegetation and flowers grow from it. But the windy cloud is full of northern air: from it, all viridity withers, and flowers fall.

Now flee these things, and remain steadfast in the pure air, and, in the kind of life unfamiliar to you, be mindful of your Creator [cf. Eccles 12.1], and do not flee from Him, because one does not know God by seeing Him. Your spirit was redolent of that life—your spirit which was designated "soul" because it came forth from the soul. For the soul assigns and approves works as good or evil, and the spirit is a powerful mill for those works.[1][a]

Raise up a building of good works so that whenever the compass of your soul is idle, it may find that building. For if it does not find it, it will collapse. Therefore, stay vigilant before the shadow of your death approaches. The fiery Holy Spirit will lend you His aid in this.

Note

1. Some distinction is being made here between "spirit" (*spiritus*) and "soul" (*anima*), but the point is quite obscure. See endnote for Latin text.

192

Hildegard to the Congregation of Nuns

Before 1153

This letter is a paean to the Holy Virgin, which Hildegard uses to encourage and uplift the daughters of her community.

The Lord says to His daughters: In ancient times the Holy Spirit inspired certain persons from a certain nation that had not yet become deceitful.[1] Oh, Oh, Oh! Afterwards, God placed Wisdom in the dawn. Ach, Ach, Ach! And He created in Himself a means to serve His purpose: a lofty mountain of justice. Woe, Woe, Woe! Now the justice of that mountain has become like a shadow because of the gluttony of those going astray. But you, O strength of the mountain, you will not crumble completely, but will rise up into the high window where many eagles will look upon you.

O how great that entity, which did not lie hidden in any thing, so that, neither made nor created by anyone, it remains forever in itself alone. O life, you arose in the dawn when the great King mercifully revealed Wisdom, which in ancient days was with the Wise Man—mercifully, because woman entered death through the hole that the ancient traitor opened up. O grief, O sorrow, O woe for those who were formed in the woman![a]

O dawn, in the form of the first rib, you washed these things away. O feminine form, sister of Wisdom, how glorious you are, for mighty life arose in you, and death will never choke it off. Wisdom lifted you up so that all creatures were adorned by you and brought into a better part than they had received in the beginning.[b] Wherefore:[2]

> Hail, O greenest bough,
> You who came forth in the mighty wind
> of the saints' searching.
>
> When the time came
> that you flourished in your branches,
> you were greeted with "Ave, ave,"
> for the heat of the sun brought forth from you
> a fragrance like the aroma of balsam.
>
> In you the lovely flower blossomed
> and sent forth a fragrance
> to all the dried-up spices.

And they all burst forth
in full viridity.

Then the heavens poured dew upon the grass
and all the earth rejoiced,
because her womb produced grain,
and the birds of the air
made their nests on that bough.

Then food was produced for mankind,
and those who feasted rejoiced with great joy.
O sweet Virgin,
joy is ever found in you.

But Eve scorned all these things.

Now, however, give praise to the Most High.[3]

Alleluia!
O branch[4] that intercedes for us,
your holy womb
conquered death
and illumined all creation
with the beautiful flower
that arose from the sweet chastity
of your unsullied modesty.[5]

What does all this mean?

O how great a miracle it is
that the King entered
into a submissive feminine form.
God acted thus
because humility is supreme over all things.
How great the felicity is
in that sex
because that malice—
which had flowed from woman—
was, later, wiped away by woman,
and she brought forth
the sweetest fragrance of the virtues,
and adorned heaven
more than woman had ever troubled earth.[6]

O radiant Virgin Mary,
illumined
by divine radiance,
infused with the Word of God:
your womb flowered forth
at the entry of the Spirit of God,
Who breathed upon you
and sucked out of you
that which Eve contracted

when she cut herself off from chastity,
infected with contagion
at the devil's deception.

You miraculously concealed in yourself
unsullied flesh
in accordance with God's plan
when the Son of God
flourished in your womb.
Holy divinity brought Him forth
contrary to the law of the flesh
which Eve had established.
He was joined to wholeness
in the holiness of the womb.[7]

Listen then, O human being, to this miracle:

Hail, Mary,
Author of life
by reestablishing salvation,
you who overthrew death
and crushed the serpent under your heel.
Eve raised herself before the serpent,
stiff-necked
and full of pride.
But you crushed the serpent
when you bore the Son of God,
come down from Heaven.

The Spirit of God
breathed Him forth.

O sweet, loving mother, hail.
You brought forth into the world
your Son sent from Heaven.[8]

What does this mean?

O refulgent mother
of sacred healing,
through your holy Son
you have poured unguents
into the weeping wounds of death
that Eve wrought
as torments for our souls.
You destroyed death
and raised up life.

Pray for us
to your Son,
O star of the sea,
Mary.

O source of life,
gladsome ornament,
sweetness of all delights,
which will never fail in you![9]

Today has the closed portal
opened unto us,
the gate which the serpent had choked off through woman.
Therefore, the flower born of the Virgin Mary
radiates in the dawn.[10]

Because a woman brought death into the world,
the radiant Virgin laid death low.
Therefore, supreme blessing is found
in the feminine form
beyond all creation,
for God became man
in that sweet, blessed Virgin.[11]

O how precious is the virginity
of this Virgin,
who kept her gate closed,
and whose womb
was so infused with the heat
of holy divinity
that a flower burgeoned in her.

And the Son of God
came forth, like the dawn,
from her secret place.

Thus the sweet seed,
her Son,
opened Paradise
through her closed womb.[12]

Let the earth hear, let the elements tremble. Why? Because all creation joyfully received the One born of the Virgin, so that the heavens glowed like the dawn at the sudden appearance of the virtues and at the radiant strength that flashed in those virtues. For the Sun of truth breathed forth the complete sanctification of souls through that Virgin.

Therefore, O my daughters, hear Me, the living fountain, speaking to you: Be filled with holy and elect viridity, not with the power of the devil that, sorely wounded, abandoned God. The good eye sees these words, the good ear hears them, but a mind of stone does not perceive them, for it abandons God and embraces the devil, thereby raising a lofty tower in hell. O wholesome and upright desires, how resplendent you are when your sweet fragrance rises to God! But how hard it is for the human race to cast off the lust for worldly things.

Therefore, let my daughters hear these words: Primordial sin rashly and deceitfully choked off human work through a woman—woman, that turreted mountain in which the proper forms of upright feelings should have appeared, but which was instead cast out into lamentation. For the malevolent thief and great deceiver came and wrapped those feelings in the blackness of swift-moving sin and the stench of pollution, so that they could not be pure. Alas, alas, alas, for creation! Woe, woe, woe, for the world! Alas, alas, alas, for that perverse desire that inclined to death when it was cut off from heaven and set in hell, where the devil vomited it forth when he choked off innocence.

But the Son of God left this darkened desire behind, and it could not pass through the light. He came by another way where there was no guileful nature, and so through Him innocence rose again. And so He brought out the sons of Adam,[13] born of perverted desire, drawing them to Himself by the wounds caused by the nails of the cross driven into His flesh. Thus He broke the bonds that bound them in the chain of the taste for wicked works, the teat of iniquity, and the delight of sin.

Therefore, O my daughters, remembering My Son, you ought always to crucify yourselves to your own concerns, so that you do not falter because of the deceitful tyrant. And, lest you fall from Me, do not let the poison of bitter wrath grow among you, nor a mind ablaze with pride, nor the vanity that rends asunder the glory of sanctification. Rather, let your joy be complete in Me [cf. John 16.24], and let your reward be the kingdom of heaven, and let holy peace be among you.

O daughters of Jerusalem [cf. Cant 1.4], the Great Physician wants you to reach up to the highest desire for good, and no one can separate you from Him. And so through the holy gift of God "increase and multiply" [Gen 1.22] over the mountains and hills of sanctification. Thus, may the earth cover with blessing whoever wishes to bless you, but whoever wishes to curse you will be cursed by the mighty Judge. For you are My mirror.

But what are you thinking in your hearts [cf. Mark 2.8]? You will find in Me that which I wish to perfect in you. What is this? It is justice. May you be steeped in the gift of God's grace so that you will not be overcome by the enemy. Therefore, do not abandon Me.

Notes

1. That is, the Jews.

2. Van Acker supplies only the first and last lines of the following musical compositions, referring the reader to Newman, *Symphonia*, for the full text. We have, therefore, employed Newman's edition for our rendering of the songs. The translations are, of course, ours. For a different rendering, see Newman, who supplies both a literal and a poetic translation.

3. *Symphonia* 19, p. 126. After noting that the first stanza of this song is "an analogous verbal icon" to the ubiquitous tree-of-Jesse image in the Middle Ages, Newman goes on to observe (pp. 276–77) how skillfully the poet further develops the basic image by biblical quotation and allusion: "Christ's parable of the green tree and the dry tree (Luke 23:31), the Advent antiphon beseeching dew from the heavens (Isa. 45:8), and the great tree of the Kingdom in which the birds of the air build their nests (Matt. 13:32)."

4. That is, *virga*, the "branch" that intercedes. Note the play on *virga/virgo*.

5. *Symphonia* 18, p. 124.

6. *Symphonia* 16, p. 120.

7. *Symphonia* 23, p. 136.

8. *Symphonia* 8, 1–16, p. 110.

9. *Symphonia* 9, 1–18, p. 112. Newman's remarks about this song (p. 271) are illuminating: "The first lines of this responsory illustrate Hildegard's taste for the mixed metaphors that give her poems some of their freshness and quirkiness. Five hundred hymnodists might point out that Eve inflicted wounds on the soul, but only Hildegard would say that she built them, and only she would hear not the victim but the wounds themselves sobbing. Such compressions seem to arise spontaneously from the intense and synesthetic character of her perceptions."

10. *Symphonia* 11, p. 116.

11. *Symphonia* 12, p. 116.

12. *Symphonia* 22, 1–14, p. 134.

13. That is, at the Harrowing of Hell, but also with the sense of breaking the bonds of sin for mortal—and, therefore, sinful—mankind.

193

Hildegard to the Congregation of Nuns

Before 1173

A letter of exhortation to her nuns in allegorical terms.

Now, listen again, my daughters, and hear the words of the Living Light, which has no darkness: Keep yourselves from evil in all things. For the whispers of the devil will come, and the whispers of many storms. Indeed, in a time yet to come the Chaldeans will grow weak, the Greeks will become stronger, the Romans with the other Romans[1] will become silent, like a blazing fire that is extinguished, and the Gauls will become new recruits.[a] But these things too will pass. A part of this transitory world runs in three directions, where kings and princes will endure a flood of disturbances. Yet a king who desires great battle will arise, but no one will help him, except an armed company of a thousand circumcised soldiers.[b] Thus humankind will grow weary.

Yet God will not destroy your monastery, O my daughters. But He will cast all arrogant and negligent beggars out of it, and He will cleanse it of schisms and terrors. Neither will the blind and lame who seek to devour it prevail, for the sparks of examination will sift them out.

Therefore, in your minds be like one who looks at a garden where flowers and apple trees grow so that he may enjoy their aroma and eat the apples. The "aroma of flowers" means a man who desires to emulate the goodness of the righteous by abstaining from sin, and "eating the apples" represents a person who faithfully governs those under his authority, and who, by the grace of God, distributes alms to the poor. Thus he merits to hear the voice of his Lord saying to him: This person touches Me by performing his duty, and he anoints Me by his compassionate distribution of alms.

This monastery stands between two paths: one of them slimy, the other bright with sunlight. The slimy path is the pleasure of this world, which all the faithful must shun lest they be destroyed by it. When one has done this, the saints join in a symphony of praise to God, saying: This person does not abide in the putridity of this world's desire. A person who stands on the bright, sunny path and looks to God by fearing and loving Him will hear his Lord say: "Well done, good and faithful servant" [Matt 25.21ff]. The person who turns aside onto the slimy path, on the other hand, will encounter a great, calamitous peril, unless he tears himself away from that path.

Praise be to the blood of Christ that dresses His faithful in the breastplate of righteousness [cf. Eph 6.14] and all the armor of the virtues. For the blood of Christ restores His faithful to their place of refreshment. And you, O Jerusalem, rejoice, for you receive those who truly believe in the Passion of the Son of God. And you, O dawn of Salvation, you are aglow with blessing, because Jerusalem preserves her sons in joy.

Therefore, the angels cry out their praises for these sons of Jerusalem, saying: We gather the vintage of your works in the winepress [cf. Is 63.3], and so we bring you into our company. For Lucifer has fled like a serpent hiding in his hole.

Note

1. With a distinction being made, apparently, between the papacy and the Roman municipal government, or perhaps between the papacy and the Holy Roman Empire. Thanks to Kathryn Kerby-Fulton and Barbara Newman for suggestions.

194

Hildegard to the Congregation of Nuns

1161–62(?)

An angry letter castigating the nuns for their moral laxity.

Poor little form of a woman that I am, I was weighed down heavily with sickness, because the Spirit of the Lord laid me low on a sickbed, and commanded me to say these words to the daughters of this monastery.

Surely, you do not suppose that you will receive the kingdom of God by feasting and drinking and wanton morals? No! You will receive the kingdom of

God through denial of the body and contrition of the mind. I have prepared My table before you [cf. Ps 22.5] adorned with My resplendent crown, so that you may set a royal banquet on it—manna, beasts of the forest, birds of the air, pomegranates—a feast for those who inherit heaven. But you are neglecting to do your duty in this respect. For, on the one hand, you are setting before Me secular morals based on mere legalistic grounds, and, on the other, the discipline of the law of those who have been joined in matrimony.[a] This is not what I seek from you, because I have chosen you not for that garden but for my choice vineyard [cf. Is 5.1f; Jer 2.21]. I have endured this for eight years now. For five years I kept silent, but for three years I have scourged those, both inside your monastery and out, who have dishonored Me in the splendor of My crown.

Here is the meaning of all this. None of the faithful should suppose that he will acquire the glory of heaven by stuffing his belly or by complete abandonment to his pleasures. For those who desire to attain that glory must beat down the flesh in humility of the heart with goodwill, not bitter malice.

My table with My resplendent crown prepared for you so that you may set a royal banquet upon it stands for those angels with radiant crown, that is, with the refulgence of God's miracles, which are so brilliant before men that they marvel at the many things that have been prepared for the beatitude of those who live holy lives. These angels offer to their Creator the diligent, sanctified works of those who aspire to the angelic order. For angels do not set before God the dregs of secular works of those people who live to gratify carnal desires. They set before Him, rather, the works of those who, abandoning carnal desires, prostrate themselves on the ground for God's sake, and who, like the angels, praise God continuously.

The manna symbolizes the obedience that God demanded of mankind, so that they might be obedient to God and to those prelates set over them by God. Also, He instilled obedience in all the other creatures so that they might serve the benefit of mankind. God, not man, created mankind, and for this reason spiritual people are to serve God obediently, like the angels. Lucifer, however, cast obedience aside and revealed disobedience to mankind.

The beasts of the forest show that those who have renounced the world are to reject all pomp along with it. Such people are like guests and pilgrims, and should, like beasts, avoid every secular way of life and all association with the world, as true hermits have done who shut themselves away from the world so that death might not enter through the windows of their eyes.

The birds of the air represent the precepts of St. Benedict and of other great teachers of the Catholic faith who drank deep of the Holy Spirit. Men live by these precepts as if they were not of the flesh.

The pomegranates declare the love of God in the hearts of those who have surrounded themselves with the aforesaid good and holy works, and who, by praying and weeping, gather unto themselves estimable virtues. These lap up the words of the saints by imitating their lives.

You, however, are not doing these things, for you turn instead to carnal desires, neglecting your proper duty. For in one way, a way that inclines to the world, you set before Me all sorts of fleshly desires like those whores who zealously and eagerly serve the world as they are trained to do, as has been said.[b] In the other way, you turn to the pleasurable desires of those who frequently sweat in carnal embraces, in which lovers please lovers. And I have never demanded this of you, neither by word, nor by writing, nor by command, for you have joined a spiritual—not a carnal—embrace. Yet you have become enslaved to carnal embraces, although I did not choose you for the vain and soon-to-fade flowers of this rotting world. I brought you, instead, into the vineyard of true election and true bliss, so that in the highest election you could receive the reward of your labors.[c]

For eight years I endured the fact that you were acting like vain children, and that then you frolicked in your vanity in a pernicious way, and, finally, that you sinned in some aspect of that vanity. As if unaware of it, I feigned silence for five years. But when at last some of you with certain signs slapped Me in the face with it, I lifted up My hand against you, and for three years I chastised with various sorrows those both inside and outside this monastery, and with an unmistakable sign I struck down the grossness of their sins, because they had neglected the beauty of betrothal to Me.

In My zeal which "slew the firstborn of Egypt" [Ps 134.8], and which drowned Pharaoh in the Red Sea [cf. Ex 14.28; 15.4]—for despite the many wonders I showed him he despised Me—I rose up and laid low a certain individual so that she became partially aware of the penalties for her sins, which, she discovered, were mixed with fire and ice. I did this as an example to them, to those, that is, who were unwilling to acknowledge Me despite the many signs I revealed to their sight and hearing.

Let that person I scourged in My zeal, and the others who dwell here, beware lest in withdrawing from My way they turn back to their former transgressions and be drowned in the Red Sea, because from now on I will not suffer those previous sins. For it is necessary that they arise to the better part [cf. Luke 10.42] because it is God's will that they not abandon His law.

Now, therefore, O my daughters, rise up to Me immediately, before I bring pressure to bear on the spiritual people who tore my tunic and divided my garments [cf. John 19.23], and who abandoned the covenant I made with them [cf. Deut 4.23]. O "woe to the sinful nation" [Is 1.4] that lies in the filthy streets and is always unchaste because of their lustful sins. In their overweening sinfulness, they are sucking the teats of pigs! Therefore, let them say: O Lord, You Who have provided food and clothing for man and have wiped away his sorrows by the blood of the Lamb [cf. Apoc 7.14; 22.14], see how a black wind mocks us and wishes to shake the seeds of holiness out of us. Cast that wind out of our midst, because the time has not yet come for schisms to run rampant, that time when the whole earth will be stripped of the garment of consecration.

Now therefore, O my daughters, look and hear and flee from this dangerous wind. Run to your King. And when you have done this, bliss will pour forth blessings upon this house and its daughters like "the early and the latter rain" [Hos 6.3], the bliss of the cherubim and seraphim and all the heavenly host as they gaze at the face of God. And virtues and the riches of the earth will multiply among them. And all who bless you will themselves increase in blessings. May God look upon this place and never be forgetful of it.

195

The Provost Volmar to Hildegard

About 1170

Volmar contemplates Hildegard's death, and the loss to the community and the Church at such an event.

To Hildegard, reverend lady, sweet mother, saintly mistress, truthful and approved confidante of God, in the convent at St. Rupert, Volmar her son, though unworthy, and the entire congregation of her maidens, along with all others who cling to her, and who serve God and St. Rupert, albeit lukewarmly. With due subjection, due obedience, and due filial affection, they offer their prayers that they may be consoled by the breasts of her consolation [cf. Is 66.11], so that they may become partakers of the heavenly country after the exile of this world.

Although, now, sweet mother, we are privileged to see you every day with fleshly eyes, and hear you with fleshly ears, and can cling to you daily (as is proper) and understand that the Holy Spirit speaks to us through you, we still have no doubt that at some time, as it pleases God, you will be taken away from us, and that, henceforth, we will no longer see you with our fleshly eyes, for there is no man that "shall live, and not see death" [Ps 88.49]. But this is a matter that we cannot even mention without tears.

When that time comes, our grief and woe will surpass the joy we now feel. Who then will give answers to all who seek to understand their condition? Who will provide fresh interpretations of the Scriptures? Who then will utter songs never heard before and give voice to that unheard language? Who will deliver new and unheard-of sermons on feast days? Who then will give revelations about the spirits of the departed? Who will offer revelations of things past, present, and future? Who will expound the nature of creation in all its diversity? We know that God's grace has bestowed these capacities upon you along with a sweet and humble character and a heart that pours out maternal affection on all around you.

O what divine mercy resides in His gifts! O how pointless are human anxieties! O "vanity of vanities" [Eccles 1.2]! Why do so many undertake difficult journeys into remote parts of the world to seek out the teachings of various men—and all in vain? Why, when afflicted with thirst, hunger, and cold, do they sweat over the profundity, or, rather, the enigma, of *sententiae*, listening to disputes in the courts and remaining awake at all hours of the night? We know for certain that they endure all these things not with a simple view to zeal, but out of the depravity of simony. Thus because they accomplish very little, if anything, they cannot grasp the commandment of the Spirit of God—nay, rather, they extinguish the spark of God's Spirit by their contempt for it, although they think that by that spark they are something important. The result is that to the embarrassment of modern scholastics who abuse the knowledge given them from above, the Spirit of prophecy and vision, revitalized in a fragile vessel and without help of secular learning, brings forth things that they cannot comprehend in any way.[a]

For the Spirit gives what instruction He will and "breatheth where he will" [John 3.8]. And so here we see the principle fulfilled that God, according to the Scripture, has chosen the foolish and weak things of this world in order to confound the wise and strong [cf. I Cor 1.27].

We say such things, sweet mother, not to put down your simple nature as if we were enflamed with the torch of envy for such a gift, a gift bestowed upon you that you might use it zealously. Nor do we speak this way so that we may boast vaingloriously, since we are the ones who are especially yours, who are with you most often, and who sedulously hear your voice. No, we do so in order to show that, compared with chaste goodness and piety, the determined exertions of such men[1] are not sufficient for investigating and comprehending the heights of true doctrine, for a teacher moves his lips, outwardly, in vain, unless, inwardly, the Spirit informs the hearts of those listening to him. In you, however, there are more signs of the virtues and more evidence of the miracles of God and the Holy Spirit than we could possibly say. Or want to say, for it is the task of others to praise you and spread your fame; it is ours to marvel at you, venerate you, and love you.

Because you know all this by your experience better than we, and because a few words are sufficient to understand many things, we refrain from saying more to the wise. We give thanks to God, for Whom all things are possible, Who gave you to us, and Who illumined you by His spirit for the glory of His name and for the salvation of many. We humbly and sincerely pray that He will bestow health of body and strength of mind upon you, so that He may abundantly spread His gift, which He has poured out upon you, for the edification of the whole Church.

Note

1. That is, the scholastics.

195r

Hildegard to the Congregation of Nuns

About 1170

Hildegard describes her confrontation with the brothers of St. Disibod over property rights. She also contemplates her own death.

O daughters, you who have followed in Christ's footsteps [cf. I Pet 2.21] in your love for chastity, and who have chosen me, poor little woman that I am, as a mother for yourselves—a choice made in the humility of obedience in order to exalt God—I say these things not on my own accord but according to a divine revelation speaking through my motherly affection for you. I have found this monastery—this resting place of the relics of St. Rupert the Confessor, to whose refuge you have fled—resplendent with miracles, by God's will, offering up a sacrifice of praise [cf. Ps 49.14]. I came to this place with the permission of my superiors and with God's assistance I gladly made it a home for myself and my followers.

Later, however, at God's admonition I paid a visit to Mount St. Disibod (which I had left with permission), where I presented the following petition to all who dwelt there: I requested that our monastery, as well as the alms accruing therefrom, be free and clear from their jurisdiction, for the sake of the salvation of our souls and our concern for the strict observance of the Rule.[1] They granted me this freedom and even promised me a written charter. Everyone—from the highest to the lowest—who saw, heard, and perceived these things displayed the greatest benevolence regarding these matters so that they were confirmed in writing, in accordance with God's will. Let all who cling to God heed and learn this and affirm this matter with goodwill, and perfect it and stand by it so that they may receive the same blessing that God gave Jacob and Israel [cf. Gen 32.26ff].

O how loudly these daughters of mine will lament when their mother dies, for they will no longer suckle her breasts. And so for a long time with groans and wails and tears they will say: Alas, alas! Gladly would we suck our mother's breasts if we but had her here with us now! Therefore, O daughters of God, I admonish you to love one another, just as from my youth I, your mother, have admonished you, so that in this goodwill you might be a bright light with the angels, and strong in your spirits, just as Benedict, your father, instructed you. May the Holy Spirit send you His gifts, because after my death you will no longer hear my voice. But never forget the sound of my voice among you, for it has so often resounded in love among you.

Now, my daughters are grieved in their hearts out of the sadness they feel for their mother, and they sigh and look to heaven. Later, they will shine with a bright, radiant light through the grace of God, and they will become valiant warriors in God's house. Therefore, if any one of my daughters seeks to cause discord and dissension in the spiritual discipline of this monastery, may the gift of the Holy Spirit root this desire out of her heart. Yet if she should do this out of total contempt for God, may the hand of the Lord strike her down in the presence of all the people, for such a one has deserved to be confounded.

Therefore, O my daughters, dwell in this place with all devotion and steadfastness, for you have chosen it as a place in which to serve in the army of God [cf. II Tim 2.4]. Do this so that, in Him, you may receive the rewards of heaven.

Appendix

And according to the true vision I received, I said this to the father, that is, the abbot, of that monastery: The Serene Light says: You should be a father to this community for the salvation of the souls of my daughters abiding in my mystic planting. The alms bestowed upon them have nothing to do with you or your brothers, but your monastery should be a place of sanctuary for them. But if it is your will to persevere in gnashing your teeth at us with your verbal assaults, then you will be like the Amalekites [cf. I Sam 30.1f] and like Antiochus, who, as it is written, stripped the temple of the Lord bare [cf. I Macch 1.23f; 6.12]. But if any among you say to yourselves maliciously: We intend to diminish their holdings—then "I Who Am" [Ex 3.14] say that you are the worst sort of despoilers. If you attempt to take from them the shepherd who applies spiritual medicine,[2] then again I say to you that you are like the sons of Belial [cf. I Sam 2.12; 10.27], and that in this matter you are not considering the justice of God, and, for this reason, the justice of God will destroy you. And when with these words, I, a poor little form of a woman, sought from that abbot and his brothers the autonomy of our monastery and the unencumbered possession of my daughters' endowments, ...

Notes

1. At this point, some MSS add the passage printed in the appendix to this letter.
2. That is, the provost and spiritual advisor, Volmar.

St. Georgen

196

Hildegard to the Abbot Withelo

Before 1153

Hildegard writes in answer, apparently, to a query from the abbot about resigning his position.

In the mirror of true vision I have seen you very troubled, stirred up like a turbid cloud when threatening air moves, caught up in wind and rain. Such are the thoughts of your mind, troubled as it is over the matter you have embraced in the core of your heart.

And I heard a voice saying of you: A man who toils with plow and oxen in arid land says to himself: I cannot endure this difficult labor because it is too hard for me. And so he goes into the desert [cf. Luke 11.24], where delicate flowers grow uncultivated by human effort, but which are being suffocated by unwholesome weeds. And again he says to himself: I will put aside my plow, and pull up these useless weeds. What is the good in this? Now, O man, consider who is better: the one toiling in the earth with a useful plow, or the one who pulls up useless weeds growing amid the flowers.

I saw also that this matter you are asking about is unwholesome for you. Therefore, stay in your position with your hand to the plow. May God help you in all your needs, and not permit you to toil in vain.

St. Nabor

197

Hildegard to an Abbot

1159–70

Another letter in response apparently to a query about resigning one's office. The abbot had also apparently asked something about the schism in the Church.

Caretakers of gardens should have advisors and counselors who carefully gather up the precepts of the law, and who do not look behind their backs at the ram [cf. Gen 22.13] but keep their eyes on the sacrifice present before them, which the Church celebrates daily, not as an allegory, but as the very sacrifice of the Son of God Himself, because He suffered in His Passion, and taught His Passion[a] [cf. Matt 26.26ff].

If you do not have a fruitful tree and matter necessary for life in your discernment of God's precepts for mankind, then withdraw to other gardens and offer them assistance in all their needs, but not so that you conceal the day in you and make yourself the night, lest your Lord find fault with you.

The Lord does not bid me speak concerning the schism in the Church, but He brandishes His sword and He bends His bow [cf. Ps 7.13], because it will quickly come to an end by the goodness of good men.

St. Thomas an der Kyll(?)

198

Hildegard to the Abbess Elisabeth

1175(?)

Hildegard advises moderation and discretion in subduing this body of flesh.

In a true vision I saw and heard these words: O daughter of God, you who out of love for God call me mother, poor little form of a woman that I am, learn to have discretion, which in all things celestial and terrestrial is the mother of all the virtues. For, through it, the spirit and the body are governed, and they are fed with proper restraint.

Let a person who, with sighs of penitence, is mindful of the sins she has committed in thought, word, and deed through the deception of the devil, embrace her mother Discretion and subject herself to her. And in true humility and obedience let her make amends for her sinful ways according to the counsel of her superiors. For just as the fruit of the earth is damaged by unseasonable rain, and just as unplowed ground produces noxious weeds rather than wholesome vegetation, so when a person labors beyond the capacity of her body, she is rendered ineffectual because of her indiscriminate toil and abstinence of spirit, for all the works of holy Discretion have been damaged in her.

When that blackest of birds, the devil, realizes that a person wants to quell illicit desire and cease from sin, then, like a serpent in his hole, he entwines himself into that person's fasting, prayers, and abstinence, and to deceive her he says: Your sins cannot be wiped out unless you crush your body underfoot with grief and tears and other immeasurable exertions so that it dries up totally. Then, that person, living without hope or joy, often loses her sense of perception and is seized by serious infirmity, and in this way is robbed of the reward for her sanctity by the deception of the devil. Moreover, she leaves uncompleted those works she had undertaken without discretion, and so her last state will be worse than the first [cf. Luke 11.26].

But a person who is bound to obedience, following the example of Jesus Christ, must be especially careful not to choose anything according to her own will, trusting more in her own self than in the good counsel of others, for then she will be overcome by that pride which fell from heaven because she wishes to be better than other good people since she believes that only what she herself has accomplished is good and holy. A person can teach herself that she ought not to give in to her own will, since she consists of two natures—body and soul—and they are continually at odds with one another, for what pleases the one displeases the other. Since this is the way it is, how could she consent to her will—a property of the body—and depend on it for the safety of her soul? A person who out of fear and love of God has despised her own will, and has subjected herself to the precepts and doctrine of the Rule and to her superiors by offering examples of good works to others in true humility, such a one makes herself a living tabernacle in the heavenly Jerusalem [cf. Heb 12.22], and the Holy Spirit rests upon her.

O blissful soul, heed these words, you who have run swiftly and bravely like a hart to the fountain of waters, that is, to the living God [cf. Ps 41.2–3]: May the mighty King preserve you in that fortitude, and bring you joyfully to eternal bliss. Amen.

St. Walburga

199

Hildegard to the Abbot Dietmar

Before 1170

Hildegard advises action, rather than simply passive reliance on God.

The Living Light says to you: Keep vigilant, and do not gather weariness in the coffer of your mind as if you were a foreigner without the ability to speak. God requires you to maintain the ability to chastise your sheepfold. Therefore, accuse yourself that in this matter you are failing to see God in the pure fountain, and only say: "God, my God help me" [Ps 69.6]. And yet by doing so, you do not touch Him.

O valiant knight, rise up now because the grace of God is hastening toward you. And you will live forever, a living stone [cf. I Pet 2.4–5] in the heavenly Jerusalem [cf. Heb 12.22].

Salem

200

The Abbot Gero to Hildegard

1165–73

The abbot writes asking Hildegard's advice concerning the disposition he should make of the office to which he has recently been elected.

To the beloved lady in Christ and his mother, Hildegard, Gero, ineffectual minister of the brothers in Salem, if a sinner's prayer has any efficacy.

Everyone who loves Christ also has the spirit of Christ, "and no man can say the Lord Jesus, but by the Holy Spirit" [I Cor 12.3]. By a special gift of the Holy Spirit that sets you apart from the other members of Christ, you, sweet mother, have been sent to witness the end of this world.[a] For truly the Holy Spirit is openly acknowledged and revealed through you and in you, as if speaking through His instrument. I have seen and read the great sacraments of God's mysteries that the Lord of all knowledge has opened up to us unworthy mortals through you in the book you have written. And so I believe and hold as indisputable that by speaking through you "the Spirit of truth, who proceedeth from" God the Father [John 15.26] and His Son, will flash out and, in flashing out, will strike against the spirit of lies, which is soon to come from its father the devil [cf. John 8.44].

Out of the anxiety of my heart, therefore, I humbly and simply seek advice from you, as from the bride and handmaid of Christ aware of the secrets of God—if, however, such a request is not contrary to His will. I have been elected abbot of the community of brothers in Salem now that the abbot of that place has died, since I had held this same pastoral position for a long period of time (although ineffectually) at Reitinhasil. God Himself, Who knows all secrets, is aware that I held that administrative position then, as this one now, against my will.

Therefore, in simplicity of heart, I ask you to enlighten me about the will of the Holy Spirit regarding this matter. That is, please deign to tell me whether it would be better for me to cast off this burden. If not, please tell me so. Whatever you decide, please send your response to me in a sealed letter through the present messenger.

Farewell in the Lord, my lady.

200r

Hildegard to the Abbot Gero

1165–73

Once again, Hildegard advises retention of the office of authority.

Whoever takes up a field or a sheepfold to see that it is faithfully tended must not let it go, but, like the head of a household, must govern it. For whoever abandons his sheepfold and takes up another is called a perverter of God's precepts.

Therefore, hold the rod of correction tight like a pious father and a zealous shepherd. The shepherd must not become a thief. Why? A thief steals what he wants and does not bother with things that do not interest him. Similarly, many shepherds choose what they want according to their own will, and reject the things they do not want. They frequently despise their perfect disciples, and seek after those who are unstable and vain. A pious father, however, chastises his son out of his complete love for him, and does not hold back from him what is good.

In your congregation I see that there are some who glow like the dawn [cf. II Sam 23.4] because of their good works and their patience. I perceive, however, that the majority are overclouded by their unstable character and vanity, and that they are bold enough to willfully make excuses for themselves. Admonish and chastise these men to the best of your ability. For God chose both the Old and New Testaments and left them for His sons, so that they might learn to live by just law through the Holy Spirit.

God wants you. See to it, therefore, that you do not withdraw from Him.

Schönau

201

The Nun Elisabeth to Hildegard

1152–56

Elisabeth of Schönau,[1] Hildegard's younger contemporary,[2] is the second most famous female visionary of the twelfth century. Indeed, given the large number of manuscripts of her works that have come down to us, it appears that Elisabeth's reputation in the Middle Ages was at least equal to Hildegard's, if not greater. In this letter, the young, tentative visionary turns to her older, more experienced and established contemporary for advice and consolation, much as, earlier, Hildegard had turned to St. Bernard (see Letter 1, Vol. 1). Recounting to Hildegard the troubles and slanders she has incurred as a result of her visions, Elisabeth seeks Hildegard's understanding and assistance in helping to quell the rumors, for, as she explains, her words have been broadcast far beyond what she herself desired, and, besides, have been distorted.

To the lady Hildegard, venerable mistress of the brides of Christ in Bingen, Elisabeth, a humble nun, sends her devoted prayers with all esteem. May the grace and consolation of the Most High fill you with joy because you have been kindly sympathetic to my distress, as I have understood from the words of my confessor, whom you have diligently advised with regard to my consolation. For just as was revealed to you about me, as you said, I have been disturbed, I confess, by a cloud of trouble lately because of the unseemly talk of the people, who are saying many things about me that are simply not true. Still, I could easily endure the talk of the common people, if it were not for the fact that those who are clothed in the garment of religion cause my spirit even greater sorrow. For stirred by I don't know what spirit, they ridicule the grace of the Lord in me, and they have no fear of making hasty judgments about things that they have no understanding of. I hear, too, that some people are circulating a letter under my name about the Spirit of God. They have slandered me by claiming that I have prophesied about the day of judgment—which, certainly, I have never presumed to do, since such knowledge is beyond the ken of any human being. But let me inform you of the cause of this talk, so that you may judge for yourself whether I have said or done anything presumptuously in this matter. As you have heard from others, the Lord has poured out His mercy upon me beyond what I deserve or could even hope to deserve. So much is this true that He has frequently deigned to reveal to me certain heavenly mysteries. Through His angel, He has frequently disclosed to me what sort of things are about to befall His people in these days unless they do penance for their sins, and He has commanded me to announce this openly. Seeking to avoid arrogance and not wishing to spread novelties, I sought, to the best of my ability, to keep all this hidden. Yet on a Sunday when I was, as usual, in a state of ecstasy [cf. Acts 11.5], the angel of the Lord stood before me and said, "Why are you hiding gold in the mud? This is the word of God that has been sent to the world to be spoken by you, because they have turned their faces away. For the word of God should not be hidden but made manifest to the praise and glory of our Lord and to the salvation of His people." And after he had said this, he lifted a scourge up over me, and as if in great wrath he struck me harshly five times, so that for three days thereafter I suffered from that beating in my whole body. Then, he placed his finger on my mouth, and said, "You will be silent until the ninth hour, but then you will make known everything the Lord has worked in you." Therefore, I remained quiet until the ninth hour. Then, I made a sign to my superior to bring me a certain little book that I had hidden in my bed, a book which contained a partial account of the things the Lord had worked in me. When I put this book into the hands of my lord abbot,[3] who had come to visit me, my tongue was loosed, and I said, "Not to us, O Lord, not to us; but to thy name give glory" [Ps 113b.1]. After this, I also revealed to him other matters that I had not wished to commit to writing, about, for example, the mighty vengeance of the Lord that, as I learned from the angel, was soon to come upon the whole world.[4] I entreated him earnestly, however, to keep what I had told him to himself. Yet he commanded me to take the matter up in prayer and ask the Lord to disclose to me whether He wanted me to keep silent about those things or not. Then, after I had devoted myself to urgent prayer concerning this matter for a long time, during the season of Advent on the Feast of St. Barbara[5] in the first vigil of the night, I fell into an ecstasy, and the angel of the Lord stood before me, and said: "Cry out mightily, and say 'alas' to all people because the whole world has become dark. And say to them: Rise up, for He Who formed you from the dust has called you, and He says, Repent, for the kingdom of God is at hand" [cf. Matt 3.2; 4.17]. Persuaded by these words, my abbot undertook to reveal this message to the masters of the church and men of religious calling. Some of them received it reverently. Others, however, did not, but spoke slanderously about my angel, saying that he was a deceptive spirit disguised as an angel of light [cf. II Cor 11.14]. Therefore, they laid an oath of obedience upon me, and commanded me, upon his next appearance, to adjure him in the name of the Lord to tell me whether he was a true angel of God or not. Believing this to be presumptuous, I received this command with great fear. Then, on a certain day, when I was in an ecstasy, he appeared before me in his customary fashion. And, trembling, I said to him: "I adjure you in the name of God the Father, the Son, and the Holy Spirit, to tell me truthfully whether you are a true angel of God and whether those visions I saw in my state of ecstasy and heard from your mouth are genuine." He answered in reply, "Be assured that I am a true angel of God, and that the visions you have seen in your ecstasy and heard from my mouth are genuine, and they will surely come to pass unless God is reconciled to man. And I am the one who has labored with you this long time." After this, on the vigil of the Epiphany,[6] my lord[7] appeared to me again while I was at prayer, but he stood at a distance and kept his face turned away from me. Perceiving his indignation, therefore, I said fearfully to him, "My lord, if I annoyed you when I adjured you, do not, I beg you, impute the fault to me. Please turn to me again, and do not be angry with me, because I was constrained by the necessity of obedience, and I did not dare to disobey the command of my superior." After I had wept profusely with words of this sort, he turned to me and said, "You have shown contempt for me and my brothers because you distrusted me. Therefore, know for certain that you will never see my face again, nor hear my voice, unless we and the Lord have been appeased." And I said, "My lord! How can you be appeased?" He said, "Tell your abbot that he is to celebrate the divine office devoutly in honor of me and my brothers." Thus after the rites of the Mass had been celebrated not just once but several times by both the abbot and the other brothers in honor of the holy angels, and the sisters had, at the same time, honored them with reading the Psalms, my lord appeared to me again, placated, and he said to me, "I know that what you did was done in love and obedience, and, therefore, you have attained pardon, and I will visit you even more frequently than before." After this, when my abbot was making arrangements to go to a certain place to ask permission of the clerics dwelling there to preach to the people the Lord's warning to repent so that the wrath of God would be turned from them, he came first to pray the Lord, along with all of us, to deign to reveal to His handmaiden whether the words that had now begun to become manifest should be more widely divulged or not. Then, while he was celebrating the divine mysteries, and we were all praying devoutly, suddenly my joints went slack, and I became dizzy and fell into a state of ecstasy. And, behold, the angel of the Lord stood before me, and I said to him, "My lord, remember what you said to me, your handmaiden, that the word of God had been sent into the world through my mouth, not to be hidden but to be revealed to the glory of God and the salvation of His people. Reveal to me now what must be done about that word of warning which you disclosed to me. Is it now sufficiently well-known or must it be preached further?" But he looked at me sternly, and said, "Do not tempt God [cf. Matt 4.7; Luke 4.12], for those who tempt Him will perish. You are to say to the abbot: 'Do not be afraid, but finish what you have started. They are truly blessed who hear the words of your exhortation and observe them, and they will not be offended at you.' But impart this to him also, that he is not to alter the method of preaching he has used so far. I have been his advisor on this point. Say to him to give no heed whatsoever to those who, out of ill will, speak doubtfully about the things that have been done through you. Rather, let him bear in mind what has been written, that nothing is impossible with God" [cf. Matt 19.26; Mark 10.27; Luke 18.27]. Animated by these words, therefore, the abbot went to the place he had arranged to go, and exhorted those who had awaited his arrival to repent. He announced that the wrath of God would come upon all unless they zealously forestalled it by the fruits of penitence [cf. Matt 3.8]. Despite the controversy in this matter, he detailed in his sermon the kind of plagues that threatened the world. And it so happened that many who had scorned this message before fearfully gave themselves over to penitence throughout the whole Lenten season, and became zealous in their alms and prayers. At that time a certain person, induced by some kind of zeal, sent a letter to Cologne in the name of my abbot—though he himself was ignorant of it, God knows—a letter in which terrible threats were recounted in the hearing of all the people.[8] Therefore, although some foolish persons mocked us, the prudent, as we hear, reverently heeded the message and did not fail to venerate God with the fruits of penitence. It happened that on the fourth day before Easter I had endured great bodily suffering and then entered a state of ecstasy. Then the angel of the Lord appeared to me, and I said to him, "Lord, what will be the outcome of this message that you spoke to me?" And he answered, "Do not be grieved or disturbed if the things I predicted to you do not occur on the day that I had set, because the Lord has been appeased by the repentance of many." After this, on the sixth day at about the third hour, I went with great pain into a state of ecstasy, and again the angel stood before me, and said, "The Lord has seen the affliction of His people and has turned from them the wrath of His indignation." I said to him, "What then, my lord? Will I not be an object of derision to all the people to whom this word was revealed?" And he replied, "Whatever happens to you on this occasion, endure it all with patience and kindness. Diligently heed Him Who, although He created the whole world, endured the derision of men. Now, the Lord is putting your patience to the test."

My lady, I have explained the whole sequence of events to you so that you may know my innocence—and my abbot's—and thus may make it clear to others. I beseech you to make me a participant in your prayers, and to write back to me some words of consolation as the Spirit of the Lord guides you.

Notes

1. This and the following letter from Elisabeth of Schönau (202/3) have been translated from Roth, *Die Visionen*, pp. 70–78. Once again, Van Acker has supplied only the numbers while referring the reader elsewhere. In this case, he defers to the edition by Anne L. Clark forthcoming in the *Corpus Christianorum* series, an edition that is still only in the early stages. Clark informs us, however, that the edition by Roth is quite suitable for our purposes. Moreover, she was gracious enough to supply variant MS readings.

2. Elisabeth's vital dates are not firmly established. She seems to have been born, however, in 1128 or 1129, and died in 1164 or 1165.

3. This is Hildelin, who was abbot of Schönau when Elisabeth took her vows at the age of twelve. As will be seen later in this letter, he had firm faith in her visions and encouraged her in her remarkable career.

4. As usual with such reports, God's vengeance was delineated in Apocalyptic terms: God would deliver to Satan the power to bring about violence upon the earth, the sun would turn a bloody red, and Christians would wail from the enormous affliction. See Clark, pp. 14–15.

5. December 4.

6. January 5.

7. That is, the angel.

8. That is, this anonymous letter, written by some overzealous believer, was apparently read to a large audience in some public forum in Cologne.

201r

Hildegard to the Nun Elisabeth

1152–56

This letter is notable for its view of Hildegard as the older, more experienced visionary offering motherly advice to her young protégée. Elisabeth's troubles come, Hildegard informs her, precisely because of her chosen status, for the devil is especially vicious against those who are singled out by God. Therefore, those so chosen must remain humble, remembering always that they are mere trumpets in the hands of Another.

I, a poor little form of a woman and a fragile vessel [cf. II Cor 4.7], say these things not from myself, but from the Serene Light: People are vessels which God has fashioned for Himself, and which He has imbued with His inspiration so that He might complete all His works in them. For God does not work as man does, but all things are brought to perfection by His command. Vegetation, forests, and trees appeared, and the sun, moon, and stars came forth, in order to serve mankind. The waters brought forth fish and birds. Herds and beasts also arose, all to serve human beings, as God commanded.

Of all creation, however, human beings alone did not acknowledge Him.[1] For although God gave them great knowledge, they elevated themselves in their own spirit, and turned away from God. God had intended to perfect all His works in human beings, but the ancient deceiver deluded them, and through the delight of an unseasonable wind tainted them with the sin of disobedience when they sought out more than they should have.

Ach! Woe! Then all the elements became entangled in the alternation between light and darkness, just as mankind did by transgressing against God's commands. But God "irrigated" certain individuals so that mankind would not be totally mocked. For Abel was good, but Cain was a murderer [cf. Gen 4.2ff]. And many saw God's mysteries in the light, but others committed multitudinous sins until the time arrived when God's Word shone forth, as it is said: "Thou art beautiful above the sons of men" [Ps 44.3]. Then the "Sun of justice" [Mal 4.2] came forth and illumined mankind with good works both in faith and deed, just as the dawn comes first, and the other hours of the day follow until the night comes. So, O my daughter Elisabeth, the world is in flux. Now the world is wearied in all the verdancy of the virtues, that is, in the dawn, in the first, the third, and the sixth—the mightiest—hour of the day. But in these times it is necessary for God to "irrigate" certain individuals, lest His instruments become slothful.

Listen now, O my anxious daughter. The arrogant deception of the ancient serpent [cf. Gen 3.1ff; Apoc 12.9, 20.2] sometimes wearies those persons inspired by God. For whenever that serpent sees a fine jewel he hisses and says, What is this? And he wearies that jewel with the many afflictions that distress a blazing mind longing to soar above the clouds, as if they were gods, just as he himself once did.

Listen again: Those who long to complete God's works must always bear in mind that they are fragile vessels [cf. II Cor 4.7], for they are only human. They must always bear in mind what they are and what they will be. They must leave to Him Who is of heaven the things of heaven, because they are exiles ignorant of the things of heaven. They can only sing the mysteries of God like a trumpet, which only returns a sound but does not function unassisted, for it is Another who breathes into it that it might give forth a sound. But let them put on the breastplate of faith [cf. I Thess 5.8], those who are mild, gentle, poor, and afflicted, like the Lamb, for they are the sound of His trumpet, and in character they are like guileless children. For God always scourges those who sound His trumpet, but according to His own good purpose, He foresees that their fragile vessel will not perish.

O my daughter, may God make you a mirror of life. I too cower in the puniness of my mind, and am greatly wearied by anxiety and fear. Yet from time to time I resound a little, like the dim sound of a trumpet from the Living Light. May God help me, therefore, to remain in His service.

Note

1. A not uncommon idea in the twelfth century. See Letter 15r, n. 2.

202/203

Elisabeth to Hildegard

1157–64(?)

Elisabeth of Schönau[1] writes in condemnation of the Cathars. See Letters 15r and 169r for Hildegard's views on the same subject.

Rejoice with me, lady and venerable daughter of the eternal King, for the finger of God writes upon you so that you may utter the word of life [cf. Phil 2.16; I John 1.1]. You are blessed, and it will always be well with you. You are the instrument of the Holy Spirit, for your words have enkindled me as if a flame had touched my heart, and I have broken forth into these words.

My lady Hildegard, rightly are you called Hildegard[2] because God's goad works mightily in you to edify His Church. Be comforted by the Holy Spirit, blessed lady, for the Lord has chosen you, and appointed you as one of those about whom He Himself says, "I have appointed you, that you should go, and should bring forth fruit; and your fruit should remain" [John 15.16]. And so you walk on the road of the contemplation of the Lord like a dove "in the clefts of the rock, in the hollow places of the wall" [Cant 2.14]. He Who chose you will

Himself crown you with a crown of rejoicing. The path of the Lord has been made straight before you. O my lady Hildegard, complete the work of the Lord, just as you have begun, because the Lord has appointed you to work in His vineyard [cf. Matt 20.1ff]. For the Lord sought people to work in His vineyard, and all those He found were idle because no one had hired them. The Lord's vineyard has no gardener, and so it has perished. The head of the Church has languished, and so its limbs have died. Alas, what will happen in this matter? For the Lord is finding few in His Church who consider this matter with burning spirit, but each person wishes to be a rule unto himself, and live according to his own will. The Lord has tested them, and found them sleeping [cf. Matt 26.40ff; Mark 14.37ff; Luke 22.45f]. As a result, a thief has come and dug through the stone of the foundation and destroyed it. He has thrown it into a dry well, and it has not been watered. The stone of the foundation is the head of the Church, which has been cast off [cf. Ps 117.22; Matt 21.42]. Thus the Church of God has withered, for it lacks moisture. Withdrawn from the love of God, it has grown cold. But I remember that once I had a vision in which poisonous serpents were about to come into the Church of God, desiring to furtively tear it apart. I understand that this refers to the Cathars, who are now stealthily deluding the Church of God. O Lord, our protector, drive them out. "And blessed is he that shall not be scandalized" [Matt 11.6] at this time. The patriarch David says, "Shall he that sleepeth rise again no more?" [Ps 40.9]. Arise! Wake up! Keep watch! For the vengeance of God calls to you. Wail, shepherds, and cry out. Sprinkle yourselves with ashes, and repent. Give no quarter to the devil, for "as a roaring lion, he goeth about seeking whom he may devour" [I Pet 5.8]. Blessed is the one who fears the Lord of all creation, and importunes the highest priest to take away the disgrace of His people [cf. Is 25.8]. Thus all Israel will be saved.

Now, My people have become perverse, and walk before Me with stiff necks, and they do not understand that they stand under My judgment. By scourging them, I show the offenses they have committed against Me and against My saints. And the saints stand before My throne every day crying out: "Lord, King of eternal glory, all things are in Your power, and no one can resist Your will. Avenge our blood, for they trample us into the earth with their pollutions" [cf. Apoc 6.10]. I the Lord, Creator of all created things, sent forth My incarnate Word from the heights of heaven into the valley of darkness to give light to those who were in darkness [cf. Is 9.2], those who thought that they were of some account although they were nothing, those who loved darkness more than the light [cf. John 3.19]. But He "was the true light" [John 1.9], like the morning star in the midst of a cloud, like the sun shining in its might at midday. He shone in the midst of His people, full of wisdom and strength, and the whole earth was filled with His teachings. But you have forgotten Him. I swear by My right hand and by My throne that it will be this way no longer.

O man, whoever you are, how will you be able to excuse yourself? You have eyes, and yet you do not see; you have ears to hear, but you do not understand [cf. Ezech 12.2]. What more can I do for you? If you destroy yourself, who, do you think, will redeem you? Remember that the only son of My heart died once and for all time for your sins, rose again, ascended into heaven, and sits in His glory. He left you the example to follow in His footsteps. How are you following Him? What kind of heart is yours? What kind of conscience? His ways are far from your ways. Do not turn aside, neither to the right nor to the left [cf. Deut 5.32], but follow in His footsteps, and then you will be able to come to Him. But now you are slipping from sin unto sin, from damnation unto damnation. Walk while the light is with you, lest the darkness overwhelm you [cf. John 12.35], for the ancient leviathan believes that he will devour the whole world. But this is still a time of grace. Repent, "seek ye the Lord your God, while he may be found: call upon him, while he is near" [Is 55.6]. Turn to Me with all your heart, and I, the Lord, will turn to you, and I will be reconciled to you. I will never desert you in time of trial and distress. And that ancient serpent will fall into great ruin, and will spill out almost all his bowels.

What is it that I said about the bowels of the ancient serpent? There are some who now have been swallowed up in his bowels, but will later be vomited out. These are murderers, adulterers, robbers, unrighteous men who have hastened their souls into death. These are the wretched Cathars, who are more abominable than any other creature. They utter flaming words from their sulfurous tongues, and the earth is polluted by their loathsome beliefs. Just as once the people crucified Me, so they, who cherish such beliefs, crucify Me every day. O how devilish is the madness of those who know that I am the Creator of heaven and earth and of all that is in them and know too that I gaze into the abyss [Ecclus 42.18], but who still lacerate My wounds when they pour forth the body and blood of My sacraments, which were offered for the salvation of all believers. If they provoke Me to wrath, I, the Lord, will wipe their race from the earth, and send it all the way to hell in My fury. Desist, perverters of justice, desist from this madness! Otherwise, I will order you to be punished beyond the limits of belief, suffering sulphur, inextinguishable fire, and the worms of hell without end. The suffering in hell is beyond all human comprehension; only that mighty leviathan, the seducer of the whole world, can comprehend it, for he is bound there.

Lest I strike you "with the sword of my mouth" [Apoc 2.16], I, the Lord, command you by My right hand—you kings, princes, bishops, abbots, priests, and all who are in lofty positions—to drive out and destroy with might and main in the Catholic faith all heresies that cause schisms in the Church that I begot in the bitterness of My spirit. You wretched and damnable hypocrites! You appear before men as if you were religious and guileless men, although inside you are full of wicked thoughts. Tell me: How can you believe in God almighty if you do not believe that all things are possible for God almighty [cf. Matt 19.26; Mark 10.27; Luke 18.27]? It was indeed possible with God to send forth His holy spirit from the seat of His great majesty into a virginal womb, and for the Word of His incarnation to come forth from it. Do you believe that God the Father created mankind in His image and likeness [cf. Gen 1.26f], and that He "put him into the paradise of pleasure, to dress it, and to keep it" [Gen 2.15]? And that the ancient serpent deceived him so that he fell into sin and was cast out because of his disobedience [cf. Gen 3.1ff]? O wretched hypocrite! How long do you think you will last in your sins if you do not believe in the Son of God, Who proceeds from the Father? Yet you do not believe that He was incarnated, or that He truly suffered, or that He was buried, or that He rose again, or that He ascended into heaven, or that He will come to judge the living and the dead [cf. Acts 10.42; II Tim 4.1; I Pet 4.5]. But you who are educated examine the books of the New Testament, take His words into your heart, and discover what kind of fruit you find there. Be renewed by the Holy Spirit, and rekindle your hearts for the edification of the Church sanctified in Christ Jesus, illumined by the sacred Gospels, and cleansed of its ancient rust. Holy Church was joined and betrothed· to the heavenly Bridegroom, the Son of the Eternal King, Who washed its sins away in the Jordan River, so that there might be one faith, one baptism, one church, one dove, and one elect bride of Christ Jesus. Therefore, O you who are the chosen race, the sacred nation, the regal priesthood, the people of increase, remember the freedom I gave you when I freed you from the yoke and captivity of the devil. "You were heretofore darkness, but now light" [Eph 5.8]. Your God says: Walk so that you may be My dear children, so that you may be children of light. And again Truth says: I planted you as My chosen vineyard [cf. Is 5.2], and caused you to recognize the whole way of truth. Why have you regressed, walking on a way that is not straight? You follow your own sinful way, and you seek peace after your own will, saying: There will be peace, but there is no Son of peace. But you are deceiving yourself.

I have been cast out, and there is no place where my foot can rest. "I stand at the gate, and knock" [Apoc 3.20], and there is no one to let Me in. "My head is full of dew" [Cant 5.2], and My bed where I desired to rest has been polluted with all manner of sins. Those who enter My sanctuary in their uncleanliness defile My bed with their depravities. My shepherds have been oppressed as if by heavy sleep—how am I to wake them up? I will raise My right arm over them. I have been patient, I have waited for them day after day, but they have totally forgotten Me. The law will perish, first from the priests and the elders of My people [cf. Ezech 7.26], because they are seeking to sell the sacrifices of My sacraments. But those who sell them are selling judgment to themselves, and those who buy a "sharp two edged sword" [Apoc 19.15]. And again I am giving paternal admonition to My pastors, who are aware of My secrets: Imitate Me and not the devil, because there are some who are not entering My sheepfold by the door, but climb in by another way like thieves and robbers [cf. John 10.1]—thieves because of their greed, robbers because they destroy the souls entrusted to them. They conceal their depraved deeds so that they will not be detected by the people. Therefore, they do not boldly speak out against every heresy, because they themselves are reprehensible in their ways. And again I say to you: Know for certain that I will require from your hands all the souls that perish from among My sheep because of your negligence, souls you undertook to govern and protect. You will render an account in fearsome judgment, and all the hardships that I brought upon them will wash over you.

Now, therefore, revive yourselves, and consider the apostles, your predecessors, and other holy teachers of the Church, who did not fear the threats of men or the scourges of executioners, but brought My word to kings and rulers. They were scourged, and they endured many tortures, but they endured all for My name. Therefore, they have attained glory and honor beyond anyone's imagination. They stand before My throne, and see Me, not in misery, but eye to eye, face-to-face, in great brightness and majesty. Blessed is the one who reads and hears the words of this text, and keeps them, because they are true. They have been sent from My throne by way of My angel for the edification of many.

As I thought of the meaning of the judgment I had made earlier, that they utter flaming words from their sulfurous tongues, the Lord set the following words in my mouth: Sulfur has such a nature that its flame does not rise up, but burns underneath with a kind of bitter darkness. It stands for the heresies that darkly bring forth poisonous words, from which comes forth a black flame igniting the hearts of the faithful. Such a flame causes them to waver in the Catholic faith.

Notes

1. Van Acker indicates two separate letters from Elisabeth at this point, but Anne Clark (who is currently engaged in editing Elisabeth's letters for the *Corpus Christianorum* series) has informed us in personal correspondence that the evidence of the MSS strongly suggests that these are not two but one single letter.

2. That is, "guardian of battle."

Selbod

204

A Provisor to Hildegard

Before 1173

The writer seeks advice about the state of his soul, for he is assured that Hildegard knows about his past, present, and future condition.

To Hildegard, the venerable handmaid of God almighty, H., humble and lowly provisor at Selbod, with his prayer that she abound with all the grace of God's bounty and that, after this life, she be united with Jesus Christ, Lord of all kings, in the heavenly bridal chamber.

Blessed be the compassion of almighty God, which in these times of iniquity has given you as a light shining in the darkness to console His faithful. I have heard of your fame for a long time now, blessed lady, and for some time I have been aware that everything said about you is true. And so I take such delight and joy in your blessedness that I always have you in my prayers—even though, because of my foolishness and stupidity, my petition has little weight in God's sight. I hope, and I pray, that the Lord will always oversee the blessings He has bestowed upon you in His mercy, and that He will increase them more and more, and make you the companion of His saints in eternal glory.

But because I am not able to come to see you in person—although I long to very much—I present myself, humble and submissive, as best I can in this present letter. Pitiable, I cast myself again and again at your feet, merciful lady, so that you will not disdain to pray earnestly to God almighty for my distress and misery. For I have no doubt that you can obtain whatever you desire from the Holy Spirit, Who dwells within your heart. And I am assured that by His revelation you can divine through this letter my condition and all that pertains to me, past, present, and future.

Therefore, if my puny condition dares to seek it and if it does not displease you, I pray, humble and submissive in heart and body, that you will not disdain to gladden my heart by apprising me of my current condition, either advising me concerning past and present matters or prophesying and giving me warning about the future and the conclusion of my life.

Siegburg (St. Michael)

205

Hildegard to the Monk Dietzelinus

Before 1170

Hildegard writes in answer to a letter that has not come down to us. Dietzelinus had apparently asked her to interpret some sign that he (or perhaps some friend of his) had received.

Concerning the sign you asked me about, that was more a matter of God's love than of His vengeance, for He saw that great fear would rise in your heart. And that person you inquired about was fortunate, because sometimes God shows His signs to men so that they may produce good fruit, like the dew that falls on fertile ground.

Your mind is like a torrent of pure water, but sometimes it is restless. Now, rise up into gentleness, like the sun that placidly and quietly maintains all its seasons. Do likewise, O valiant knight, and establish the light of your soul, lest you dry up from excessiveness in any thing, for Jesus loves you and desires your sacrifice.

206

A Congregation of Monks to Hildegard

1164(?)–70

The monks of St. Michael in Siegburg chose Hildegard as their spiritual mother, and wrote her letter after letter, but never received a reply. Here, once again, they write expressing their special reverence for Hildegard, and begging her, once again, for a letter.

To Hildegard, beloved lady and mother, the brothers of Saint Michael in Siegburg of one accord offer whatever servants owe to their lady or sons to their mother.

He Who knows all secrets is aware with what an extraordinary feeling of love we have chosen you as our spiritual mother and have brought you into the circle of our prayers, and you yourself, beloved lady, have been able to observe this from the sheer number of messages we have sent to you. Yet you have never shown us any sign of motherly affection. And despite our desire, you have never even sent us a letter of admonition, which you should have done even against our will, just as a mother gives wholesome advice to her children.

But, as we have begun, we do not cease knocking at the door of your heart, so that if you do not arise because you are our mother, you may nevertheless arise because of our importunity, and give us what we need [cf. Luke 11.8]. For we petition that, taught by a true vision, you reveal to us some information about the state of our monastery, and that you send to us words that advise and chastise.

These are the matters that we particularly desire you to look into, beloved mother, humbly beseeching you to inform us in writing about these and other matters that you know to be even more essential for us. We also implore you to make us a partner in your prayers, even as we have made you a partner in ours. Farewell.

206r

Hildegard to the
Congregation of Monks

1164(?)–70

Hildegard encourages the monks about the state of their community, encouragement accompanied, however, by the warning that some grow weary in the good
fight. She stresses discipline and stability in the governance of the monastery.

In a spiritual vision by which I frequently see, I saw and understood these things.
I see this monastery like a cloud suffused with the kind of light that occurs when
day becomes dusk, and night approaches. And I see that there are some among
you who shine like stars in their good intent, but that there are others who grow
weary, overshadowed by fatigue. Arise, therefore, and "embrace discipline, lest
at any time the Lord be angry, and you perish from the just way" [Ps 2.12].

I also saw something like a crown with two circles, one above and one below,
both filled with angels. And in the middle of this crown the archangel Michael
stood like a tower so that these two circles clung to him like two walls. On his
breast shone the image of the Son of man, and around it was written, "The Lord
will send forth the rod of thy power out of Sion: rule thou in the midst of thy
enemies" [Ps 109.2]. With his right arm stretched out, he held a shield in his hand.
And next to him was a cloud like golden smoke arising from a censer, in which
the meritorious prayers and holy works of this congregation shone. And I heard
him saying to this congregation: As long as I see the radiance of holiness in you,
I will fight for you against the black, flaming spears that I have seen hurled by
impious tyrants against your monastery.

Then I knew that this rod of power was the rod of Aaron that blossomed [cf.
Heb 9.4] with those branches of power which God had set in the angel on the
first day. But through his pride, that angel cut himself off from felicity. But God
saw the rod of his inheritance on Mount Sion [cf. Ps 73.2], for it blossomed like
the power of greatness in mankind when God almighty arose in virginity. And
this flower came forth from Sion, from which many waters flow, exhaling a sweet
breeze. These waters are the powerful works of holiness flowing into the hearts
of mankind so that man sees God in all things. Wherefore God's countenance
radiates among them when they renounce the devil's deception. Thus, equipped
with two wings, they wage war against the devil as if in the midst of their power
so that they love God more than themselves and do holy works. And then they
stand like pillars of cloud [cf. Ex 13.21f] "in the midst of their enemies," striking
them down on all sides, that is, by loving God and doing holy works, for He shines
like the sun "in the brightness of the saints" [Ps 109.3].

The first angel, however, longed to overcome God and to assume His honors rather than to love Him and do good works. But man is different, for, de-

spite his potential for doing evil, he honors God's divinity by overcoming himself through virginity (which abides in him under the banner of the King) or, for those who have tasted sin, through turning aside from the millstone of iniquity and abandoning the world. All of this is found "in the brightness of the saints" whom the word of God brought forth in accordance with the will of the Father.

And so the following is said clearly through the Holy Spirit to this community: "The blessing of the Lord be upon you" [Ps 128.8] "in the brightness of the saints." And may all who bless you be filled with blessing. And may blessing flee from those who curse you.

Springiersbach

207

The Abbot Richard to Hildegard

Before 1162(?)

Troubled by his feeling of inadequacy in his office, the abbot requests Hildegard to consult the Lord about the possibility of his resignation.

Richard, unworthy servant to the servants of God in Springiersbach, to Hildegard, most holy administrator of the congregation of St. Rupert and worthy steward of God, with his prayer that she become a denizen of the heavenly country after she has passed from this life.

I have instructed the present messenger to stand before you in my stead and to speak with you, holy lady, through this letter. Although I have wanted to, I have not been able to come to you for myself, but I have, I confess, spent many days, even years, vainly considering the matter. Indeed, in all sincerity and without deceit, I call God Himself to witness, to Whom "all things are naked and open" [Heb 4.13], how much I have desired from the beginning to speak with you face-to-face, magnificent and saintly lady.

Appointed ("unhappy man that I am" [Rom 7.24]) to manage and oversee in my pastoral position, I realize that I am completely useless, weak, and unequal to the task, for I am now almost completely bereft of strength, both of mind and body. Thus I desire more and more to lament, weep, and be freed "from the body of this death" [Rom 7.24]. And so, O holy lady, blessed among women, with you as my intermediary, I wish to put my situation before the Lord, and consult Him in the matter. Through you, I wish to question and discover whether it is possible for me to resign from my position.

For God's sake, please inform me as quickly as possible of the upshot of this matter and gladden my grieving heart with your advice and aid in the Lord.

Tholey

208

Hildegard to Her Brother Hugo

Before 1170

It is interesting to see the mundane affairs that the saint had to deal with. Hildegard writes her brother beseeching him to treat his brother with more civility.

The Church frequently recounts miracles, but sometimes they move beyond truth into derision. Therefore, I admonish you not to accuse your brother Roricus unjustly in your heart and not to move beyond the bounds in speaking evil words about him. God knows that you are not acting correctly in this matter.

Therefore, beware lest the Lord find you guilty in this wrath of yours and other similar matters. May God have mercy on you in all your sins.

Trier (St. Eucharius)

209

The Abbot Bertolf to Hildegard

1148–59

The abbot Bertolf was present at the famous synod of Trier, when Pope Eugenius read from the *Scivias* to the assembled prelates. Here, he writes a letter of praise for Hildegard, and requests her prayers for himself and his community.

To Hildegard, refulgent pearl, Bertolf, poor servant of Christ and unworthy abbot of St. Eucharius, with a prayer that, dedicated to virginity, she be pleasing to the Bridegroom of virgins.

We have heard of and fully believe in the fame of your virtue, nay not just the fame but the real virtue that is active in your fragile vessel [cf. II Cor 4.7] of divine piety. We heard and fully believed, and immediately we knew that the following prophecy was fulfilled in you: "It is good for a man, when he hath borne the yoke," et cetera [Lam 3.27]. Indeed, you have far exceeded your sex by having surpassed with manly spirit that which we were afraid even to approach, and you have made it such a part of your calling that you can say with the Apostle, "Our conversation is in heaven" [Phil 3.20].

Although, saintly lady, we have failed to greet you for a long time, impeded as we have been by the vacillations of this unstable age, you must not believe that the fire of love for you that once blazed in our hearts has grown cold. Therefore, blessed lady, please be no less mindful of us, puny as we are, in the presence of Him with Whom you are one spirit [cf. I Cor 6.17]. Likewise, please instruct the sisters entrusted to you to pray without ceasing both for us and for our community.

We also desire to hear words of admonition from you, and with all our hearts we wish you to be always in good health. Farewell.

209r

Hildegard to the Abbot Bertolf

1148–59

Hildegard advises the abbot on the duties of an administrator, stressing love and mercy.

"He Who Is" [Ex 3.14; Apoc 1.4] says: O man, you have put on the breastplate of faith [cf. I Thess 5.8], and you are girt with the belt of sanctity. Yet you are like a person who takes no joy in looking at his face in a mirror, because he sometimes doubts whether or not his face is comely. For your mind is like a building seen from afar that is sometimes covered by a cloud. And just as a porter quickly carries off a bundle to sell it, you are hasty.

Therefore, consider which of the following is the more useful: an ox or an ass, a fertile field or an arid one, a family name or a given name, a mountain or a valley situated between a man and his enemies. But the upright administrator is more useful than all the rest, just as air is beneficial in producing various kinds of fruit. Without the oversight of an administrator, a person's works do not come to fruition.

Now, beware lest you grow weak in your governance, as long as you have even one eye in your head. But hold out the light for your subordinates with maternal gentleness, cleanse their wounds, and fear to be regarded a tyrant. For the good Physician is not slow to mercifully anoint the wounds of mankind. For He gave a kiss to His own sheep, and He washed it in His blood.

You, therefore, O man, set Mercy, the beautiful friend of the King, in the bridal chamber of your mind, and in sweetest love put on sanctity like purple and a crown. Also, gather sweet aromatic herbs into your lap, and you will live in eternity, like the mountain of myrrh and incense [cf. Cant 4.6].

Be watchful, therefore, as you bear your burdens with the key of restitution,[a] so that when the sun shines over all things with no hint of whirlwind or storm, you may regard yourself to your benefit.

210

Hildegard to the Abbot Bertolf

1161–62

Hildegard gives advice to the abbot on the election of his son—spiritual son?—as abbot.

O father and consoler, I looked to the True Light about the burden soon to be imposed on your son, and I saw that this is something neither hot nor cold [cf. Apoc 3.15f], but rather lukewarm with no beneficial consequences. For I saw in the vision that that burden—if he were to take it on—would be like a withered tree with only one or two half-dead branches, which could never bring viridity back to the full tree again.

This tree represents the calling and life of those very few who can be found verdant in the love of the holy way of life and good counsel. Therefore, that burden would not be productive for him or for others, because he would falter altogether since he would get no help or wholesome guidance from them.

God does not embrace the election to that office with His love, but neither does He direct His anger against it. He merely allows it, just as He allows many other things that are done by His permission. Therefore, it would be much better for that man if he could refuse the office.

211

Hildegard to the Monk Gerwin

1161–62

A brief letter of admonition to the monk.

God in His wisdom seeks the sacrifice of your heart offered up in simplicity, for He is true [cf. John 3.33; Rom 3.4], and He will not tolerate duplicity on the one path that is faith among one's neighbors. For the eye of God looks upon the felicity of mankind in simplicity.

May God grant you this, and free you from the storms of flagrant sins. Therefore, purify the eye of your heart.

212

Hildegard to the Monk Gerwin

1162

Hildegard responds to the monk Gerwin, who has apparently written her troubled by the fact that he has been elected as abbot. She warns him of the dangers of accepting the office.

O beloved son of God, I will respond to you. This is God's view of that election: God did not wish you to fall into perdition and into dangerous sins, as the human will frequently causes a person to do. You are not, of course, obliged to accept the results of that election.[a]

Still, I do not see that it is God's wrath that has placed you in that position to which you were called by men.[1] Your discipline will be of this kind: You will not, during your tenure in office, be able to fulfill your will as you would like to do.

May God watch over you, and rule over all things with regard to you, in both body and soul.

Note

1. Apparently in answer to Gerwin's own response to this unwanted election.

213

Hildegard to the Abbot Gerwin

1162–64

This letter seems to justify Hildegard's fears about Gerwin's acceptance of the administrative position. Hildegard offers him advice on the duties of his new office.

The time for your healing [cf. Jer 14.19] has not yet come, for the earth cries out for God's vengeance, and heaven has been overclouded by unrighteousness. And again: not long from now heaven will resound with God's praise, and the earth will be released from its captivity.

The streets of the monastery where you live and hold the rod of correction are darkened by the instability of precarious morals, and they exhale, as it were, the poison of vice and disobedience. This is why disquieting battles arise. But later, when God so wishes, the first dawn will provide an example for you.

O lofty person, do not in your arrogance regard yourself as lofty. Do not rage against the sheep of your flock in the heat of your anger [cf. Ecclus 45.23]. Rather, anoint and correct them to the best of your ability. Then you will live forever.

214

Hildegard to the Abbot Ludwig

1168–73

Ludwig became abbot of St. Eucharius in 1168, and served in that capacity until 1173, when he resigned to become abbot at Echternach. Hildegard writes the abbot a general letter of advice about his duties as administrator. Early on, Ludwig became a close friend and confidant of Hildegard's, and, later, he was to be instrumental in enlisting Theodoric of Echternach to complete Hildegard's *Vita* begun by Godfrey of Mount St. Rupert.

In a true vision I saw and heard these things: A certain man carefully tended his garden, but a cloud passed over it and caused it to wither. Therefore, the man let the garden go untilled. Later, he dug up the garden and planted roses and lilies and other sweet-smelling plants in it. But, again, a whirlwind came over those plants and ravaged them. Then the man said to himself: I will turn this garden into a field, and plant wheat and barley in it.

Now you who bear the name "father," listen. That garden was your beginning, which, at first, was somewhat overclouded by instability, but heeding the admonition of the Holy Spirit, you turned it to the better part [cf. Luke 10.42]. Then, you delighted in the Holy Spirit as in wholesome plants. Still, from time to time you became weary, just as the whirlwind beats down the flowers. Now, God has decided to make you a farmer, as it were, so that you may look all about with due concern and plow properly, for it will do you no good to become slothful from your weariness.

You will become a good farmer by following the example of the saints, and by observing their character you will learn the nature of the righteous Father. Love good and upright men, and chastise those who are vain and neglectful. Endure with patience those who are as hard as stone, and do not, like an eagle, fall on them in hardness of heart or in the heat of your anger. Instead, do all things in moderation. Act in this way, lest you scatter Christ's flock.

Therefore, restrain yourself and live in accordance with the Rule of that most learned master.[1] And take instruction from that mighty Man, Who brought forth the waters and divided them into streams [cf. Gen 1.7], and Who causes the earth to put forth shoots and flourish [cf. Gen 1.11ff], and Who has raised up the mountains, setting them over the valleys, and Who established the firmament with all His ornaments, and Who caused the winds to blow and the air to fly with fire.

That Man is blessed because all blessing flows from Him. He is called "Man" because He created all things, and He manfully brought forth all things that are strong and mighty.[2]

Therefore, imbue your perception with streams of water from the Scriptures and with the calling and way of life of the saints. Restrain your body so that it will not cause the riches of the devil to put forth shoots, but so that virtues will blossom through wholesome doctrine. And so climb the mountain of virtues. Do this in humility, and bring forth flowers from your brothers as from trees. Be their sun through your teaching, their moon through your disputation, their wind through your uncompromising governance, their air through your mildness, and their fire through seemly exposition of doctrine.[a]

Begin to do these things in the beautiful dawn, and perfect them in the radiant light. Persist with might and main so that you will live for ever.

Notes

1. That is, St. Benedict.
2. It is impossible to render the Latin wordplay here into English. Hildegard plays on the words *vir, virtuosa,* and *viriliter,* which we have rendered as "man," "manfully," and "strong."

215

The Abbot Ludwig to Hildegard

1173

The abbot expresses the strength of his friendship for Hildegard.

To the holy virgin dedicated to God, Hildegard, his beloved mother, Ludwig, abbot in name only of St. Eucharius, greetings. My affection for you is so great that nobody except me could fully understand it.[a]

How ludicrous it would be for butterflies to greet eagles in a letter; or fleas, harts; or worms, lions. Just so, it would be strange, even laughable for me, a sinner, who has little, if any, capacity in any divine or human skill, to presume to write you. For adorned with the miraculous privilege of chastity, you have been endowed by God with such lofty and remarkable sagacity that you surpass the insight not only of modern philosophers and logicians, but even the prophets of old.

And yet with your customary kindness, saintly mother, you will surely not deny pardon to my rash presumption, for our friendship has made me bold to write to you again. And I will not be deterred from writing you or coming to see you frequently by the hardship of the road, for the benefit obtained from hearing you is all the more to be desired the greater the effort it requires to do so. For we possess those things more gratefully that we acquire by exertion.

Therefore, my lady, do not let our wickedness distress you, for compassionate love will lend you the strength that your physical infirmity denies you. I greatly long for the letter you promised to send me. So please do not delay sending it by the present messenger. I pray you to write back what seems to you best regarding the matter entrusted to you.

215r

Hildegard to the Abbot Ludwig

1173

Hildegard writes the abbot to thank him for his sympathy and understanding in her time of need, and she adds that since her helper (Volmar) has been taken from her by death, she will send the book he had helped her write to the abbot for review and correction, as soon as it is finished.

In regard to your request I looked to the true vision I see in my soul, and I saw and heard these words: You were chosen to govern that church with the rod of chastisement, an election not improper in the sight of God. Therefore, labor in that church to the best of your ability with God's help, for God's justice has grown cold among many who run on the narrow path of spiritual life, because they long to follow their own will. This time will not show you the perfection of holiness that the Holy Spirit first planted in that community. Therefore, restrain yourself, lest, led astray by the esteem acquired by an honorable name or by secular inclination, you fall short of the stability of your good intentions.

Imitate the gentlest Father in humility, patience, and mercy so that you will deserve to hear Him say to you for your good labors, "Well done, good servant" [Matt 25.21ff], and so that you may live blissfully in eternal beatitude. I and all my sisters zealously commend to God the infirmity of your body and all the pressure brought to bear on your heart. Therefore, fear not, because God, by Whose grace you are endowed with wisdom and knowledge, will never abandon you.

Gentle father, I give thanks to God, and to you, because you deigned to sympathize with me, a poor little form of a woman, in my infirmity and pain. Now, like an orphan I toil alone to do God's work, because my helper has been taken away from me, as it pleased God.[1] The book that I wrote with his help through the grace of the Holy Spirit according to a true vision is not yet finished. As soon as it is completely written, I will offer it to you for correction.[2]

Notes

1. That is, Volmar, who died in this year. Volmar had served as Hildegard's secretary and provost for some thirty years. It is scarcely a wonder that she feels like an orphan.

2. The book referred to is the *Liber Divinorum Operum*, which was completed in this year. After Volmar's death, Ludwig, along with Hildegard's nephew Wezelinus, served for a short time as Hildegard's advisor.

216

Hildegard to the Abbot Ludwig(?)

About 1173(?)

After a disquisition on the varied humors of mankind, Hildegard applies the theory to the abbot's present circumstances: those in his community are of a humor that conflicts with his own.

The secret mysteries of God cannot be comprehended or known by those things which came forth at the beginning.[a] Yet all His judgments are just, because there is no lack in Him, for just as He was and is, He is. And just as a man is compacted of the elements, and the elements are joined into one, with none being of worth without the other, so too the dispositions of mankind are of varying kinds although they all arise from a single breath.

The dispositions of mankind exist in four modes: hard, airy, stormy, fiery. The man who is "hard" is bitter in all his affairs. He consults no one else, but is pleased to handle all his affairs by himself alone. The mind of the man who is "airy" is always vacillating, and, therefore, he fears God and shows restraint in sin, because he is displeased with everything he does. The "stormy" are unwise, and they act foolishly in whatever they do. For they are not edified by words of wisdom, but shudder at them with indignation. And, last, those who are "fiery" give themselves wholly over to the secular, and alienate themselves from the spiritual. They shun peace, and, wherever they see it, they do violence to it with their secular ambition.

But God takes note of the presumption of those who do not look obediently to Him, but, as if they do not need Him as helper and lawgiver, take all their affairs into their own hands. Yet God will sweep them with the broom of tribulation and adversity until, through penitence, they recall that they have not cherished and observed His commandments.

But God gathers all people of whatever disposition to Himself when they at last come to an understanding of those things that are contrary to their salvation, and turn once again to God: those who fear Him at last, like Saul [cf. Acts 22.1ff] and many others.[1][b]

O person, you who are called "father" after the highest Father, your sickness is the "airy" kind, and so you fear God greatly. Those in the sheepfold that God has committed to you, however, are "hard" and "stormy" and "fiery," and, therefore, they oppress you. There, you have no consoling ointment.

Rejoice, however, because God loves you, and He cleanses your soul through that sickness of yours, and He will establish your soul in His inheritance. God is not unmindful of your community, but He will purge it of those unstable dispositions that displease Him. You never knowingly sought to do harm to your monastery, but all that you did you did for its good. Now, therefore, rejoice in the salvation of your soul, for you will be a living stone in the heavenly Jerusalem [cf. I Pet 2.4; Heb 12.22].

Note

1. There is a lacuna in the MS at this point. We translate following Peter Dronke's conjectural emendation. See endnote for Latin text and Dronke's suggestion.

217

Hildegard to the Abbot Ludwig(?)

1173–74(?)

Although Schrader and Führkötter (*Echtheit*, p. 146, n. 91) express some uncertainty about the recipient of this letter, whether Ludwig or some other abbot at a later date, Peter Dronke (*Women Writers*, pp. 312–13) argues that the letter is a follow-up to 215r in which Hildegard indicates that she will send her book (the *Liber Divinorum Operum*) to Ludwig for correction. Here, Dronke is convinced, is the cover letter for the manuscript that Hildegard is now sending. The similarity of language here to that of 215r, unquestionably addressed to Ludwig, as well as the echo of the language of the *Liber Divinorum Operum*, serves to support Dronke's contention.

The sun rises in the morning, and from its appointed place it suffuses all the clouds with its light like a mirror, and it rules and illumines all creatures with its warmth until evening. Just so, did God fashion all creation—which is mankind—and, afterward, vivified it with the breath of life and illumined it.

Just as morning first arises with damp cold and shifting clouds, so also man in his infancy is damp and cold, because his flesh is growing and his bones are not yet full of marrow, and his blood does not have its full vigor. As the third hour begins to grow warm with the course of the sun, so also man begins to chew his food, and learns to walk.

In his youth when infancy is over, man, becoming bold, happy, and carefree, begins to think of what he will do in life. If in the light of the sun he chooses the good by turning to the right, he will become fruitful in good works. But if he turns to the left to pursue evil, he will become black and corrupt in the evil of sin. When he reaches the ninth hour while doing his work, he becomes arid and weary in his flesh and marrow and the other powers through which he earlier grew and advanced. So also the great Artisan set in order the ages of the world from the first hour until the evening.

Therefore, O father, you who take your name from the Father, reflect on how you began and how the course of your life has proceeded, for in your infancy you lacked wisdom, and in your youth you were happy and carefree. In the meantime, however, you were seeking the affairs of the unicorn, all unbeknownst to yourself.[1]

This is the subject of my writing, which resonates of the fleshly garment of the Son of God, Who loved a virginal nature and rested in the lap of the Virgin like the unicorn, and with the sweetest sound of beautiful faith gathered all the Church unto Himself.

Be mindful, O faithful father, what you have often heard of that aforesaid garment of the Son of God from this poor weak form of a woman. Now, because the almighty Judge has taken my helper from me, I submit my writing to you, humbly asking you to preserve it carefully and correct it diligently. Then, your name will be inscribed in the book of life. In this you will imitate the blessed Gregory, who, despite the burden he bore as bishop of Rome, never ceased from his writing, which was infused with the sound of the lyre of the Holy Spirit.

Now, put on the armor of heaven like a valiant knight, and wash away the deeds of your foolish youth. In the angelic vestment of the monk's habit, labor strenuously at noon, before the day ends, so that you will be received joyfully into the company of angels in the heavenly tabernacles.

Note

1. Schrader and Führkötter (*Echtheit*, p. 146, n. 91) believe that this sentence refers to a question asked by the person to whom Hildegard's letter is addressed, which, on the face of it, seems unlikely. There are, in fact, so many meticulous connections (*interim, tamen, tunc*) to the preceding sentence that it seems, rather, that the reference is to the ignorance of foolish youth. The point being made seems to be that the person was seeking God even before he himself was aware of it.

Endnotes

Letter 91

a. *presentia tangere, reuoluere preterita, futura preuidere.*

b. *Visitauit enim nos oriens et iam ruenti seculo supposuit manum suam.*

c. *cuius interuentu et ueniam peccatorum et remedium laborum et consolationem dolorum obtinere, atque diuine dispositionis secretum cognoscere gaudemus.*

Letter 91r

a. *Nunc enim sunt tempora in obliuione Dei et lassa in certamine Christi. Sed fama uolat in mendaciis per uicissitudinem uanitatum quasi Deum uideant, sed tamen nesciunt eum.*

Letter 92

a. *Mens etenim tua aliquando est uelut in tanta sanctitate quod eam sustinere non potes, aliquando etiam in lassitudine et in ceteris similibus.*

b. *quamuis quocumque modo sacrificium eius constringas, quoniam constituit te quasi oculum suum.*

Letter 94r

a. *O filia Dei, cum caritate Christi circumdata es, sed tamen cum amaritudine tui corporis constricta es bellis et rebellas contradicendo diabolum. Et constructionem populi, cum quo es, Deo placitam uideo et etiam in meliorem partem strenue ascendentem, et in bona conuersatione plus edificari quam institutus sit.*

b. *Sed tamen nescis nec cogitare potes uincula ligatorum dirumpere, eorum scilicet qui in inuio irrisionis ambulant. Quomodo? Quidam homo ad magnam turrim aspexit ne se moueret, sed tamen hoc prohibere non potuit et in inquietis clamoribus clamauit: Ve, ue. Et sic in irrisionem populi ductus est dicentis: Quid proderit tibi semper contra eos bellare qui te nolunt?*

Letter 98

a. *Nolumus etiam uos ignorare nomen uestrum, personam uestram simulque cum salute super omni diligentia uos amplecti atque honorari, Deumque pro uobis pro posse nostro die noctuque interpellari.*

Letter 98r

a. *Illa scilicet que mihi molendinum corporis mei exhibuit.*

Letter 100

a. *Bruto ergo animali iure inferior habebitur qui bene dulcia minus bene amplectitur.*
b. *societatem fraternitatis tue.*

Letter 102

a. *Et o mirandam indesinenter et predicandam circa genus humanum benigni pietatem Redemptoris, qui per eum quo mors intrauerat sexum in matre ipsius uita restituitur, et de qua manu pestifer potus perditionis illatus nobis fuerat, de hac eadem manu in te salutaribus doctrinis antidotus recuperationis nobis refunditur.*

Letter 103r

a. *quoniam in speculatiua scientia honorifica opinione caret.*
b. *et quod propter liberationem hanc qua Deus ipsum liberauit, omnem malam consuetudinem peccatorum suorum conterit, omnemque miseriam et paupertatem quam in celestibus diuitiis habet, supra petram illam, que firmamentum beatitudinis est, proicit.*
c. *quoniam nullam securitatem ullius possibilitatis in me scio.*
d. *Spiritus uero meus, prout Deus uult, in hac uisione sursum in altitudinem firmamenti et in uicissitudinem diuersi aeris ascendit, atque inter diuersos populos se dilatat, quamuis in longinquis regionibus et locis a me remoti sint. Et quoniam hec tali modo uideo, idcirco etiam secundum uicissitudinem nubium et aliarum creaturarum ea conspicio.*
e. *illudque umbra uiuentis luminis mihi nominatur.*
f. *Quod autem non uideo, illud nescio, quia indocta sum.*
g. *Dextera ala scientia bona est et sinistra mala scientia est, et mala bone ministrat bonaque per malam acuitur et regitur, atque in cunctis per illam sapiens efficitur.*

Letter 104

a. *qui in splendoribus sanctorum ex utero Patris ante Luciferum genitus est.*
b. *Nec opinor, inquit, uim et altitudinem quorundam uerborum, in hac epistola positorum, summos huius temporis Francie magistros, quantouis polleant acumine ingenii, ex integro posse consequi, nisi eo spiritu quo dicta sunt reuelante.*

Letter 109

a. *Presentes litteras et quascumque hactenus uel fratrum Villarensium diuersis et temporibus et cartis tibi sparsim transmisi, michi nunc sedulo rogo retransmitti. Volo enim omnia, et tua ad me et mea ad te, sub uno scripta colligere et ad consolationem meam et ad eos, qui forte legere dignabuntur, diuine ammirationis pro muneribus eius excitandos michi in posterum reseruare.*

Letter 113r

a. *Sed et ipse sacerdos fuit, cum se ipsum in ara crucis pro hominibus immolauit.*

Letter 114

a. *uelutique humana fragilitas diuine ultionis est ceca, si ob benefactorum increscentiam in morbum seu temptationem inciderim non noui.*

Letter 115r

a. *Lux uera in lumine dicit per os sapientie.*

Letter 121

a. *Hauris enim, mea domina, et effundis et in formas specificas et practicis in theoriam uis et motus exsistis.*

Letter 122

a. *Animam autem abbatis tui uideo aliquantulum dissolutam in cruribus eius, sed tamen in uentre et in pectore, ac in cerebro ipsius est adhuc in inquietudine.*

Letter 144r

a. *Pessimus enim accusator retro deiectus est et abscisus ab omni beatitudine. Et quia retro proiectus est, ideo cogitauit in malignitate cordis sui ut hominem duceret retrorsum in contrarium peccatum. Sic relinquit homo formam coste, unde et formatio hominis ibi perit in huiusmodi effuso semine.*

Letter 146

a. *in extrema ungula schedule rescribere.*

Letter 148r

a. *et millenis artibus uentris sui circuit.*

Letter 149

a. *non solum operari bonum, uerum etiam prophetare uentura, contemplari celestia.*

Letter 149r

a. *"Quare fremuerunt gentes, et populi meditati sunt inania? Astiterunt reges terre, et principes conuenerunt in unum"* [Ps 2.1–2]. *Nam permissione Dei super uos in iudiciis suis fremere incipient plurime gentes, et multi populi de uobis meditabuntur inania, cum sacerdotale officium uestrum et consecrationem uestram pro nihilo computabunt. His assistent in euersione uestra reges terre, cum terrenis rebus inhiabunt, et principes qui uobis dominabuntur conuenient in hoc uno consilio quatenus uos de terminis suis expellant, quoniam innocentem Agnum a uobis per pessima opera fugastis.*

b. *Cum enim Deus hominem creauit, omnem creaturam in ipso signauit, quemadmodum in paruo loco membrane tempus et numerus totius anni describitur. Et ideo Deus hominem nominauit omnem creaturam.*

Letter 150

a. *Adduco mecum nobile par, monialem scilicet laudabilem, perfectissimarum sororem acceptabilem, quam Spiritu mihi generavit celestis Pater, non minus illi quam mihi cupiens tui notitiam, veneranda et omni laude dignissima mater.*

Letter 156

a. *Mementote quod pergamenum ea de causa uobis nuper transmisi.*

Letter 158r

a. *Deus opus suum fecit, sed illud uno modo non constituit.*
b. *Spiritales quoque populos Spiritus Sanctus inflauit, qui seculum in semetipsis finiunt et angelicum ordinem colunt.*

Letter 170r

a. *quam non tetigit uiriditas terrenarum causarum, sed supernus calor in secreto suo.*
b. *quia caro eius suauiter sudauit de Virgine et non de femore viri.*

Letter 174r

a. *quia sepe lutum luto abicitur, sicut etiam magister per discipulos et discipuli per magistrum abluuntur.*
b. *Nam propter metum discipulorum se affliget et a tortoribus inquietorum discipulorum punitur, et summum magistrum qui eum precessit sic imitatur.*

Letter 178r

a. *Quidam uero uentosi sunt et de uiriditate et humiditate terre, ac de aere et aquis comprehensionem per sensualitatem habent.*

Letter 185

a. *Si modus et locus uobis seruiendi mihi adimitur, eo tandem remedio affectus meus utitur ut utriusque hominis uestri incolumitatem per transmissas quantocius litteras experiar.*

Letter 185r

a. *Sed cum in tedio es, ita quod naturalis motio te concutit, exsilium huius uite attende, et quod etiam ad aliam uitam exspectando anhelas.*

Letter 186r

a. *O filia Ade, Deus rationalitas illa est que nec initium nec finem habet et per quam homo rationalis est; et eadem rationalitas in ipso animata uita est que numquam deficiet.*

b. *Deus uero hominem illum numquam perdet, qui maiorem partem peccatorum suorum ipsi offert, sed aliam partem minorem peccatorum illi remittit.*

Letter 187r

a. *Respice quod in oculo Viuentis in magno studio preuisus es, sicut mitissimus pater ouem suam requirit.*

Letter 188

a. *Verum, quia meminisse te cupimus, Deo dilecta, quemadmodum ad uicissitudinem huius instrumenti in quo uelut rudes ac delicati milites uersari cupimus, recta spe properamus, idcirco te, mater sancta, adiutorem "in opportunitatibus, in tribulatione" instanter pro nobis interpellare ut uias nostras in te post Deum confidentium dirigat, suppliciter exoramus.*

Letter 191r

a. *De uita etiam illa spiritus tuus redolebat, qui anima nominatus est quando anima de ipsa processit. Anima namque opera ponit et probat, et siue bona siue mala sint, et eisdem operibus spiritus fortissima ui molendinum est.*

Letter 192

a. *O magna res, que in nullo constituto latuit, ita quod non est facta nec creata ab ullo, sed in seipsa permanet. O uita, que surrexisti in aurora in qua magnus Rex sapientiam que in antiquo apud uirum sapientem fuit, misericorditer manifestauit, quia mulier per foramen antiqui perditoris mortem intrauit. O luctus, ach meror, he planctus, qui in muliere edificati sunt!*

b. *O aurora, hec abluisti in forma prime coste. O feminea forma, soror sapientie, quam gloriosa es, quoniam fortissima uita in te surrexit quam mors nunquam suffocabit. Te sapientia erexit, ita quod omnes creature per te ornate sunt in meliorem partem quam in primo acciperent.*

Letter 193

a. *Sed et adhuc in aliquo tempore Chaldei infirmabuntur, Greci robustiores efficientur, Romani cum ceteris Romanis silebunt ut ardens ignis qui cadit; et Galli tirones fient.*

b. *nisi millenarius armatus numerus illorum qui preputium non habent.*

Letter 194

a. *Nam in altera parte mihi affertis quosdam seculares mores obseruationis legalis discipline, in altera parte disciplinam legis eorum qui sub coniugio iuncti sunt.*

b. *secundum obseruationem iuuencularum illarum que mundo studiose et diligenter uelut disciplinate seruiunt, ut prefatum est.*

c. *In altera autem parte conuertentes uos ad constrictionem et ad placitum uariorum studiorum illorum qui carnalibus copulis frequenter insudant, quatenus amantes amantibus placeant—quod nec dicto, nec scripto, nec mandato a uobis postulo, quia spiritali copule adhesistis nec ad oculum famulantes—carnali amplexioni uos subiecistis, ubi non in uanam et mox cadentem floriditatem putredinis mundi uos coaptaui, sed in uineam uere electionis et uere beatitudinis induxi uos, quatenus in summa electione mercedem laborum uestrorum recipiatis.*

Letter 195

a. *Spiritus prophetie et uisionis in organo masse fragilioris absque adminiculo instrumenti exterioris resuscitatus.*

Letter 197

a. *Hortorum pigmentarii auctores et consiliatores boni consilii habere deberent qui diligentius precepta legis colligant, non aspicientes retro sui arietem, sed uictimam coram se presentem et diurnam quam Ecclesia habet non facta significatione, sed Filii Dei, ita quod ipse in passione sua doluit et passionem docuit.*

Letter 200

a. *Tu uero, mater dulcissima, speciali a ceteris Christi membris dono Sancti Spiritus finem huius mundi uisitare missa es.*

Letter 209r

a. *cum claue remunerationis.*

Letter 212

a. *Illa electio Dei est ita: Deus noluit ut in perditionem et in periculosa peccata ires, sicut propria uoluntas hominis frequenter postulat. Et ista electio non est officii tui.*

Letter 214

a. *Sol quoque esto per doctrinam, luna per differentiam, uentus per strenuum magisterium, aer per mansuetudinem, ignis per pulchrum doctrine sermonem.*

Letter 215

a. *tante deuotionis affectionem quod, si quis preter me sciret, uel nihil uel ea que non sunt scibilia sciret.*

Letter 216

a. *Secreta Dei mysteria ab his comprehendi uel sciri non possunt que per principium exorta sunt.*

b. *De omnibus uero istis qui tales mores habent, Deus ad se colligit, cum in scientia sua illa que contra salutem anime eorum sunt ad Deum pertimescunt, ut in Saulo et aliis multis factum est.* There is a lacuna in the MS after *Deum*. Peter Dronke (*Women Writers*, 261, 264) suggests adding the following words between *Deum* and *pertimescunt: conuertunt—eos qui tandem eum.*

Supplemental Bibliography

Adriaen, Marcus, ed. *Sancti Gregorii Magni Homiliae in Hiezechihelem Prophetam.* In *Corpus Christianorum*, vol. 142. Turnhout, Belgium, 1972.

Blume, Clemens, ed. *Analecta Hymnica medii aevi*, vol. 53. New York: Johnson Reprint Corporation, 1961.

Bruylants, P. *Les Oraisons du Missel Romain.* Louvain: Centre de Documentation et d'Information Liturgiques, 1952.

Clark, Anne L. *Elisabeth of Schönau: A Twelfth-Century Visionary.* Philadelphia: University of Pennsylvania Press, 1992.

Constable, Giles, ed. *Religious Life and Thought (11th–12th Centuries).* London: Variorum Reprints, 1979.

Derolez, Albert, ed. *Guiberti Gemblacensis Epistolae.* In *Corpus Christianorum: continuatio mediaevalis*, vol. 66. Turnhout, Belgium: 1988.

Jones, Charles W. *Saint Nicholas of Myra, Bari, and Manhattan: Biography of a Legend.* Chicago: University of Chicago Press, 1978.

Junod, Eric, and Jean-Daniel Kaestli, eds. *Acta Iohannis.* In *Corpus Christianorum: Series Apocryphorum.* Turnhout, Belgium: 1983.

Lindeman, H. "S. Hildegard en hare Nederlandsche vrienden," *Ons Geestelijk Erf* 2 (1928), 128–60.

McDermott, William C., trans. *Gregory of Tours: Selections from the Minor Works.* Philadelphia: University of Pennsylvania Press, 1949.

Rissel, H. "Hildegard von Bingen an Elisabeth von St. Thomas an der Kyll." *Citeaux* 41 (1990), 5–44.

Roth, F. W. E., ed. *Die Visionen der hl. Elisabeth und die Schriften der Aebte Ekbert und Emecho von Schönau.* Brünn: Verlag der Studien aus dem Benedictiner-und Cistercienser-Orden, 1884.

Schaller, Dieter, and Ewald Könsgen, eds. *Initia carminum Latinorum saeculo undecimo antiquiorum.* Göttingen: Vandenhoeck & Ruprecht, 1977.

Van Acker, Lieven. "Der Briefwechsel zwischen Elisabeth von Schönau und Hildegard von Bingen." *Instrumenta Patristica* 23 (1991), 409–17.

Van Acker, Lieven, ed. *Hildegardis Bingensis: Epistolarium, Pars Secunda.* In *Corpus Christianorum: continuatio mediaevalis*, vol. 91A. Turnhout: Belgium, 1993.

Scripture Index

Frequency of Scripture cited or alluded to is indicated in parentheses.

Acts 2.2; 2.3; 2.3–4; 2.11; 9.15 (3); 10.42;
  11.5 (2); 17.28; 22.1ff
Amos 5.4–6
Apocalypse 1.1–2; 1.4 (7); 1.11; 1.16; 2.16;
  3.15f; 3.15–16; 3.20; 4.4ff; 4.6; 6.5; 6.6;
  6.9; 6.9f; 6.10; 7.10; 7.14; 8.3–5; 9.9;
  9.13; 9.19; 12.4; 12.6; 12.9 (2); 12.10;
  12.14; 13.6; 14.14; 15.1ff; 19.15 (2);
  19.16; 20.2; 20.12; 21.5; 21.10f; 22.14

Baruch 4.6; 4.36; 5.5

Canticles 1.1 (2); 1.2; 1.3 (2); 1.4 (2); 1.6;
  1.14; 2.2; 2.3; 2.4; 2.4–5; 2.12; 2.14 (4);
  3.6 (3); 3.7–8; 3.11 (2); 4.4 (3); 4.5;
  4.6; 4.11; 4.13; 4.15 (2); 5.2 (2); 5.9;
  5.14; 7.1; 8.5; 8.13
Colossians 1.12; 2.3
I Corinthians 1.27; 1.31; 3.8; 4.16; 5.3; 6.17;
  6.18; 6.20; 7.7; 7.26; 9.24 (2); 10.13 (2);
  11.5ff; 12.3; 12.4; 12.11; 13.1; 15.9 (2);
  15.10; 15.44ff; 15.47–49
II Corinthians 1.8; 1.22; 2.14–15; 2.15 (2);
  2.16 (2); 3.18 (2); 4.7 (3); 5.5; 10.18;
  11.1; 11.14; 11.25; 12.2–3; 12.11

Daniel 3.19ff; 3.55; 12.3
Deuteronomy 4.23; 5.32 (2); 6.16; 8.11;
  31.6ff (2); 32.2; 32.33; 33.2

Ecclesiastes 1.2; 12.1
Ecclesiasticus 1.11; 1.26ff; 2.13; 16.11;
  18.1; 18.5; 18.6; 18.20; 24.8; 24.12;
  24.19; 39.8; 42.18; 44.16; 45.23; 47.16;
  51.20
Ephesians 3.8; 3.18; 4.1; 4.7; 4.15; 5.2; 5.8;
  6.14; 6.14ff; 6.17
Exodus 3.2; 3.8; 3.14 (6); 13.21f; 14.13;
  14.28; 15.4; 18.16; 19.18; 24; 29;
  32.4ff
Ezechiel 1.18; 3.1ff; 3.13; 7.26; 12.2; 18.23;
  33.11; 45.10

Galatians 1.4; 4.26
Genesis 1; 1.1ff; 1.3; 1.3ff (2); 1.7 (2);
  1.11ff; 1.22; 1.26f (2); 1.26ff; 2.6; 2.7
  (2); 2.15; 2.16–17; 2.17; 2.21; 2.22;
  3.1ff (3); 3.1–6; 3.6 (2); 3.8; 3.15; 3.17;
  3.22; 3.24; 4.2ff; 4.4 (2); 4.8; 4.8–16;
  4.24; 5.24; 8.20; 9.5; 9.6; 9.11–17;
  12.1ff (2); 17.23–24; 18.1ff; 18.27;
  22.9ff (2); 22.13 (2); 22.15ff(2); 23.8–
  9; 24.9; 25.9–10; 27.27; 27.36; 32.1ff;
  32.26ff; 42.1; 47.29; 48.15ff; 49.29

Hebrews 3.13; 4.13 (2); 6.4; 9.3–4; 9.4;
  9.10; 9.15; 10.9; 11.1; 11.5; 12.22 (9);
  13.5
Hosea 2.6; 6.3; 6.6 (3); 7.11; 14.2

General Index